The
ADD
Answer

The
ADD
Answer

How to Help Your Child Now

Dr. Frank Lawlis

VIKING

VIKING
Published by the Penguin Group
Penguin Group (USA) Inc., 375 Hudson Street, New York, New York 10014, U.S.A.
Penguin Group (Canada), 10 Alcorn Avenue, Toronto, Ontario, Canada M4V 3B2
(a division of Pearson Penguin Canada Inc.)
Penguin Books Ltd, 80 Strand, London WC2R 0RL, England
Penguin Ireland, 25 St. Stephen's Green, Dublin 2, Ireland (a division of Penguin Books Ltd)
Penguin Books Australia Ltd, 250 Camberwell Road, Camberwell Victoria 3124, Australia
(a division of Pearson Australia Group Pty Ltd)
Penguin Books India Pvt Ltd, 11 Community Centre, Panchsheel Park,
New Delhi - 110 017, India
Penguin Group (NZ), Cnr Airborne and Rosedale Roads, Albany, Auckland, New Zealand
(a division of Pearson New Zealand Ltd)
Penguin Books (South Africa) (Pty) Ltd, 24 Sturdee Avenue, Rosebank, Johannesburg
2196, South Africa

Penguin Books Ltd, Registered Offices: 80 Strand, London WC2R 0RL, England

First published in 2004 by Viking Penguin, a member of Penguin Group (USA) Inc.

10 9 8 7 6 5 4 3

A NOTE TO THE READER: Every effort has been made to ensure that the information contained in this book is complete and accurate. However, neither the publisher nor the author is engaged in rendering professional advice or services to the individual reader. The ideas, procedures, and suggestions contained in this book are not intended as a substitute for consulting with your physician. All matters regarding your health require medical supervision. Neither the author nor the publisher shall be liable or responsible for any loss, injury, or damage allegedly arising from any information or suggestion in this book.

LIBRARY OF CONGRESS CATALOGING-IN-PUBLICATION DATA
Lawlis, Frank.
    The ADD answer : how to help your child now / Frank Lawlis.
      p.   cm.
    Includes index.
    ISBN 0-670-03336-7
      1. Attention-deficit hyperactivity disorder—Popular works.   2. Attention-deficit
    disordered children—Popular works.   3. Child rearing—Popular works.   I. Title.
    RJ506.H9L39 2004
    618.92'8589—dc22   2004040851

This book is printed on acid-free paper. ∞
Printed in the United States of America

To
Lorri,
my wife and partner
in my life adventures

Foreword by Dr. Phil McGraw

Attention deficit disorder (ADD) is a major challenge for many families in this century. The needs and unresolved challenges of children with ADD are affecting virtually every school in this nation, and a high number of adult issues in the workplace have been linked to adult ADD. Children are our most valuable asset, yet many of our children with the greatest potential are being left on the sidelines.

There is good reason to believe that there are multiple reasons for the upsurge of ADD. The growing toxicity of our nation, the breakdown of family stability, the increasing distractions of technology and video games, and the possible role of various viruses are all areas of concern. However, regardless of the cause, I have seen few solutions or approaches that hold out much promise or hope to the families who are overwhelmed by the diagnosis. I hear the despair and frustration expressed by parents as they go from one source to another with the same result—failure. Too often the label of ADD becomes a stigma of long-term problems that will never go away.

We are not doing enough as a nation to help children and families overcome the challenges of ADD. The majority of our convicts in prisons can be diagnosed with ADD, yet we have no programs for children to avert this outcome or to offer adequate treatment. Most teachers and parents do not know what to do for children with ADD, although they are bright and eager to learn. Some parents are so frustrated in their dealings with the educational system that they have decided to homeschool their children.

Most people know me by some of my pet phrases, and one is very appropriate to the current ADD situation: Is this working for you? The fact is that no one fully understands the problem of ADD, only the symptoms. I feel that as a psychologist with a specialization in behavioral medicine, I should be able to read the literature and determine whether someone has nailed down a cause-and-effect. But what I have discovered is that there are a lot of people trying to stick their finger in the dike, hoping the flood of questions will go away.

What Dr. Lawlis is trying to do in this book is to help families understand their own child and what ADD means to them. He has recognized that this condition can mean many things and have many causes. Parents do not need academic explanations. They do not need prescriptions for a medication that may not work. And they certainly don't need prescriptions for a medication that can have tragic side effects. Parents need an understanding of what their child is experiencing personally and a plan for the whole family to implement. Dr. Lawlis offers a step-by-step approach focused on accurate assessment and individualized solutions. In this way, progress can be measured and reinforced. He offers ways and methods to meet the educational and practical needs of children who suffer the academic and social stigma of ADD whatever their strengths or deficits. He supplies the biological and psychological basis for each approach, and he has also applied them in his own practice to be sure they are safe and effective.

But more than a gentle plan and personal assessments, this book offers the most advanced approaches available for the treatment of ADD. Perhaps it takes someone with a research background and clinical passion to be able to address and appreciate the progress that most people simply do not know about. Most of the innovations Dr. Lawlis describes have been widely used in the world of behavioral medicine, but they may take ten years or more to become common throughout the educational, psychiatric, and psychotherapeutic fields. But for the reader, they are accessible now in this book. Not all the paths Dr. Lawlis suggests are required for any one individual, but through concerted effort, the parent can become the expert and the child the hero.

When I am placed in a position to help people, I try to ask myself what it is that has caused a person to try and fail in the past, and what it is it that can be offered to change that outcome. I am not known for being a theoretician and for making global statements about the theoretical scope of the human brain. But I am known for putting things in understandable terms and giving people a way to use that information in their lives on an action-oriented basis. I like approaches that have *verbs* in the solutions. And that is exactly what this book about ADD offers.

My approaches are based on how well people find solutions to the goals they set and then how effectively they act on those solutions. I want you to ask yourself: Are you and your child making measurable progress in dealing with ADD? Are your family interactions improving? Is your child modifying his temper in the classroom or his acting out at the teacher? If not, I would ask you to investigate other paths and seek out new skills and methods.

As I observe the situation of children with ADD and think about everything Dr. Lawlis says within the book, I come to one immediate conclusion: the family has to step up to meet this challenge. Parents cannot remain in the denial stage one day longer. Although I suspect that it can be very scary rubbing elbows with all those doctors and teachers, you have to reach down and bring up the courage to make your child's needs known and become an active participant from now on. In order to do that, you need cutting-edge knowledge. The book you are now holding, in my personal and professional opinion, holds that knowledge.

To tell you the truth, I was not surprised to see this book written by Dr. Frank Lawlis. He was my major professor in my doctoral studies program at the University of North Texas. He has been a trusted friend and mentor for almost thirty years. I have reveled in the innovations he has pioneered in his clinical work, which have earned him the coveted title of "Fellow" in two divisions of the American Psychological Association for his scientific contributions in the field. Dr. Lawlis has created many of the behavior medicine protocols for chronic pain, rehabilitation, and cancer that are practiced throughout the world, and his new clinical research efforts are concentrating on neurological impairments, such as ADD.

Based on my trust in Dr. Lawlis and my respect for his integrity and unselfish desire to help people, I have every confidence that you will find powerful answers in this important book. Make a plan, as Dr. Lawlis proposes, and create a purposeful direction. Make it work for you with a purpose.

Nothing comes easy that has true value, and your family is vitally important. I believe that what Dr. Lawlis promises is a path of success. But you are going to have to find it. It will not be given to you, and it is unlikely that you will absorb all the answers you need in one reading or while you sleep. Take this book seriously, and I believe that your returns will be tremendous.

Preface: Sharing the Journey

I did not begin to write this book last year or the year before that. I started this book when I was born, and I have edited it ever since.

My birth was an ordeal for both my mother and me. She was given too much pain medication, by accident. Her labor was halted, and I was declared dead while still in the birth canal. A few hours later it was clear the doctor was wrong, but that did not stop him from issuing another diagnosis that was equally dooming: I was mentally defective due to oxygen deprivation. He told my parents there was no hope that I would progress in school, and he warned that sooner rather than later, I would cease to learn.

Being unaware of my limitations, I found that in a variety of settings, I could fake it until I made it. I developed ways of compensating for my problems much of the time, such as avoiding handwriting by means of self-imposed bruises on my right hand and requesting oral tests. I could not—and still cannot—read my own writing, though I finally developed my own style during my internship. During most of the third, fourth, and fifth grades, my world was like Mardi Gras. The letters would dance off the page when I tried to focus on my reading. When the teacher presented some topic for learning, my mind played tricks on me, such as counting every other word in her sentences, or making up new sentences, or finishing her sentences with my own version. I cannot tell you how many times I got busted for laughing at my own internal comedies. Church represented a host of materials for my imagination, especially from the hymnals.

I suspect that what kept me out of juvenile detention, especially in later years, was my parents, my sister, and the typewriter. All were teachers to me then, and later in my professional life, so I was very, very lucky. With the patience of Job, my father spent endless nights teaching me how to befriend numbers rather than fear them as my enemies. I remember one of the first things he told me: "Write your numbers big enough so you can read them." That was an amazing concept to me because I had been writing them in small little messes, with the thought of saving paper or for some other crazy rationale that escapes me. That task required some basics in organization, too, because he also made me line my numbers up in some order.

My sister brought in her typewriter when I was in the fourth grade, and I found that I could actually make out my own words. Finally I could reread what I had written, and I could begin to understand the mechanics of a sentence. *Wow!* (I cannot tell you of my rebirth when word processors arrived.) My mother was my cheerleader. Whether or not I would ever be a high school graduate did not matter to her as long as I had a mission to be the best person I could be. If this sounds like Forrest Gump, it may be accidental, but I sure identified with that character.

Many of the paths in this book are examples of things I learned as a means to "make it through." My highest goal in school was junior college, but I survived college, with a major in mathematics. (What else?) Then I began to explore the world of books, and could actually read one all the way through. What a concept! But I learned that I needed to read fast in order to keep my mind from wandering into some interesting story of my own. Two master's degrees and a Ph.D. later, with over a hundred research articles written and multiple books, I am still creating more stories in my head than Stephen King, and juggling at least four projects at one time.

But this book is not about my journey. This book is based on the hope seen in the faces of thousands of children and adults I've met on their pilgrimages in the miracle we call life. One of the most incredible blessings in my life has been to witness people on their healing journeys. I do not have to try to convince myself that individuals can be successful at any challenge. I have seen and known the spirit that lies within each of us that pushes us onward toward our destinies.

I have rarely seen people who are happy all the time, and just as rarely have I seen people who are sad all the time. The goal of life is not to be happy, because that is a transitory state. Regardless of what our circumstances are and what our challenges are, I believe that we learn to live our lives according to the unique contributions we make for one another and for ourselves. It may be difficult to witness your child attempting to cope with the challenges of ADD. It may trigger your own confrontation with what it means to be a parent. But you do have a choice in your reactions. You can choose to label yourself and your child as victims of a harsh and stupid disorder, or you can actually embrace the challenge to become a hero and a star who can model the best possible response. You can learn to trust yourself and your creative senses. You might even learn that you are truly beloved by God.

Acknowledgments

As the reader will quickly discover, this book has many dimensions and levels of understanding, none of which could have been realized without the wonderful personal and professional support and consultations I received as I was writing it.

The person who has always been there as a colleague and friend is Dr. Phil McGraw. Dr. Phil and I have been friends for more than thirty years, and ours is a relationship in which I have learned the true meaning of commitment and trust. He has shared his loyalty in more strange circumstances than I want to mention or explain. He may have been my student at the University of North Texas, but I cannot take credit for his genius. I owe Phil McGraw a huge debt of thanks for his encouragement and for his willingness to write the foreword to this book.

Jan Miller, my literary agent and adopted sister, has generously given me of her enthusiastic direction and editing. At times she has been more impassioned about this project than I, and her advice has always been nothing less than helpful.

Cindy Gallaher was the first to see how I could "make a difference" for the parents of ADD kids with my alternative medicine background and experience. She read the manuscript from the perspective of a family's needs, and her relationship with other parents enabled her to make recommendations for the direction of the book.

But I would be the first to say that this book has been the result of consultation with many experts in medicine, nutrition, and neurobiofeedback. I have been consulting with physicians all my career, and I think that Andrew Messamore, M.D., is the smartest doctor who knows more about the causes of disease as opposed to just treating symptoms than anyone I know. He obviously was a major help with the medication and detoxification issues in this book. Maggie Greenwood-Robinson, Ph.D., has written more than twenty-five books about nutrition and was my coconsultant (as was Dr. Phil through his book *The Ultimate Weight Solution*). Besides knowing just about everything there is to know about this part of ADD, she is a brilliant writer and consultant. I have found her to be a wonderful friend and a major contributor to the wisdom of this book.

Barbara Peavey, Ph.D., is my partner in the specialized clinics for ADD and wrote the protocols based on this book. Being friends for twenty-five years says a lot for loyalty, but being partners in a business venture says a great deal about the trust. She has established her own international reputation as a leader in biofeedback and knows this stuff forward and backward.

Nanciruth Autin, retired school counselor and favorite sister, contributed insights into the school perspective and was also instrumental in editing her brother's scrambled wording. Besides being an educational expert, she is the most courageous person I know, and she has always been my best friend.

Janet Goldstein has been the helmsman of this book. Even when her patience has been tried and frazzled by my "Texan" writing, her voice has been like a beacon of hope in this bold endeavor to change the lives of children and families. I have West Smith to thank for translating my words into meaningful sentences.

Contents

The
ADD
Answer

ONE

Taking a Step
on the Healing Path

This book was written from my heart, soul, and mind for the sake of our children, because we are on the edge of crisis. I have seen too many children and families suffering because they lack plans and solutions for managing the realities of ADD. No one has been giving families tools they can use to take charge of the problem themselves, but I will. No one has been giving families the means to understand and assess the specific problems their child faces as a result of ADD, but I will. No one has been giving families clear action plans that will guide them toward success, but I will. It is with these goals in mind that I have written this book.

As a researcher and someone who is personally invested in helping people, I want you to know that I base all therapy on truth. And I will tell you the truth about why I am so passionate about writing this book. My interest in medicine and healing began when I was a child, growing up with a mother who had numerous surgeries, spread out over many years. Being a good son, my first career choice was to be a traditional doctor. However, I soon became aware of the limitations of medicine, and I eventually chose to become a psychologist who worked in the medical field. I quickly discovered that there are often a number of approaches to diseases and conditions that are very effective and scientifically valid but that never see the light of day. Many of these alternative treatments take longer than the typical seven minutes currently allowed in the doctor's office, so the traditional medical solution—a pill—is usually prescribed without even a brochure explaining the medical alternatives.

In all truth, ADD cannot be treated in seven minutes or in seven days, and probably cannot be treated in a doctor's office. It has to be approached in the home, where there is a higher calling than just getting a child to be quiet and conform to the rules for a while. This book, then, is written for the family. It offers new and exciting approaches, with action plans as well. But this is not a gift that cures the problem by itself. It is a path—a healing path that with effort and focus can and will shift the impact of your child's ADD from disaster to growth as your child becomes the human being he or she is truly destined to be.

It is critical for you to keep something in mind from this point forward: you and your family can beat this thing. It will not destroy your lives, your values, or your dreams. God did not invest ADD with that kind of power over you. ADD is challenging. It is confusing. But I've helped thousands of patients find hope and renewal.

Your job will be to stay strong and to keep things in perspective. This is a considerable challenge, but it is one you and your child can handle, just as others have. Remember, the measure of our character is how we respond to life's challenges.

If you are a parent who is new to the challenges of ADD, you need to begin this journey with two guiding thoughts:

- *You must commit yourself to a long and deep study of ADD.* It impacts every realm of experience for you and your child—social, educational, and spiritual. So you must become both an expert and an advocate.
- *You must be willing to reach out for help and support.* Even the most determined people can do only so much. We all have limits to our reserves of courage and energy. Do not be too proud to ask for help or to vent your exasperation. The important thing is to protect your own mental and physical health because your child needs you.

If you are a parent who has been on this merry-go-round for a while already, I want to offer hope. By now you've realized that there is no quick fix—no healing gurus, no miracle cures. But there are scientific approaches that will offer relief. I am going to share with you my proven strategies for helping those afflicted with ADD.

I encourage you to begin this new journey of treatment and healing by making a promise to yourself, your spouse, and your children. Pledge to open your heart and mind so that you can understand and meet this challenge. Make this a positive journey of accomplishment for you, your child, and your family. Every parent wants to find the easiest path. But the reality is that life rarely allows for easy travel. As in the children's tale *The Velveteen Rabbit*, it is only in wearing off our fur that we become real. In facing the challenge of ADD together, you will experience the privilege of truly getting to know your child and yourself. Believe me, that is a gift, regardless of what life throws at you later.

Many of the accepted treatments for helping kids with ADD put parents in the role of clowns in a three-ring circus. Physicians say one thing, teachers say something else, friends and family have their own opinions. Suggestions, recommendations, and diagnoses fly at you from all directions, but no one seems to fully grasp what works and doesn't work. Every day I am amazed at how even the most intelligent and dedicated parents miss out on important resources available for helping their children with ADD.

Parents of ADD children often talk of the emotional roller coaster they experience in searching for answers and in trying to determine what is right and what is wrong for their children. Many have endured criticism for trying different approaches when the recommended treatments appear to fail. They feel trapped in a no-win situation when an approach that has worked for others does not help their own children. At times when they most need support and praise for their efforts, they feel ashamed and damned.

This disorder often disrupts the normal life of a family. Certainly not every ADD family is dysfunctional, but the insidious nature of this condition can disrupt basic communication. Even the most loving family relationships can be thrown dramatically askew. Sometimes parents tend to focus so much on the needs of an ADD child that the needs of other siblings are neglected. When a family becomes dependent on outside expertise from psychiatrists, psychologists, teachers, and school counselors, that can undermine its healthy sense of self-reliance and disrupt its decision-making processes. Never knowing what to expect from an ADD child from day to day also disrupts a household. Trust can erode.

ADD can tear at the fabric of a family by undermining parental authority and creating suspicion and doubt. Yet we know, too, that challenges like ADD often strengthen familial bonds. Having worked with hundreds of clients, I've seen some horrific family crises arise because of ADD, and I've seen family members rally around one another with compassion and dedication. This book will give your family the tools and the guidance to make the best of your experience with ADD.

The Diagnosis

The scenarios of discovery don't vary greatly from one family to the next. Often a teacher sounds the first alarm by alerting parents to the fact that a child is disruptive in class. Within the first month of a school year, the label *attention deficit disorder* becomes associated with the child. The parents are given behavioral reports from the school and are encouraged to consult a physician or psychologist. Over the course of the next six months the child is put under a microscope and the family is subjected to an overload of stress as they attempt to grapple with this new development.

In the majority of my cases, the family quickly begins to experience conflicts and doubt. Their conventional understanding of what constitutes good and bad behavior for a child is tossed out. The child once seen as beautiful and precious is suddenly cast as abnormal. The blame game begins soon thereafter. Parents and teachers are often at odds over their responsibilities. This is a dangerous time. When the adults in a child's life become completely focused on negative behavior, the youngster's self-image deteriorates. The child can give up hope of ever being good or normal when his parents and teachers seem to perceive everything he does as bad or aberrant. You cannot allow this to happen.

A Disorder, Not a Disaster

The modern terms *attention deficit disorder (ADD)* and *attention deficit hyperactivity disorder (ADHD)* are often used interchangeably, but they have subtle differences. Actually, *ADD* is typically used for the lack of attention abilities, while *ADHD* usually refers to the hyperactive behavior often attributable to the lack of concentration. The condition has undergone many name changes over the past century. First described by Heinrich Hoffmann in the nineteenth century, in a poem about Fidgety Philip, the disorder and its implications have not been fully appreciated until the last ten to twenty years. Today, attention deficit disorder is understood to be a neurological disorder. It is typically mild as far as direct brain symptoms, such as seizures or paralysis, are concerned, and the child functions normally in most daily activities and has age-appropriate skills. But ADD has extensive ramifications for a child's learning processes.

An ADD diagnosis means that the child's brain is not functioning normally. ADD is not a sign of inferior intelligence. It is not a handicap. It does not result in a damaged personality, criminal tendencies, or immoral behavior. And it is not necessarily a learning disability or a mark of mental immaturity, although such conditions can coexist with ADD. Much of the time, the problems of ADD are related to the brain performing at lowered, subdued ranges.

Brain performance is usually discussed in four ranges of measurable electromagnetic activity. These output ranges, called "states," are *Beta, Alpha, Theta,* and *Delta.*

Beta State. This is the highest range of brain activity. This brain state measures greater than 13 hertz (or cycles per second), and this is the output that occurs during most of the day. You are producing Beta waves when you are problem solving and actively thinking.

Alpha State. This is called the relaxation or calm state (8–12 hertz) because there is a perceptible tranquil sense that you experience as you enter this state. You may remember the Alpha machines that were popular a few years ago as aids to help people relax and fight stress.

Theta State. When you are in a trance, similar to that period just before you fall asleep, in a kind of "twilight" time, you have entered the Theta state (4–8 hertz). This is the state of hypnotic effect, where realities blur and the imageries of dreams are created. Consequently, this is the state when creativity is highest, because the obstacles of rationality and objectivity no longer restrict you.

Thomas Edison used an unusual technique to achieve a Theta state for solving his problems. It sounds awkward, but he would hold pebbles in his fists while supporting his head on his wrists above a bowl of water. Just before he dozed off, his fists would relax enough so that the pebbles would fall into the water. The water would splash up into his face and keep him just close enough to the waking state, while still in the Theta zone, for him to view a problem in more insightful ways.

Delta State. This is the slowest range (0.5–4 hertz), but you are fully asleep during this phase. There are lower levels within the sleep stages, but suffice it to say that Delta is not usually a state that psychologists consider as related to the issues of ADD.

The Brain Stuck in Overdrive

With attention deficit disorder, the brain is functioning in the Alpha and Theta ranges most of the time, even when it is more appropriate to be in the higher ranges, such as when the child is at school and solving problems.

Your child's ADD brain, then, is like a car stuck in overdrive. Your child can't use the power of the engine to get over the hill. He may feel as if he is caught in mud up to his knees while being expected to run a hundred-yard dash. No wonder he gets frustrated and acts out!

ADD children are hyperactive *not* because their brains are operating in high gear, but because they *can't shift* into high gear. Their mental engines are bogged down. Their normal methods for stimulating the brain aren't working, so they try other ways to step on the gas. They engage in risky behaviors, get into fights, and challenge authority—anything they can do to create an excited state. They create stress, and then their adrenal glands kick in and raise the brain activity to a higher level.

Children love to run and play. Movement gives them pleasure. This is especially true for children with ADD. They crave excitement as a means for stimulating their lethargic brains. They eat gobs of sweets because sugar offers a quick fix. Unfortunately, their energy drops rapidly once the sugar high fades.

For some children, certain parts of the brain connections in the administrative and memory parts run at a lower rate than normal; but they may not feel drowsy, because their muscles and organs are still charged with energy. Children experiencing this condition do not feel particularly unpleasant, but their conscious thoughts are in that dreamlike state of free association, with the boundaries between reality and dreams broken down. We've all experienced a similar state of consciousness as we drift off to sleep.

An Imaginative State

Tune in to the internal dialogues of two children in geometry class. Jane's brain is in a normal state, conducive to learning. Jill's is in an ADD mode.

As the geometry teacher explains how to find the area of a circle, Jane follows the teacher's process of calculation without being distracted: *I see the circle and I can visualize that there is a line crossing through the center. That is called the diameter, and half of that is called the radius. OK, I understand the diameter and radius, and all I have to do to find the area inside the circle is to mul-*

tiply the length of the radius by itself, and then multiply the result by pi (π), or about 22/7. I just do that to get the answer. I got it!

But if you were to tune in to Jill's internal dialogue, it might sound like this: *I see the circle, and the circle reminds me of that ring I saw on Molly's finger. I wonder where she got it. That reminds me, I have to get a new top to wear to Joe's party. Oh yeah, Joe is sitting over there and he is looking at me. I wonder if I am looking stupid again. Oh darn! The teacher is looking at me. I probably missed the lesson again, and she is going to call on me. Oh darn! Let's see. Radius squared times pi. What was pi again? Maybe it is called pi because it looks like a pie. That reminds me, I am getting hungry . . .*

Jill, the child with ADD, is in an imaginative state. But it is not the proper time to be creative. It is the time to focus and learn in very precise steps. If Jill misses a step, she becomes anxious. She then tries to focus and regain lost ground, but she is unable to break free of the free-associative state. This inability to control mental tracking explains why a child with ADD is forgetful, cannot concentrate, becomes bored quickly, and is easily distracted. Since most of us do not have trouble focusing our minds, we assume a child who is so easily distracted is simply inattentive, lazy, or lacking in self-discipline.

Treatment for ADD

When your child has a neurological problem, you might expect that you'd find a doctor who could assess the problem and prescribe a treatment plan to remedy it. A parent might also expect that teachers would have specific methods for helping children with memory and concentration problems, since it is estimated that 3–6 percent of all students have a form of this problem. In most areas of medical treatment and in most schools, there are specific therapies and organized programs for helping children with special needs. But as parents of ADD children have discovered, specific therapies and organized programs too often do not exist for them. No wonder there is so much anger and frustration expressed by families dealing with ADD.

Does Your Child Have ADD?

Parents of children with ADD can become exasperated very early on because it is often difficult to determine if a child truly has attention deficit disorder. According to a widely accepted checklist, ADD should be considered if the child often

- fails to pay close attention to details or makes careless mistakes in schoolwork or in other activities
- avoids, dislikes, or is reluctant to engage in tasks that require sustained concentration and effort
- does not seem to listen when directly spoken to
- does not often follow through on instructions and fails to finish schoolwork, chores, or duties
- has difficulty organizing tasks and activities
- loses things necessary for tasks or activities
- is forgetful in daily activities

These recognizable symptoms have been accepted as indicators of ADD for a number of years now as part of an effort to standardize the diagnosis. I've used them in my practice as a clinical psychologist. However, the same symptoms also relate to the following conditions:

delirium, dementia, amnesic and other cognitive disorders
mental disorders due to a medical condition
disorders related to substance abuse
schizophrenia and other psychotic disorders
mood disorders (including depression, dysthymia, and bipolar disorder)
anxiety disorders

dissociative disorders
sleep disorders
adjustment disorders
personality disorders

I do not want to imply in any way that your child is suffering from a mental disorder. The point I'm making is that *ADD* is merely a name assigned to a long list of dysfunctional behaviors. It does not refer to any specific cause for the behavior. The paradox of scientific medicine is that a diagnosis does not guarantee a cause-and-effect. All children have these symptoms at times, especially during high-stress periods. What child hasn't become distracted and lost concentration at one time or another? Every boy and girl is forgetful at times. Every child has experienced difficulty getting organized, following instructions, or focusing on the task at hand. And that is exactly why identifying and treating children who are truly afflicted with ADD is such a challenge. Far too many children are labeled as suffering from ADD without scientific justification. In fact, very few students ever get assessed with anything more than a behavioral checklist similar to the one I just provided. The symptoms in that checklist can apply to a whole host of kids who may just be slow to mature or have poor stress management skills.

There is a very real possibility that your child was checked off as a troublemaker by a teacher faced with the daunting task not only of educating each student to her full potential, but also of meeting the political goals of the school system and its standardized-achievement testing system. There are many demands on teachers, and most teachers have too few resources. They are often pulled in opposite directions. As an educator myself, I respect dedicated teachers and I place a high value on the educational system.

Still, I'm afraid that many teachers mislabel young people as having ADD because they don't have the time or the resources to develop real expertise. When a teacher is trying to educate thirty-five students and one of them is working against her by acting out, the understandable temptation is to apply a label, to solve the problem by categorizing the offending student's behavior. But it is dangerous to label a child without a scientific basis for the diagnosis, and too often the treatment that follows treats only the symptoms and not the person afflicted.

In the pages that follow, I will give you tools and direct you to resources that will help you get a much better handle on your child's deficits and the treatments that are available for it.

You Are Not Alone, and There Is Hope

The first fact parents of ADD children should know is that they are not alone. There are an estimated 17 million children diagnosed with ADD in the United States, and the number increases every day. Generally, this is not a condition that can be outgrown. Nor can it be prevented by vaccination or cured simply by making lifestyle adjustments.

The second helpful fact parents should know is that while there's no treatment approach that works for all children, there are strategies that *do* work and that can be combined to create an effective program for their child. *ADD* is a grab-bag, catchall term for a series of troublesome problems, just as *the common cold* is really the name we have given to a series of symptoms that include a runny nose, stuffed sinuses, sneezing, coughing, and body ache. And just as one person's surefire cold remedy may have no effect on another person's symptoms, I've discovered that there is no one remedy for ADD. But there are treatment methods that work in specific cases. The good news is that although ADD raises many questions, this book has many answers. My promise to you is that if you dedicate yourself to meeting this challenge, I will give you all the tools available. Together, we will find the solution for your child.

Medication Is Not the Long-term Answer

Americans are living longer and in better health than ever before. So why is ADD on the rise? I suspect that one day we will find some environmental pollutant responsible for most of the symptoms. But right now, I am more concerned with the dangers inherent in the way we treat those symptoms.

Far too many children are being drugged as a solution to the symptoms of ADD. Medications may be necessary for short-term goals, but I believe they are dangerous. I do not advocate the use of drugs as the fix for ADD because of the very real possibility that they will lead to severe complications, toxicity, and even death. We are a society addicted to quick fixes and magic pills. It's one thing to do that to ourselves, but now we seem to be doing it to our children too. Sales of prescription drugs such as Ritalin and other medicines for childhood neurological and psychological disorders are huge. Ritalin sales alone increased by 122 percent, and depression medications for children increased 5 percent, in one year alone (2000–2001).

In 2003 the National Institutes of Health (NIH) announced that Americans spend more on medications for their children than for the elderly. Are we using drugs to control our children's behavior instead of being responsible parents? When we teach our children at a young age to rely on medications, I fear that we are in danger of creating a generation of pill poppers as a result. Do we want our young people to rely on the magic of chemistry to regulate their behavior, or do we want them to naturally develop the discipline and focus necessary for them to contribute to society?

Most responsible school counselors and pediatricians feel that drugs for ADD should be used only as a last resort, and they recognize that even if they do work in younger children, their effectiveness will be minimized by the teenage years. In other words, drugs are not the total answer. They cannot remedy negative environmental factors, family conflicts, or educational failures.

The risks of poor treatment are real. If your child has ADD, it is certainly a personal problem for you. And it is a crisis for your child's future. Without effective treatment, the risks associated with ADD are very great. Children with ADD can fall out of the mainstream of positive social, educational, and emotional life with their peers and family members. ADD is also a problem for society as a whole. The challenges associated with this affliction have enormous implications. The following numbers are taken from the

Attention Deficit Disorder Association and from material provided by Children and Adults with Attention-Deficit/Hyperactivity Disorder (CHADD):

- 35 percent of students with ADD never finish high school.
- Individuals with ADD have significantly more hospital visits than those without it.
- Parents of ADD children divorce three times more often than the general population.
- 50 to 75 percent of incarcerated inmates in prisons have some form of ADD.
- 52 percent of ADD sufferers abuse drugs at some time in their lives.
- 43 percent of male ADD students are arrested for a felony before the age of sixteen.

The costs of ADD and ADHD are reflected in the entire family medical profile. According to a study published in 2003 in the *Journal of the American Academy of Child and Adolescent Psychiatry*, "Attention Deficit/Hyperactivity Disorder: Increased Costs for Patients and Their Families," families who had a child diagnosed with ADHD had the following results:

- Family members (not counting the patient with ADHD) had 60 percent more medical claims, and twice as many were treated for some type of psychiatric disorder.
- Direct annual medical care costs per family member were twice as high ($2,060 vs. $1,026).
- Indirect costs for disability and absenteeism in ADHD families were 61 percent higher.
- Patients with the diagnosis had 2.6 times more medical claims than non-ADHD patients.

The statistics are staggering, but you and your child can avoid being included in these numbers.

The Plan

I've created a step-by-step plan for dealing with your child's ADD. It is based on three approaches: audit, action, and assessment. Each chapter introduces a new step on the path, and each includes an *audit,* to help you clarify potential sources of your child's behavior; *action,* or activities that offer specific strategies of change that can be implemented immediately; and *assessments,* to help you evaluate whether the plan is working.

The chapters are organized so that important pathways can be charted and easily reviewed. Since every child is unique, any treatment plan needs to be specially fitted to the individual. In my experience most children benefit from the use of more than one approach. In the following chapters I will introduce you to the theories and practices found useful through clinical research and over thirty-five years of actual practice.

This book combines the best of what traditional and alternative medicine have to offer at this time. I am a scientist in my heart—a curious one admittedly, but I have made a serious effort to evaluate the efficacy of these approaches. I also take my responsibilities very seriously (Hippocrates: "First, do no harm") when I recommend the approaches that might be best for a child. I'll offer my advice and suggestions on methods that include drugs and medications, counseling and biofeedback, electromagnetic treatments, biocleansing, nutritional adjustments, strategies for sleep disturbances, neurotherapy, and self-development management. I will also touch on spirituality and examine how families can engage *their own* faith and beliefs in dealing with ADD.

Together, we will create an individualized assessment of the ADD symptoms for your child. Together, we will create a plan for treatment. I have researched these methods, and while some may appear to be unusual and nontraditional, they've all been used successfully and all are based on scientific methodology.

Family Healing

Throughout this book, I call upon the family to be part of the healing process, which will also include assistance from professional caregivers and the school system. Please note, however, that I make no promises that any one method will cure all of your child's symptoms. ADD is very complex, and I caution you to be patient as you try these approaches. It may take time to find a treatment or a combination of treatments that work for your child. A parent's impatience with treatment can be misinterpreted by the ADD child as a criticism. You don't want your child to fear that his parents have lost hope.

I confess to being very optimistic in treating ADD. But I have a good reason to think that each child's symptoms are treatable. I have seen what families can do when they rally around a child. The treatment path you follow on this journey to a better life for your ADD child may very well bring your family closer together than it has ever been. I've seen it happen many times. At some junctures the important challenges may be related not to the symptom resolutions of ADD, but to the personal or interpersonal growth of the family. If that is all that happens, that is enough, because that is what will endure.

The Healing Home

L ynda, at age ten, was the youngest of three sisters and enjoyed being the baby of the family. Her older siblings had
strong personalities. Judy, who was five years older, was a
star volleyball player; Lorri, three years older, excelled in academics,
particularly math. Being the youngest among high-achieving siblings had advantages and disadvantages. On the downside, many
of Lynda's teachers expected her to perform at the same level as
her sisters. They set the bar high for her, based on the sisters' performance, but Lynda had unique challenges.

She would sometimes solve difficult problems and complete
complex assignments, but then completely fail on other assignments that were no more difficult. Lynda also was easily distracted.
Her teachers complained that she talked to girlfriends rather than
listened in class. She often came home from school lamenting that
she didn't understand the homework assignments or the lessons of
the day.

Lynda's parents did not pressure her to get high grades, but
they assumed that she would have success in her areas of interest,
which were drama club and the debate team. But Lynda struggled
even there. Her parents had been conditioned to expect their
daughters to be self-motivated. They reacted to Lynda's lack of
success by accusing her of being spoiled and unmotivated. They
decided to fire up the parental engine to motivate her.

Lynda's dad, John, identified himself as a "Molder" type of parent because he had high expectations of his children and demanded that they live up to them. Not surprisingly for someone of this personality type, he was the CEO of a large department store. He conducted his business in a direct, no-nonsense manner. He was performance and results oriented at work and at home.

He told Lynda's mother that it was now time to directly engage Lynda about her responsibilities as a member of the family—before she got any older. Talks would begin on a daily basis, said John.

Lynda's mother, Gloria, had a parental style that complemented her husband's. She was more permissive and she was comfortable letting him play the family leader, although she was very effective as a behind-the-scenes power broker. Normally she remained passive while John dictated how the girls were to behave. His demands required adherence to a code of standards usually inappropriate to the generation in which Lynda and her sisters were growing up. Often, when John was not around, Gloria would help the girls find ways to do what they wanted without upsetting their father. In some ways she was acting more like an older daughter, conspiring to circumvent the strict rules of their demanding father.

Within this context Lynda lived out a highly personal internal war. Instead of adopting the social role her parents expected, she began to live out a private life, withdrawn from the public eye. She felt different from her sisters and other kids, and was not interested in much of what they talked about. Her inner world was one of chaos and confusion, and it was only due to her high intelligence that she was able to keep just enough focus to get by in school and in the other parts of her life. But school tasks were getting harder, and she knew that sooner or later she would be discovered. She was terrified of the day when the world would realize that she was mostly faking her way through, and she had a real fear that her family would abandon her when she was found out.

One of her teachers thought that Lynda was depressed and recommended that she see a counselor, but Lynda was afraid of taking off her mask. She claimed to be upset about the death of her dog and promised to do better. Lynda's mother had similar concerns about her at the time. She'd attended one of my presentations and she called me to ask if I would speak to her daughter.

When we met, Lynda was at the edge of panic. But after ten minutes or so, she began to feel safe. She asked me to commit to an ironclad promise never to tell *anybody* the story that she was going to confide to me. Later she released me from this promise in order to discuss the issue with her parents. We spoke for nearly three hours. She told me how her mind would seem to jump from one unconnected idea to the next, and how it took great effort to remain focused on any one thing for very long. She said that her mind would drift off during class and that when the bell rang at the end of a class period, it often seemed as though she'd been far away the entire time.

Lynda told me of losing her way when she walked or rode her bike to school because her thoughts would keep her from concentrating. She would forget the names of her girlfriends. She'd feel embarrassed when they talked about things she did not remember doing with them. In class, she was often frustrated. She might know the answer to a teacher's question but then forget both the question and the answer. She stopped participating in class as a result of her concentration problems.

In short, she thought—no, she *knew*—that she was going crazy, and she feared that it was only going to be a short time before some men with white coats came to take her away forever. Lynda's fears were very real to her. I tried to help her understand that she was not going wacky, but she was fragile. I arranged to give her some tests. The results showed that Lynda had concentration and memory problems consistent with attention deficit disorder. Although she was pleased to learn that she was not "nutso," she was still frightened, particularly about how her father would respond. He had screamed at her for forgetting the keys to the house, she said. What would he do now?

When I explained the problem to Lynda's parents, I was not prepared for their expressions of disappointment in her. It was as if they had just discovered that Lynda had lied and cheated on them.

They felt shamed by the diagnosis. They had no clue how to help her. Initially, it seemed they simply wanted to walk away and leave her to me for repair and salvage, like some damaged appliance.

Their disappointment and shame seemed out of proportion to my descriptions of Lynda's situation. Her case was not all that severe. But I've encountered similar reactions from the parents of children diagnosed with ADD.

Some parents grow emotionally distant when confronted with the ADD diagnosis for their children. They feel frustrated, and if they believe they cannot help, they withdraw. Then they will turn to a doctor, a psychologist, or someone else from outside—not as a consultant, but as a savior. Unless they reinvest in their child's future, the family's problems deepen.

Thankfully, Lynda's family avoided that fate. Lynda, John, and Gloria pulled together instead of falling apart. With some guidance and after reflection, they became open to working together as a team. They worked at communicating. They identified the best ways, based on their individual strengths and weaknesses, to deal collectively, as a family, with Lynda's challenges. Her parents accepted that she was different from her high-achieving sisters and that she was not a mere projection of their desires. Along the way, they learned to accept not only Lynda but each other, embracing strengths and weaknesses too.

The family found ways to help Lynda function much more effectively. Her acupuncture points were stimulated with sound, a treatment that has been found to be very effective (see Chapter Eleven). Her body was cleansed of lead, and she undertook a changed nutritional program. But the true healing was in the relationships that were at the very foundation of their family. That healing produced new and deeper understanding for them all. It was such a life-changing experience that each family member told me independently during the treatment process that Lynda's ADD diagnoses may well have been the best thing that happened to them.

The Challenge for Parents and Siblings

The treatment of an ADD child begins in the healing home—not at school, not at the psychologist's or doctor's office. If a child's parents and other family members do not invest their time, effort, and love in his treatment, there is very little doctors or teachers can do.

A child's response to ADD treatment reflects the family's dynamics. That is not to say a family must be perfect and without conflicts. There are problems in all families, whether they are the Osbournes or the Osmonds. There are no perfect families, and each generation has its own challenges. Your parents raised their children in a different world from the one your child is growing up in. To a great degree, you have to rely on your own instincts and judgment in raising your children. And in the same manner, every family finds its own way to cope with a child with ADD.

Sadly, some families do fall apart because they lack needed guidance and support. The demands of a child with ADD can expose flaws in a family's structure or they can provide a foundation for building an even stronger one.

Certainly, the problems of a child with attention deficit disorder can transform a household into a battlefield. How the parents respond to the disorder and the disruptive behavior will have a strong influence on the attitudes and behaviors of other children in the family. Siblings may be sympathetic to a brother or sister with ADD, but the disruption can seem like a problem that will never go away. They may also experience jealousy over the extra attention their needier sibling receives, and be quick to note and respond when they are held to a stricter code of behavior. They may sense that all kinds of allowances will be made for the sibling who acts out in ways that would never be tolerated of them.

On the other hand, the child with ADD must deal with always being *the sick one*. No one wants to be labeled a problem child or otherwise socially isolated. We all prefer to be distinguished by our talents and strengths rather than our flaws and weaknesses.

The parents must also cope. New mothers and fathers often joke that they wish each child came with a set of instructions because no two children have the same personalities, needs, or capabilities. Children with ADD present unique and substantial challenges. Frustration and fear will dog parents who feel they have no clue—no prior knowledge, background, or personal experience—how to handle such a child. It's not like treating the measles or mumps. You can't recall what your own mother did for you and follow the same remedies.

For most of us, the first step in handling a child's behavioral problem is to search our own experiences. (*If I had acted like that, I would have had extra chores for a week.*) But for most parents, ADD is a mystery outside their realm of experience. Often they feel guilt and anger because they don't know how to help or control their child on their own. That guilt and anger can cause turmoil in even the most loving families, which is one of the reasons why the divorce rate for parents of children with ADD is three times that of the general population.

Taking Control of the Healing Process

ADD affects the whole family. Too often, the impact is more destructive than positive (this is a fact that cannot be denied), but that does not have to be *your* family's reality. The decision you have to make before you turn another page is whether you are going to control and guide the healing process for your child. Your dedication and determination are essential. Without them, the information and guidance I'll provide are useless. But if you are willing to take responsibility for your child's future success and happiness—and that of your entire family—this book will equip you to do that.

You may not feel that you are ready for this challenge, and that is understandable. We rarely feel adequately prepared for the biggest challenges in our lives. I am asking only that you accept responsibility and commit to taking positive action. You cannot take a pass and expect your child's teachers, doctors, or anyone else to step up. As the parent you must be fully engaged in the treatment process. When parents have been committed and dedicated, I've seen incredible results that last a lifetime, not only for the child with ADD but for the entire family.

The Family Dynamics Audit

To plot the course of any journey you must first take note of your starting point. In determining how your family will best respond to the challenges you are facing, you need to begin with an understanding of your parenting style and your family's dynamics. The idea is not to make a judgment of what is right or wrong, or best or worst, in parenting styles. There are many family structures that work well. There will be no attempt to force a new parenting style on you or your family. The audit that follows is offered to help you gain an objective understanding of the underlying influences within your own home. Often parents tell me that they don't know what their style is, and that's understandable. They can easily recognize patterns in other families but they may need outside assistance in assessing their own. This audit can give you the tools you need to bring that outside perspective to your own life and situation.

Step One (for Parents Only)

From the following words (or more created by the family), each parent privately assesses his or her parenting strengths by circling the most descriptive (these perceptions might be reflections of your own self-image or of how the family has identified you in the past):

I.	II.	III.	IV.	V.	VI.
Assuring	Supportive	Judgmental	Mother hen	Needy	Stern
Patient	Watchful	Traditional	Surrendering	Dependent	Tense
Determined	Listener	Directive	Sympathetic	Manipulative	Self-absorbed
Helpful	Indirect	Expectation	Permissive	Limited	Director
Coach	Negotiator	Structured	Nonthreatening	Sick	Whimsical
Teacher	Equal	Impatient	Moral	Receiving	Funny
Lecturer	Partner	Ambitious	Accepting	Baffled	Dramatic

Step Two

In a family meeting, allow the children to decide which descriptions pertain best to each parent, using examples if possible. It might also be helpful for the children to voice how they react to the parent's trait or expression. Again, this is not about blaming anyone or criticizing anyone. The goal is to assess how a family functions so we can later determine the best approach to handling the needs of the child with ADD. Please note that there is no need for consensus or agreement for each description. This is simply an opportunity to communicate observations within the family.

Step Three

Determine which of the following parent types describes your style, based on at least four traits circled in one category. It is permissible and recommended to have your family help you judge between these six types for which best matches your parenting style, either in a group discussion or from a personal survey. There may be more than one style, since there are overlapping approaches, and it is possible to have as many as three at different times.

DESCRIPTIONS OF PARENTING STYLES

I. The Teacher. This style is based on a perception that the parent adopts the role of teacher of his or her children. This teaching includes specific values and philosophy, cultural attitudes (such as relationships between the sexes and other groups), as well as the proper ethics and manners for the accomplishment of goals. The parent maintains this role for life.

II. The Supporter. Most parents can be described as supportive, but this parenting type maintains the attitude that the child's destiny is beyond one's control. The parent sees himself or herself in the role of supporting the child as he develops his talents and abilities. The Supporter truly reveres the child and may offer advice on achievement strategies, but there are few or no expectations as to the final outcome of the child's direction.

III. The Molder. This type of parent has specific expectations and hopes regarding what the child will become and how he will behave. The parent may have formed career or cultural expectations for the child before the child was even born, and has determined the roles to be played by a child of the family.

IV. The Guide. This permissive type of parent feels a child should be free to grow and express her talents with minimum interference or control from the parent. The parent may employ punishment or guilt to motivate the child to maintain values and behave in acceptable ways, but mostly this parent plays a more passive role. The overriding concept is that if the parent helps the child develop strong values and moral guidelines, they will serve to guide her throughout life. The underlying concept is that control infringes on creativity and individuality, so this parent avoids overt controls in order to reduce the risk of rebellion, resentment, and anger from the child.

V. The Dependent. This parenting style effectively reverses the traditional role of parent and child. At an early age the child has to learn to serve the parent's needs. The child, then, becomes caretaker to the parent, who, for whatever reason— poor relationships, childhood issues, health problems—has a dependent personality.

VI. The Monarch. This type of parent covets center stage in the family. His or her needs are primary. The needs of every other family member are secondary. Often, this type of parent experiences dramatic mood swings that require constant adjustments from other family members to avoid conflict. Every day is a crisis for this parent, and every change creates turmoil because the parent feeds on being center stage.

Implications of Parenting Styles for ADD

Our parenting styles develop based on our temperament, personal experience, and education derived from schooling, readings, observations, and discussions with other adult parents. We often use our own parents as models, even if we disagreed with their parenting styles as children. What parent hasn't had the thought *My God, I sound just like my father/mother?*

Our parents are our primary role models, for better or worse. This tends to promote a parenting style lineage. Of course, our spouse's parenting style influences us too. It can reinforce, modify, or cancel out the influences from our own mothers and fathers and other sources.

Still, at any point in our lives as parents, we can learn new methods and approaches that help us change unhealthy or ineffective parenting patterns. The following information, then, may help you adjust your own parenting style so that you can be more effective in dealing with your child's ADD:

I. The Teacher. The strengths of this style offer some very good opportunities for the child to manage his or her ADD conditions. The Teacher parent will tend to view ADD as a challenge but not an insurmountable one. This optimistic and proactive approach can be a wonderful asset for the child.

The downside to the teaching parent's approach is that such parents may tend to form unrealistic expectations of the child. The best approach with an ADD child is to understand both her potential and her limitations without putting undue pressure on her to perform beyond her capabilities. I will offer more in-depth guidelines on educational strategies in Chapter Fifteen.

II. The Supporter. The Supporter parent tends to accept without qualification a child's strengths and weaknesses. That is a blessing when dealing with ADD children because it allows them to develop to the best of their abilities without being pressured to live up to parental expectations. In raising my three children, I was often struck by how they developed talents and interests that I'd never anticipated them developing. It has also struck me that if I'd pushed them into areas that I chose, I probably would have frustrated them and stifled their creativity. This is especially true in the case of children with ADD, who do not respond well to being pushed beyond their abilities or to being closely controlled.

Most children do inherit certain characteristics and traits from their parents, but each child is much more than the sum of her genetic parts. By acknowledging that children with special skills and limitations have special needs and unique goals, we can help them exceed their own expectations and even ours. This is not to say that parents cannot make demands or set goals for children with ADD, but the best approach is to encourage these children to look for opportunities within their grasp.

The limitations of this parenting style may be the willingness to accept the child's performance based on her motivation, rather than the parent's expectations. The ADD child needs more guidance than most.

III. The Molder. This demanding style of parenting has the advantage of providing a clear structure for development. This is especially important for children with ADD because they are often confused by more flexible boundaries. All children need boundaries and clearly defined expectations. Often they act out in inappropriate ways because no one has made the boundaries clear to them.

Yet there is danger in the Molder style because such parents may tend to have expectations that the child cannot fulfill. The problems of high expectations are compounded when a child has a diagnosis of ADD because he often learns in ways unfamiliar to his parents. Without a path that can be usable to the child, any goal appears unattainable. Too often we, as parents, forget to teach the steps and remember only the end results.

Most of the children I have worked with and assessed have expressed the emotional pain of not living up to their parents' expectations. There is a deep desire in every child to make his parents proud. But more troubling to me is that the children's despair is often justified by their parents' disappointment in them.

IV. The Guide. With this permissive parenting style the strength is the bond of loyalty between parent and child. A child with this type of parent often is blessed with the sense that whatever she does, the Guide parent will be there to offer forgiveness, sympathy, encouragement, and support. The downside is that children with Guide parents often act out because of the lack of enforced boundaries and guidelines. In some cases, such children may develop the attitude that they can do no wrong because the parent is so nonjudgmental.

While it is valuable for a child to feel unconditionally loved, this type of parent can place the child in a difficult position. Such parents abdicate too much control, particularly in the case of the child with ADD, who needs distinct guidelines. In my experience, Guide parents are afraid to discipline their children, especially one with ADD, because of their confusion between structure and punishment. Theirs is the child with ADD that everyone learns to dread because of the lack of boundaries.

V. The Dependent. Interestingly enough, children who grow up under this parenting style often learn how to give and nurture in their adult lives. They have relationship skills and, often, deeply held spiritual beliefs. Children with ADD who've been raised by a Dependent parent usually put the needs of others before their own.

Basically, the Dependent retreats from his or her responsibilities and forces the child to act in the role of parent, enacting a role reversal. For example, an ailing mother becomes dependent on her daughter for care. This may be merely convenient in the short term, but it can be harmful over the long term.

The parental pattern promotes the *sickness concept* in a child, in which symptoms serve as sources of power. In other words, attention can be directed to the one with disease, and ADD can become a basis for attention instead of a set of problems to overcome. If this dynamic continues unchecked, the child has no motivation to overcome the challenges of ADD and may even hold on to the condition as a source of power. This result is not invisible to siblings, who are also in need of power. The disastrous outcome is the continuance of the behavior into adulthood.

VI. The Monarch. The strengths of the Monarch parenting style lie in the command-and-control decision-making process. Often quick and decisive direction is vital in dealing with a child with ADD. The Monarch is decisive and generally not afraid to delegate or to put together a team when confronted with a problem, and that can be of great benefit to the child.

However, problems can arise when the Monarch parent is self-involved, which tends to be the case. The ADD child's needs are such that they often require a parent's full attention—and Monarch parents are often incapable of maintaining that sort of focus on anyone other than themselves. Interestingly, this type of parental style often occurs when one or both of the parents is also afflicted with ADD.

The benefits of this parenting style lie in two regions, correctness and concern for the child. If the parent is using his assertions with correct information, there can be a very favorable outcome because there is so much investment and focus, even if it is the parent who is making the decisions "for" the child. It reminds me of the story of the old man who "taught boys how to be men," in which he asserted responsibilities and courage. The boys who he taught had high praise for his teaching; however, if he had given them wrong information, it might have been disastrous, as it has been for many emotionally disturbed children. The second consideration is that the focus of concern needs to be the child and not the goals of the parent. Even very obsessive parents can be important when their child needs such a warrior for their needs.

Parenting the Child, Not the ADD

Hopefully, this exercise has provided you with some insight into your own leadership and parenting style. It is not meant as a critique or as an indictment of past behavior. The idea is to look inward and to be honest in your appraisal. Examine both your limitations and your strengths and then build on the strengths.

It is important for parents to develop and tap into supportive relationships, whether with friends, family, community resources, or spiritual beliefs. Although this book will provide you with techniques I believe in, you shouldn't rely solely on them. Don't let your relationships suffer because of the ADD challenge in your family. Do your best to stay in touch with your own support team.

One other cautionary note: be careful that you don't depersonalize the child with ADD. You are dealing with a disorder, but more important, you are protecting a child. That person may have ADD, but he is *not* ADD. Respect and love the person even as you take action to make his life better. There will be times when you will lose sight of the distinction between the person and the ADD. Anger, frustration, and irritation will get the best of you from time to time, but it will help you to deal with your child as he is rather than as what you think he should be.

Actions to Promote Healthy Family Patterns

A healing home is the secret to treating a child with ADD. I've seen miraculous and inspiring things happen when families rally around a child with the diagnosis. I've also seen terrible, traumatic examples of what can happen when family members run from the challenge. Although dealing with a family member with ADD can be daunting, it can also be a journey to enlightenment and to a deeper and more powerful family bond.

If you haven't done so already, take concrete steps now to assess your parenting style. Identify and document your strengths and limitations. Use the audit provided as a starting point. Begin to write down your own observations of your values and beliefs about yourself and your reactions to one another. Don't focus only on the child with ADD. Take a look at your whole family and at others who may be closely involved. Get the input of other family members so you have an honest understanding of yourself and your impact on your children and spouse. (You may feel that you behave consistently as a team player and Supporter, but everyone else may see you as authoritarian and a Monarch.) This action alone can set your family on a new course.

Second, have a family meeting and discuss the positive aspects of each family member.

- Each person takes a turn in the hot seat. That person becomes the focus of the family and cannot say anything until after his or her turn is over. The other members each express three *positive* perceptions of the person in the hot seat, with at least one example of each perception. Remember the perceptions must only be positive (no one learns from negative perceptions).
- After the full round is over for the first person in the hot seat, the person can respond to the perceptions in terms of how meaningful they were and how accurate they seemed.
- Another person takes the hot seat and another round is completed as before. This continues until everyone has been in the hot seat at least once.
- This exercise is intended to develop a sharing of perceptions so that everyone can learn from one another

and discuss their reactions without defensiveness and regression into anger and denial.

The third action you must take—this is truly an essential action—is to begin to select individuals to be part of your healing team. Find and identify persons from within the family circle, which can include nonblood relationships and trusted friends, who will be available for the following needs (one person can be identified for more than one need):

1. Someone with whom you can let down your defenses and show your vulnerabilities, your frustrations, and your disappointments.
2. Someone who can be trusted to understand the technology and medical information presented so that she can explain it to you when you don't understand or remember.
3. Someone who will provide inspiration for you regardless of how badly things seem to keep going.
4. Someone who will tell you the truth about yourself from an honest and nonnegative perspective.

This is your support team. From here on out it's up to you to let each person know how they can help and be sure that they will seriously attempt to fulfill the roles that you have assigned. Congratulations! You are on the threshold of a journey that will bring healing knowledge from sources of creativity and strength that you may never have known existed for you.

One of the most interesting families I worked with through the family dynamics process was the Robinsons. Of course, I cannot share the details of their encounter, but the outcome was impressive. The father was very defensive when he was on the hot seat because he sensed a loss of power, but I will never forget the tears that came when each member expressed how much his love and support had meant to them. Instead of the anger he had expected (due largely to the anger he felt for his own father), he discovered that his family truly loved him.

In fact, the expression of love appeared to be the main focus of the overall experience, which was sorely needed. As with many families, communication of love often becomes a low priority when each person is overwhelmed with confusion and low self-esteem. Family meetings focused on the positive can help families recognize their shared values and their strong connection to these values, which in turn can lead to the resolution of many issues.

Assess Your Family Interactions Every Day

ADD is a challenge to your family as a whole and to each of you individually. Each of you can be more loving and more loved. Attention deficit disorder can be managed. It can also bring your family members closer. The success of any therapy depends on the willingness of people to seek more productive behavior. The definition of *neurosis* is to keep doing the same things while expecting different results. Your child cannot expect better results if his parents keep doing the same things. All members of the family must be willing to change their behavior patterns so the outcome can be different. Every day you can assess your own actions and attitudes: Are you expressing your love of and confidence in your family members? Are you providing enough structure? Are you accepting when you are setting goals for the future? Are you getting the support you need?

Family patterns are fascinating to me, especially when confronting a crisis like ADD. Some families seem more naturally equipped to deal with the new demands, and others seem to falter. It is important to remember that your family can thrive. Family dynamics are not necessarily dependent on personalities and can be altered with greater support. Family patterns may be habitual (even if they are destructive) because they appear to be the only choice we know. Just as overcoming a medical crisis can make a person stronger, so the diagnosis of ADD can bring new life and better communication for everyone in the family.

THREE

Ending the Child's ADD Game

F rank's mother looked hopeless as she asked me, "Why can't I get him to do his homework? He just looks at it, and I explain it over and over again. But he never completes it."

"What usually happens?" I asked.

"Oh, I finally talk him through it all and he goes on about his business."

"So you end up doing the homework while he looks on? Is that what happens, Frank?" I directed my question to the twelve-year-old redhead.

Frank smiled and nodded, being careful not to explain his actions or motivations—because that was exactly what had been happening for the last four years, I later learned.

Frank and his mother were locked in a situation that is all too typical. The parent becomes so involved in taking responsibility for the homework that the child's need for power and manipulation exceeds the need for academic performance. And there is a good reason. Frank gains little if any satisfaction from his constant sense of failure, but a lot from the knowledge that he can use his mother's involvement to meet his own needs of power. A great deal of this child's motivation is based on the fact that he becomes very stressed at failure. There is a strong tendency to dispel the anxiety as soon as possible, which leads to impulsivity during the interaction with his mother. That makes the situation explosive, with highly emotional outbursts and anger.

I refer to this kind of behavior as *ADD games.* This term seems to me to describe the nature of the relationship that exists when one individual changes the implicit rules in order to gain power over the other. In our example, Frank's mother was operating on the assumed rule that her son's intention was to complete his homework if he had some extra help. However, Frank's goal was quite the opposite. He was using the opportunity to gain some level of self-esteem by manipulating his mother's need for his success into having her work for him. He was compensating for his lack of success in school performance and was finding a way to "win."

Games are natural for children, and for the most part, they are not indicative of psychopathology. These familiar tactics are not particularly unique to children with ADD, and some of them can seem like fun—delightful maneuvers. However, when a child meets with constant frustration, he will attempt to find some way not to be defeated. Parents, in their own desire to help and even to protect themselves, can become unsuspecting participants in a game.

One of the marks of ADD is the persistent failure of a child to conform to expectations, so it is highly likely that your child will be facing more failures than successes—and far more than the average kid does. Therefore, it is critical that you, as the parent, prepare for the probable stress and even depression that comes from these disappointments and find constructive avenues for your child to have success, in at least one arena of life. Otherwise, you can be sure that your child will find other ways of achieving some means of personal power, and these means may not be in the best interest of your child or the family.

Basic Human Needs

All people are driven by basic emotional needs, including the need for

- *survival*—wanting to exist
- *trust*—having security
- *autonomy*—having control
- *love*—feeling valued
- *effectiveness*—having a power for self and the world
- *curiosity*—the need to explore
- *identity*—having a crystallized self-concept
- *intimacy*—the ability to commit to others and receive support in return
- *contribution*—contributing to a greater good
- *self-esteem*—holding a sense of personal integrity and well-being
- *creativity*—expressing oneself and one's ideas
- *spirituality*—being part of something greater than the self

Our mental health depends on the degree to which we fulfill these needs. When someone's efforts to do so are thwarted by ADD or another circumstance, that individual may resort to destructive methods to get the desired rewards. A young woman who feels that she can't control other aspects of her life, for example, may fulfill her need to be in control by binge eating or by dieting in excess. A youth may take risks, such as driving too fast, trying to achieve a sense of mastery. These may be destructive behaviors, but they fulfill a basic need for self-determination.

Your child is no different from any other. We all want a sense of satisfaction and the ability to have our needs met. When we see little or no opportunity to achieve these goals, depression can set in. Consequently, we become desperate to have even a small bit of satisfaction, however destructive the means may be. Frank hollers back at his mother and causes her to feel guilty and even fearful of her child. Another parent might become enraged and react with harsh words, causing more frustration and stress. The end result is usually another slip in self-assurance and a deeper sense of pessimism.

Purposeful Behavior

Nearly all human behavior is purposeful even when it seems otherwise. Children and adults behave as they do for a reason, whether good or bad, consciously or unconsciously. We act the way we do because there is a payoff. A loud and boisterous child likely seeks the payoff of attention. A quiet and inactive child may prefer the payoff of solitude, or he may be avoiding people for some reason. If someone is chronically late, it is because there is a payoff derived from that. Someone who is constantly complaining of poor health has learned to seek whatever payoff that provides. These payoffs drive most human behavior.

The payoff of control and power over our lives is one of the strongest motivators of human behavior. Some behaviors meant to establish control may be constructive, while others may be destructive. If a boy sees his father get his way by being angry and hostile, he might adopt this method for getting his own way. A girl may see her mother assert control by feigning dependence or weakness and adopt the same behavior. Parents are the primary models for children learning to seek control and power.

ADD can be an obstacle for a child seeking to fulfill the basic need of identity or control, but children are highly adaptive, and some learn to use ADD to their advantage. If the child is attempting to gain a sense of identity by being the smartest kid in his class, ADD would thwart his effort, perhaps causing him to act out as a class clown or rebel. On the other hand, he may adapt by using the ADD diagnosis as a sort of badge of honor or as a license to act out even more.

How your child responds to a diagnosis of ADD determines how difficult or easy it will be for his basic needs and goals to be met. If the family is to find remedies and solutions to the ADD symptoms, you have to understand your child's behavior and the payoffs she seeks. If you can find the payoff, which is a psychological currency, then behavior can be channeled accordingly.

The Power of Illness

I was nine years old when I discovered that there is power in being needy. My friend Tom and I enjoyed being together but we didn't enjoy being in school. So the payoff we sought was to stay home together. Our mothers both worked, so if one of us got sick, the other was allowed to stay as caretaker so that neither mother would have to miss work. Tom and I figured that being sick was worth the payoff, so we arranged to get exposed to the mumps, measles, and chicken pox during that one school year. We were professional patients.

But then I came down with something that didn't pay off. It was highly contagious, which meant that Tom wasn't allowed to stay with me. In fact, none of my friends were even allowed to visit. It started with a high fever and pain in my legs. Our family doctor paid a visit—they did that in those olden days—and I heard him tell my mother that if I didn't improve quickly, he'd have to put me in an iron lung to help me breathe.

Things were definitely spiraling out of my control. Being confined to an iron lung without my pals was definitely not the payoff I wanted. Maybe there were health factors or powerful prayers in play that I wasn't aware of, but I do know that I decided that I no longer wanted to be sick. And the next day, I was up and at 'em. From that point forward, I rarely missed school because of illness, real or otherwise.

As debilitating and maddening as ADD can be, there are children who use it to achieve payoffs they desire just as my boyhood buddy and I used illness to get what we wanted. Have you ever looked closely at your own behavior to see what you do to achieve the payoffs you seek? In some cases, achieving a payoff becomes so important that individuals will undertake destructive behavior. The heroin addict puts his life in danger for the payoff of a narcotic high. The abused spouse stays with a violent husband because the payoff of the relationship—as dysfunctional as it is—is worth the pain to her. It usually takes intervention, or a crisis that finally makes the payoff no longer worthwhile, to break such destructive behavior patterns.

The Nature of Payoffs

It's not always easy to examine a behavior and then determine what the payoff is, particularly with children with ADD. Some payoffs are quite subtle. The rewards may be buried within a broader context. Some may be far beyond our conscious awareness. I worked with Jimmy, who was raised by an embittered father who felt that his intelligence and worthiness never led to the recognition he deserved. Jimmy seemed to take on his father's bitterness and lack of trust in the world. As his ADD symptoms began to affect his performance in school, Jimmy showed resentment to anyone who offered help. It puzzled his teachers that the boy appeared to take pride in failing grades.

When I talked to him, Jimmy told me that he did not want to do well in school because his teachers weren't capable of recognizing his intelligence anyway. By purposely doing poorly, he could claim control, fulfilling the basic human need of self-determination. I spent some time building trust and rapport with Jimmy. Then I worked to help him find a more positive way of fulfilling his need to feel respected and valued for his intelligence. I helped him recognize that his declining performance wasn't really giving him the payoff he wanted. "Is this attitude working for your own good, or is it just making the school assume more control over your life?" I asked him.

Children get the point quickly when the right questions are asked. They also respond well if you let them play a role in their own treatment. Together we planned a strategy in which Jimmy would *act* as if he was cooperating with the school's plan until the end of the year. This put him in a position of control. It was our little joke on the school when he began performing much better. I cannot say that he became a straight-A student, but he graduated with his class. Later, he became well known for his inventions.

This child learned to fulfill his needs, or get the payoffs he desired, through constructive behaviors that also helped him become a successful adult who made a positive contribution.

The Payoff Audit

The following audit lists possible games your ADD child may be playing to regain lost power and esteem. Review them carefully and note those that seem familiar.

Cover-up Game

Most children do not like being diagnosed with ADD. It is not something they take pride in. Most see it as a stigma. It is not at all uncommon for children to respond to the diagnosis, which was beyond their control, by manufacturing a crisis, or a whole series of them, as a distraction, restoring their need for control.

A child might stop doing his homework, grow abusive toward other family members, vandalize property, or shoplift. The payoff of controlling his destiny—even if it means punishment—can be extremely powerful for an ADD child who feels stigmatized by the diagnosis.

The Question: What cover-up payoffs might your child be using? (List them on a separate sheet of paper.)

The Rumpelstiltskin Game

For some children there is emotional relief in being labeled with ADD. They see it as preferable to being accused of laziness, insanity, or stupidity. This is what I call the Rumpelstiltskin syndrome. In the Grimm brothers' fairy tale, a little man helps a miller's daughter spin hay into gold in exchange for her firstborn son. According to their pact, the only way the miller's daughter can break the deal and keep her child is to discover the little man's real name. She cleverly does that, foiling his plan. For the miller's daughter, putting a name on the little man, who represents an evil force, saved the day.

The same holds true for some children plagued by the symptoms of ADD. Those symptoms are an evil that they can't understand. Why are they doing poorly in school? Why can't they seem to perform as well as other kids? It's not unusual for children to suffer depression and fear because they do not understand what is happening to them. They may have mysterious pains or nervous habits. It's not unusual for a child to say that he is worried he is going crazy. It doesn't help either that his teachers and parents may charge him with being lazy or unmotivated before the ADD symptoms are recognized.

When the diagnosis does come, then, it may be a relief regardless of how severe the case. At least now the child has a name for the evil that has overtaken him. Now the child—and those who care about him—can identify with a *real* problem that afflicts many others.

The game starts when the child and the family begin to hide behind the diagnosis as an excuse for all the problems. For example, I have heard so many individuals explain that they cannot compete for the softball team or complete their homework, that they miss appointments, and that they even lose their tempers because they have ADD. A diagnosis is no excuse but can become a blank check for any problems that come up if this game is allowed to blossom.

The Question: What are some names you have used to describe your child's condition? Have you taken comfort in the fact that the affliction—and not some character flaw—is responsible for his behavior? Have there been times when you have used the ADD label to cover up problems and excuse behavior? (List them on a separate sheet of paper.)

Joining-a-Group-as-a-Victim Game

The desire for acceptance is perhaps the most common emotional need. There is an abundance of emotional satisfaction that comes from the security of being a part of something larger than our individual selves—a marriage, a family, a social clique, a community organization, or a group of professional peers.

It should be no surprise, then, if your ADD child has acted out in search of an acceptance payoff. In every school where I have consulted there has been a losers' gang—kids who feel like outcasts. The glue that unites these individuals is the sense of being a victim. It's not unusual at all, particularly in the case of teens with ADD, for a young person to say that he feels like a loser because of his diagnosis or the symptoms he experiences.

Parents should pay attention to that kind of talk and to the actions that accompany it. Street gangs feed upon that sort of alienation among young people. Their recruiters understand basic human needs. "We're all losers here, but together we get respect," they'll say in recruiting members. In one school there was the Blue Club, whose members were all diagnosed with ADD, and they went so far as to wear blue shirts as uniforms. The teachers dreaded them because they refused to do any schoolwork—because they were "special"—and they were never suspended because the administrator was afraid of potential legal repercussions.

The Question: Has your child expressed feelings of alienation or rejection? Has he found an acceptance payoff outside the family with a group involved in antisocial, dangerous, or criminal activities? Examples of payoffs include

- acceptance of him- or herself as a disenfranchised person
- power base as a part of a group like him- or herself
- elitist separation from others as part of "the exclusive" group

- special attention because of the unique designation and focus
- increased freedoms or excuses for low performances
- identification with the victim role and the externalizing of responsibilities
- more validation for expressing hostility and creating power battles
- ways of avoiding goal achievement

The Power-of-Being-the-Victim Game

If you've ever watched children—or adults—squabble over the television's remote control, you've observed one of the basic truths of human existence. Control is power. That holds true whether in a family, on a sports team, or in a corporate setting.

Attention deficit disorder is an upsetting and serious diagnosis. A child diagnosed with ADD can potentially assume a high degree of power because of the magnitude of the diagnosis and the implications for the family. In this case, control means having the power to focus the family's attention in a particular direction. It also means having the power to direct the family toward meeting his needs.

This dynamic is certainly not limited to children with ADD. Many adult male patients have told me of feeling empowered after they'd had heart attacks or otherwise been removed from the work world because of illness. Their debilitating illness finally made them the focal point after years of working to pay the bills and caring for the needs of their children. Who is going to argue with a man who might die tomorrow? Certainly there are women who've done it too, trading pain for power by playing the victim and requiring the husband or children they once waited on to wait on them instead.

The child with ADD can dominate a family's daily life in many ways. He'll create emotional scenes or trigger crises with manipulative or high-risk behavior. Reckless acts (such as climbing on rooftops or up towers) and disruptive aggressive or irrational behavior are common methods used to divert attention from problems in school or other issues. Promiscuous behavior by girls is common when they want the power of attention.

Siblings of children with ADD frequently complain to me that the afflicted brother or sister gets all the attention. If one of the spouses is particularly focused on the ADD child, the other is likely to express feelings of being neglected or marginalized.

The Question: What power has come from your child's experiences with ADD? Examples of power sources include

- achieving special status in the family
- garnering more time and resources from the family and school
- motivations and problems being recognized above those of others
- receiving more attention, especially for positive events
- achieving equality in power with parents in terms of decision-making (daily agendas, special events, educational goals)
- gaining more assistance by expressing incompetence
- being allowed more negative expressions of self and others

These are examples to take into consideration as you go about identifying and writing down personal games. Think about the following: How is the diagnosis of ADD working for your child? What are the payoffs for her that are resulting from this diagnosis? Does the diagnosis provide a way of getting pleasure or emotional relief? Does the diagnosis protect your child by insulating her from others? Does your child reward herself with reckless behavior? As you think about these questions, don't get discouraged. Don't give up. If you do some honest probing, you will discover what your child is actually receiving as payoffs from the attitudes both of you hold.

Teaching Children to Get What They Need

Children with ADD need to learn how to meet their basic human needs—or receive payoffs—with productive, safe, and beneficial behavior, as opposed to the negative and often dangerous behavior they might typically adopt. Negative behaviors—such as bullying, arguing, disrupting in class, and more serious responses like drug or alcohol abuse, promiscuity, and criminal activity—are known as *illusionary* because they give the illusion of satisfying basic human needs but in fact do not. There are *positive* behaviors that offer the same payoffs as the illusionary behaviors. It can be helpful to show the ADD child that negative behaviors only appear to have a payoff.

Optimizing Options

Psychologists have found that children and teens who have chronic behavioral problems consistently lack the ability to identify legitimate ways to get the same payoffs that they derive from destructive activities. There is a simple test for measuring a person's tendency toward destructive thinking patterns. You begin a story but stop before the ending with the request that the person complete the story. The story might begin, "There was this boy named Johnny, and he always felt that he was different from everyone else because he was born with yellow eyes. He could have considered himself *special* because most people told him that his eyes were very mysterious and had a special intensity. But Johnny hated this feature about himself . . .

"Now complete the story."

The way the individual completes the story is rather predictive of how that person responds to challenges. The next step in the assessment is to ask the test subject to add a second ending; when that is concluded, another ending is requested; then another. A person with a healthy approach to life generally can come up with at least three different endings. This implies that the individual has the ability to find alternative behaviors to deal with challenges and stressful situations. Psychologists call this *cognitive flexibility.*

Children and adults who have trouble following the rules, whether at home, in school, or in society, have difficulty coming up with more than one ending. These individuals have difficulty finding socially acceptable ways to get the payoffs they want. Your job as the parent of an ADD child—or any child, for that matter—is to help the youngster learn to identify multiple acceptable options that meet his needs.

The I-OPT Approach

In my clinical practice and teaching, I have found that children can quickly learn to choose alternative behaviors with a method I call the I-OPT approach. The four steps that give this method its name are

1. **I**llusionary behavior
2. **O**bjective feeling, or payoff, sought
3. **P**ossible alternatives
4. **T**rial

Suppose your ADD child is angry and resentful toward a teacher. The anger and resentment qualify as *illusionary behavior* because they are not helping Johnny get the payoff he wants in an acceptable manner.

The first step in the I-OPT method of treatment for this negative behavior is to describe the illusionary behavior: "Johnny, you seem to be very angry with your teacher. Can you help me understand why you feel that way?" Johnny might answer, "Ms. Smith makes me so angry because she expects me to do all those math problems, and it takes me forever. She is so unfair."

If children have few coping skills (not many do), they usually react to stress and threat in one of two proactive ways: fight or flight. In the first way, they try to escape these situations by avoiding, denying, or running away—hence the word *flight.* In the second type, they become angry, stubborn, and hostile—hence the term *fight.*

The next step is to inquire about the *objective feeling*—the payoff—the child really seeks. "OK, Johnny, let's just pretend for a minute that you've just gotten really angry at the teacher. When you get to this point, how does it make you feel?"

Johnny might say, "I would feel good because I would get rid of my frustration and she would understand how I feel."

The next step is to have the child consider *possible alternatives* that would give him the desired objective feeling. For example, "OK, Johnny, so you want to feel two ways. You want to feel less frustrated and you want to feel that Ms. Smith understands you better. Besides blowing up, can you think of any other ways you could behave, and feel those things?"

Johnny gives some thought to the question. "Well, I could write her a letter and tell her, or I could just tell her how I feel."

You can help the child find more possibilities. One idea parents can teach their children over time is to take the focus off blaming others and put the focus on their own efforts. Johnny's mother introduced the idea. She explained, "Maybe you could try something called *focus techniques,* which they teach in martial arts, to help you use all your powers of concentration. That way you won't have to worry about anyone but yourself. It will put you in control of your life. Doesn't that sound better than being angry all the time?"

Johnny liked the notion that these techniques were called martial arts, because he had seen these concepts acted in movies. I taught him that the first step in these approaches was to remove his emotions from the situation in order for him to focus all his intentions on strategies. He grasped an immediate understanding after some rehearsals with various scenarios, such as a bully threatening him or a person calling him names. (Youngsters are usually quicker to learn this principle than adults because youngsters' worlds are simpler.)

Once Johnny had mastered the concept, we rehearsed focusing techniques that would involve a teacher model. The next day I phoned his teacher and explained our plan to have Johnny practice this approach with her, and I also explained that Ms. Smith would be playing her part as "practice" for that day. Ms. Smith was great in her understanding; and with full knowledge that the first *trial* would be a practice run, they had an encounter the next day.

Johnny was excited in his first practice run with the teacher (thanks in great part to the teacher's reinforcement), and he continued to "practice" his focusing techniques, thus becoming a teacher to other students.

Not all dialogues with ADD children go as smoothly as that, but you'd be surprised how many actually do. This is a solution-based approach to destructive behavior. In summary:

- **I**—Consider the *illusionary behavior* without critique and as a method the child has chosen to achieve legitimate emotional needs.
- **O**—Consider the *objective feelings,* the payoff, the child seeks.
- **P**—Consider *possible alternative options* that would achieve the same payoff.
- **T**—*Try* them out.

As examples, some of the most frequent behaviors, feelings, and alternatives I have observed for children with ADD are listed below.

Illusionary Behavior	Payoff	Behavioral Alternatives
Lying	Self-esteem	Achieving success through physical challenges
Passive aggression	Power	Controlling internal dialogue and learning techniques of positive self-talk
Drug abuse	Independence	Learning altered states of consciousness
Bullying	Attention	Assuming responsibility for others (for example, as a traffic supervisor)

Assess Your Child's Evolving Behavior Patterns Through Trials

Most people react automatically to stress, and even with time, some irrational behaviors cannot be explained when examined. The first step is to monitor those automatic responses to discover what payoff the individual derives from the behavior. Once the payoff is determined, other destructive behavioral patterns can be recognized. The most difficult step in treating ADD is to get the child to try new behaviors offering the same or better payoffs.

Jane seemed like the meanest girl in school although she was only ten years old. If someone made a comment about what Jane did or did not do, she would immediately start degrading that person. When I talked to Jane about this response, she explained that she anticipated that people would not like her, and would often begin humiliating them even before they had a chance to speak.

In an inquisitive approach, I asked her if that helped her feel better about herself. It seemed to me that, in her own mind, she was doing the work for those who might criticize her, and was rebuffing those who wanted to befriend her. I was frank with her— I couldn't see that she was going to find what she wanted by this reaction, and I was concerned for her.

Jane listened and did not respond immediately. She finally whispered, as if it was a secret, that she was afraid of people hurting her, and if she was tough, no one would get the chance. I agreed that she was tough, but what did she really want, and what could she do to get it? Being a pretty bright girl whose only limitation appeared to be ADD symptoms, she asked if I had any suggestions for how she could act if she wanted people to be nice to her.

We discussed several options, including treating others the way we wanted to be treated ourselves and making positive comments to others first, to take control of the situation in the beginning of an interaction. Jane liked the second option best since she knew how to take control from a negative perspective. For a ten-year-old girl she was very clever and exercised her payoff games well.

In working with children of all ages with ADD, I tell them that they will be doing things that they haven't done before and that they may feel uncomfortable and frustrated initially. That is to be expected as it is human nature to prefer the old ways of doing things even when the results you've been getting aren't satisfactory.

The attitude of parents in this process is important because the child with ADD will pick up on their demeanor. Parents need to be *willing spirits* so the ADD child will be willing to try new things and abandon the old ways. Change can be stressful, but the exercises I've designed will bring change for the better.

Assess Your Child's ADD Games and Identify Replacement Strategies

Now it is time to compile a list of the inappropriate, out-of-control, victim-talk activities and behaviors you have observed from your child. Sit down with your child and go through the I-OPT approach. Write down alternative behaviors to meet her emotional needs. (Writing things down helps to drive home the need for doing them.) Then consistently act on them when you're confronted by cues.

A child's impulsive behavior is usually a reflexive response to anxiety, an attempt to stop panic. It is important to manage the impulsive behavior during the treatment process because children with ADD can quickly backslide into destructive routines. That is why you need a strategy worked out in advance. When your child is seeking a certain payoff, such as reduction of stress, the negative behaviors that have become automatic and impulsive can make it difficult for her to practice more positive approaches.

First, *audit* your child's day in order to figure out when moments of high stress and low self-esteem are most likely to hit. That way, you're in a better position to avoid them by changing your child's routine or environment. Second, *plan very carefully* what you are going to do at those moments when your child has the urge to overreact to little issues. Relax and anticipate the power-seeking behaviors with at least two approaches to distract or quell the stress-producing circumstances.

The Challenge of Changing One's Response Styles

Children diagnosed with ADD have an underlying fear of losing control of their lives. Many parents also have tremendous fear that their children's development will be stunted and they will never reach their potential. Bitterness and resentment often build in families because there is a sense of lost opportunity and of being cheated. Family members may resent others who are more fortunate.

Joey, a seven-year-old, demonstrated all of these responses after he was diagnosed with ADD. It turned out that the "disorder" part of his attention deficit disorder was not that problematic. His memory was the only cognitive function affected; it could be argued that Joey's anxiety about "being different" was the chief factor hindering his performance on various tests. His initial diagnosis was autism. It was based on his bizarre behavior, including an intense aversion to displays of affection made toward him. When I first saw this troubled child, he was holding his legs tightly to his chest. He resembled a little ball rolled up on the chair.

He wouldn't speak and he shrank from my touch. When I put my hand on his shoulder, he jerked away as if I had pinched him. Rather than press him, I sat down with my guitar and began picking a few chords. After a while I told him a story about a wolf that had a diagnosis of ADD. The wolf had to take a long journey through the feelings of anger and secret despair. As I told the story Joey began to listen, not to my sloppy guitar playing, but to the story. I stopped halfway through the story and kept strumming that guitar, and waited. Finally Joey asked, "What happened to the wolf?"

Still focusing on my music, I said in my exaggerated Texas drawl, "I don't remember exactly. How do you think he ended up?

I imagine he had some rough times, but this wolf is a hero. Remember that when you finish the story."

Joey finished the story, although it took four weeks, and his wolf *was* a hero. The thing Joey's wolf was so mad about was that he desperately wanted to become a musician and have a band. His father was a musician, until he was killed in a train crash, and the wolf still had his saxophone. But he would never be able to play the horn or anything else because he was retarded.

When I corrected the perception that ADD was mental retardation and said that the wolf could be a musician just like his father if he worked hard at it, the story took a different turn. We talked about the reaction of anger and the feelings of being out of control that come with the loss of dreams. We found better responses so that Joey could develop better relationships, and he developed skills he knew he would need for success. I gave him a statue of a wolf when we finished what we had to do.

One of the key decisions a person has to make in order to be successful is to accept what can and cannot be controlled. Regardless of what physical obstacles your child faces, there are always opportunities to satisfy emotional needs. Some of these options eventually have destructive results, such as social isolation, more severe physical problems, or legal action. You have to ask yourself what options you have and what steps you are willing to take. You can choose to become bitter and create more limitations than you have, or you can learn and grow from the situation.

Attention deficit disorder is a great challenge. But every person faces challenges. Your child's challenge—your entire family's challenge—is ADD, but as with any challenge, this one can make your child and your family stronger, wiser, and more resilient. The choice is yours and your child's to make.

FOUR

Taking Charge of the Diagnosis and Labels

One of the most damaging side effects of ADD in young people is that their parents come to see them as defined by their symptoms rather than as the unique and worthy individuals they truly are. This distortion is tragic for both child and parent. The restricted view of the child can limit not only the child's view of himself but also the contribution the child can make to the family and the world.

What we *think* we know about ADD and our child often prevents us from learning what we *should* know. To be blind to our own ignorance is a common human failing. I happen to know someone who offers a good example of that. Someone very close to me. Me, in fact.

I was raised in west Texas, where football is a second religion. My early life was dedicated to mastery of the left tackle position. I earned a football scholarship and even considered playing at the professional level before turning to coaching at a public school. By every measure of success, I was a failure as a football coach. My team lost every game—for three straight years. Oddly enough, during those same three years, I had a great deal of success coaching two sports that I'd never been much good at myself—basketball and track. My basketball and track teams had winning records, and two of my pole-vaulters became state champions.

I eventually figured out that I had more success in the two unfamiliar sports because, in contrast to football, I hadn't assumed I knew all there was to know about them. In football I took a lot for granted and I expected my players to perform at my level. When they didn't, I immediately labeled them failures. But in basketball and track, I was a great cheerleader. I had no preconceived expectations of what a player could achieve. I rejoiced at each success. I hadn't projected my own beliefs and experiences onto my basketball players and track team members. Instead, I looked into their hearts and learned what drove and inspired them.

Too often, parents of children with ADD are blinded by their supposed knowledge of their child's symptoms just as I was blinded by my knowledge of football. Thinking I knew it all, I felt I had nothing to learn. As a result, I never developed true knowledge. Whether you are a football coach or a parent, it takes humility to help others achieve superior performance. To help your child find himself, you have to set aside what you think you know about your child and start anew.

Your child is an autonomous human being whose ability to rise above his disabilities depends, to a great extent, on how you perceive your child's gifts and potential. How we perceive our children has a tremendous effect on how they see themselves.

The Case That Should Never Happen

Jesse was one of the brightest and most popular kids in my high school. He was president of the student council, witty, and clever. He seemed to be one of those golden teenagers. But Jesse was really a very good actor. He played the role of a happy and outgoing teen. He took great care to always be upbeat and outgoing in school because he didn't want anyone to see the emotional turmoil going on inside.

For years, Jesse believed in himself. He had trusted that he was every bit as popular and successful as he seemed. But then he overheard his mother talking with a friend on the telephone. He was at a highly impressionable age. Her negative depiction of him destroyed his self-confidence and his view of his own potential.

He was listening to his mother talk to the friend on the phone when she said, "I would have a good life if it wasn't for Jesse. I could sell this house and go to Dallas for a good job. I could start over, but I have this kid I have to raise. He's dragging me down, like some kind of parasite, and I can't really live my own life because of him."

Those hurtful words changed Jesse's life. He'd done so well in school. He was so well liked by his peers. Yet his own mother considered him an annoying burden.

The schism within Jesse became obvious four years after high school graduation as he sat in jail with a serious drug habit, facing charges for driving while under the influence. Directed to rehabilitation, he finally found himself unraveling his social façade and facing the deep wounds of his mother's message. The good news is that he recognized that he could not keep up his destructive self-dialogue and have a life. When I ran into him ten years ago he was the CEO of his own computer consultation firm, and it looked like he had grown into himself.

Each of us begins life dependent upon someone else. Our self-perceptions are very much a reflection of how our parents see us—or at least how they say they see us. You cannot underestimate how important it is to your children that you believe in them and their potential. Even when they are acting out and rebelling and failing, they need to know that you can look into their hearts and have hope for them.

The Developmental Snowball

Children generally do not have a well-formed sense of self, so they tend to place a higher value on how others describe them. And while they occasionally rebel or test authority, they instinctively want to submit to authority because it gives them a sense of security. It makes them feel protected in a world that they do not fully understand. I have yet to meet the parents who are perfectly consistent and totally wise in all the aspects of child rearing. (I include myself in that assessment—but not my wife, of course.) As

Saint Luke writes in the Bible, even Jesus Christ was neglected at one point in his life. His parents took him to the temple and lost him for three days. The child Jesus was surprised at his parents' distress when they found him, and Mary said: "Son, your father and I have been searching for you in sorrow." After all, he was only engaged in high discourse with a group of holy men.

Joseph and Mary did not mean to undermine their son's self-confidence by expressing concern that he might be in danger on his own at that age. I'm certain that Jesse's mother had good intentions too. But her words had a powerful effect on his developing self-image.

As hard as we try to protect them, children experience failure and frustration as they grow. Their self-concept seems to change or shift with each passing day. While school yard slights and other childhood insults probably won't have a long-term impact on the development of a child's self-image, the judgments and evaluations of authority figures often weigh heavily and for longer periods.

Labels of Destruction

As children grow and mature, they search for their identities. This manifests itself clearly in junior high when kids begin to identify each other with labels such as *popular, jocks, preps, brains, geeks,* and *skaters.* The names they choose for themselves are early indicators of their evolving self-awareness.

The names we receive at birth are our first labels, and the ones that stick for a lifetime—except for Puff Daddy (aka P. Diddy), Prince, and a few other notable exceptions. The meaning you attach to your name can affect how you feel about yourself. If a boy is named after an alcoholic uncle, he may feel that he has to prove himself by being an achiever, or he may feel that he'll never live down that association. If a girl is named after a beauty queen, she may either incorporate or reject the behavior that she associates with that particular image.

In many cultures, newborn children are given a generic name, such as *Firstborn* or *Male Number One,* until they are old enough to decide what they want to be called. We would certainly gain some information about a child's self-concept if we adopted this tradition. The chosen name could be quite revealing, and would provide valid clues to the child's self-concept. I've received interesting responses when I've asked children in our culture, "If you could, what name would you choose for yourself?"

Sometimes the labels children accept or place on themselves become so much a part of their self-image that they affect the children's inner dialogue and, in many cases, their behavior over a lifetime. I had a friend who was known as Beanpole by his grade school classmates. That nickname became such an ingrained part of his self-image that he still thought of himself as Beanpole at his thirtieth class reunion, even though he never grew beyond average height. Interestingly, he still walks in the manner of a self-consciously tall and skinny boy—with his shoulders slumped forward awkwardly—a strong indicator that Beanpole is more than a nickname for him.

I can understand his behavior because for the first seven years of my life, I was called Shorty. I adopted a little man's edgy attitude and never lost it even when I was playing college football as a lineman at six two and 250 pounds. I played with the attitude that my opponents were bigger and stronger, so I had to be faster and smarter. In this case, my somewhat skewed self-image worked in my favor because I never took it for granted that my sheer bulk would give me an edge.

Yet labels are always restrictive, even if they are semantically positive. Even being known as *beautiful* restricts a person. An acknowledged beauty will tell you that she feels pressured to always live up to that image. To a greater degree, many diagnostic labels can be extremely limiting. They can make limitations seem insurmountable even when they are not. Children, in particular, may feel that once they've been labeled by an adult authority figure they'll never shed the label or the behavior associated with it.

The ADD Label

Children and adults associate a wide variety of images and feelings with the diagnosis of attention deficit disorder. It might surprise you to know that some contradict others. I've had parents and children say they were relieved. Others have said they felt restricted. Still others have said that the ADD diagnosis gave them a sense of having safe boundaries established, although there were those who said they viewed ADD as an excuse.

Relief is a very common feeling associated with the ADD diagnosis. For many people it helps to have an explanation for the frustrating behavioral symptoms that have been disrupting their lives. Parents often say, "If there is a name for it, there must be a cure for it." And children with the ADD diagnosis often remark, "Well, now at least I know I'm not crazy." For families, the diagnosis can mean an end to blaming and the beginning of treatment.

For some, labels such as ADD are seen as providing a welcome clarity. Finally they can define their child's success or failure within the accepted ranges for the disorder. If the parents understand that ADD children have short attention spans, they can accept without frustration or guilt that their ADD child won't be able to focus as long as other children. The downside is that a parent or child may decide that the ADD diagnosis is a convenient excuse for accepting limits and then resist treatment efforts as useless.

I call this the "lost keys" syndrome. Once you find your car keys, you stop looking for them. If you are searching for the reason your child can't master basic math, you might be tempted to stop searching once he is diagnosed with ADD. If the child hears, "You are disabled and you will always have trouble in math," he may give up too. The child can legitimately ask why he should continue trying to learn math if his disability prevents him from ever mastering it. But the parent, teacher, or counselor can legitimately respond, "You can improve your skills well beyond what they are now"—by finding new ways to learn that take into account the impact of ADD on traditional learning processes.

Labels can also distort a child's view of the world. A child labeled as ADD might tend to see everyone else as smarter or more worthy. It's understandable, but it is also a distortion. ADD is a limitation, but so is poor eyesight or dyslexia. Both can be overcome and neither limits true intelligence. Even if a teacher tells a child that, he may refuse to believe it because other children seem to have an easier time with their studies. Some children may take on a victim's mentality or develop anger instead of accepting the challenge of treatment.

Sadly, the damage we do to ourselves with these imprecise labels can outweigh the cognitive problems caused by the affliction itself. Human beings are capable of overcoming extraordinary challenges. We scale mountains, we explore the bottom of the ocean, we've walked on the moon. The most serious limitations many have are those they place on themselves unnecessarily.

Auditing for Labels

For every individual who has accepted false limitations because of a label, there are ten who've gone on to achieve wonderful things. I've known hundreds of individuals who accepted the ADD label and then defied any limitations associated with it. They've gone on to full, rich, and authentic lives. They are courageous warriors who eagerly take on life's challenges. They chart their own destinies in spite of the labels put upon them.

When I begin working with a child with an ADD diagnosis, I find it useful to assess her perceptions of the disorder and its symptoms. The audit that follows is a tool that can help you identify your child's self-perception and some of the restrictions that may have resulted from the label of attention deficit disorder.

These questions have open-ended responses. Encourage your child to write down the answers or have your child dictate them to you. Save them, because we'll refer to them for a later comparison. Honest responses will benefit your child the most. Approach this as a learning experience that will help your child break free of boundaries and limitations.

Ask your child:

1. If you had to describe yourself as an animal, what animal would you choose? Why did you choose it?
2. Describe three strengths of your animal.
3. If you had to describe yourself as a vehicle, such as a car or airplane, what would it be?
4. Name three characteristics of that vehicle.
5. Select a heroic figure that you identify with, such as a comic book hero like Spider-Man or a historic figure like Eleanor Roosevelt.
6. Come up with three characteristics of that hero that you would like to have.
7. Has anyone in the family or a friend ever called you something or described you in some way that has made you feel different about yourself, either in a good way or a bad way? Write down what they said.
8. List five characteristics that *you* feel you have. Include attention deficit disorder if you've been told you have it—and if you agree that you have it.

Note: The parent should now compare the labels that the child mentioned in 8 with those mentioned in 1 (animals), 3 (vehicles), 5 (heroes) and 7 (family labels). How are they the same or different? List them.

9. Have you observed how friends, family members, or others have labeled themselves? Do you see any ways in which those labels have limited them? (Examples: "I am just a kid. I am just an idiot. I am just an eighth-grade student.") List some.
10. Do you recall any examples of labels such as ADD that have affected your behavior or attitudes? List them with explanations of how you have been affected.

This audit can also aid in broadening the self-concepts of the whole family. Remember that labels like *mother of an ADD child* and *sibling of an ADD child* can be restrictive too.

Consider all the adjectives and descriptions you or your child have used anywhere in the above exercise, and circle them. Compare the ones that are associated with ADD or other limiting labels. Determine the limitations imposed upon yourself or your child by these labels. Most important, which labels does your child recognize as important and want to retain, and which ones does she wish to release? Start a list here. Feel free to come back and add to this list as you read further.

Action Plan to Break the Bonds of Self-restriction

There are experts who understand diseases, works of art, and mechanical processes, but it is difficult to find a person who claims to truly know him- or herself. It doesn't help that modern consumer marketing creates labels and then does its best to channel people of all ages into marketing categories. They do this in an attempt to convince us that we need to purchase certain consumer goods and brands. Those labels are derived from the popular culture, and we are almost powerless to stop their insidious intrusion into our daily lives.

The point for parents of a child with ADD to understand is that there are multiple forces at work that affect their child's attempt to forge an identity. Recognize that your child may buy into any one of those influences, consciously or unconsciously, and that her behavior will reflect that.

Encourage your child by recognizing her assets and strengths. Play the cheerleader for your child so that she learns to recognize her value and potential. The greatest power comes from within, but parents instill that power—they fuel it by helping a child build a strong foundation of security and confidence.

Parents should never mislead a child or give a child false information, but it is certainly better to follow the advice of the old tune and accentuate the positive rather than dwell on the negative.

A child who is shorter than his classmates and not likely to ever be more than average height certainly should be encouraged to look beyond height as a measure of his worth. In the same manner, once your child has been diagnosed with attention deficit disorder, you should stress that thousands of men and women who share the symptoms have achieved success in their lives.

If you want your child to be successful, you have to help him find the tools to create his own success over a lifetime. You can't create it for him. You can only prepare him for success by helping him learn how to learn in the most effective manner. Some people learn best by trial and error, some by rote memory, others by rational reasoning.

I am always inspired when I see the innovative methods devised by successful people to overcome their limitations. Texas had a governor in recent years who had such a reading problem that he had all of his notes written on large cards with broad black one-inch-high letters. A well-known opera singer could not read the words on the score and had to memorize each note and word by listening to her coach repeat them. One very wealthy businessman still does not know the order of the alphabet.

I have observed CEOs of major organizations develop specific strategies, such as acupuncture, massage, and music, to prepare for important staff and board meetings. Professional athletes use rituals and creative imagery to prepare for each event—to remove specific obstacles in their thinking or focus to ensure success and high achievement.

A Three-Step Action Plan to Achieve a Goal

We have heard of twelve-step, seven-step, and even five-step action plans. It's time to step up with the three-step plan. I want your child to step faster than others. My mother used to say, "Inspiration without perspiration makes you a fan, not a player." So I'm putting your child to work so he can get in the game too.

STEP ONE: IDENTIFY A GOAL

Labeling usually occurs when we confront a challenge en route to a goal. The operative word is *a* goal—not *many* goals or *all* the goals for your child's whole life. For this exercise, the *entire* family must participate. Your child with ADD shouldn't be made to feel like the family project. If everyone participates, then everyone can gain empathy for the demands of the exercise. More important, participation shows that this is as much about family unity as it is about the ADD child.

Call a family a meeting to define one goal for this exercise. Some examples:

- Read a book, one chapter per day. (This helps extend attention span and develop good study habits.)
- Memorize a poem, book passage, speech in a play, or short story. (This helps develop memory skills.)
- Learn to sing a song with all the verses. (Believe it or not, this can help stimulate the brain as well as induce healthy breathing patterns.)
- Dig a ditch or take a ten-mile hike. (The physical act of performing even a monotonous task for an extended time stimulates the brain to pace itself.)

STEP TWO: IDENTIFY INNER DIALOGUE THAT LIMITS YOUR ABILITY TO PURSUE GOALS

As Yoda might say: *This is inner homework, Jedi trainee.*

Your child might fight it, but it is important to show him how his inner thoughts can be reprogrammed for more positive results. After you have identified the limiting inner dialogue, write down some healthy alternatives. Talk to your child about the importance of finding positive options both for his inner dialogue and for his actions.

What follows is an example from the family workbook of one

of my patients, named Bobby, containing family members' thoughts on a goal—digging a ditch in the backyard:

Thoughts	Alternative Healthy Thoughts
Bobby's Thoughts: *This is dumb.*	*I am just scared of doing something else stupid, but this might help me improve my abilities to focus on a task.*
Father's Thoughts: *I don't want to dig another ditch. I did enough of that in the army.*	*This might help my relationship with Bobby.*
Mother's Thoughts: *This is his problem, not mine.*	*I am kind of proud of what I have done, and it does help the garden.*
Younger Sister's Thoughts: *Not another thing to do for my big brother.*	*I can see that my family would help if I needed it. I like my family better.*

STEP THREE: ASSESS YOUR CHILD'S EXPERIENCE

Step three is an ongoing process that requires that your child look within himself in the context of the experiences. How does your child feel about his self-concept? Did the exercise lead to any changes in the family's perceptions of themselves?

Bobby's family experiences:

1. Bobby: *I learned that it feels good to do something physical once in a while, and dumb as it seems, you can at least see you have done something.*
2. Bobby: *It was strange that once I got into it, I could think better after digging for a while. I got some pretty good ideas while I was working.*
3. Bobby's father: *I did not like digging, but I liked the activity with my family. We had some fun.*
4. Bobby's mother: *I liked getting my hands in the dirt, and for the first time we were doing something together.*

5. Bobby's sister: *I thought it was cool, and I could see how this was more fun than I thought it was going to be.*

It is helpful to discuss what positive behaviors or attitude changes became visible to the group. These can be valuable for validation, especially since someone with ADD rarely gets positive support. Some of Bobby's family's thoughts about each:

1. Bobby: *I saw my family trying to help me instead of preaching at me.*
2. Bobby's father: *I saw Bobby want to give up a time or two, but he kept at it. I was proud of him.*
3. Bobby's mother: *Bobby worked hard, and he tried. That is all that I asked—that he would try.*
4. Bobby's sister: *I was surprised that Bobby did it, and he seemed to appreciate me pitching in. That made me feel good. So I appreciated him back.*

The critical accomplishment is not that your child digs a good ditch or likes the book, but that he recognizes that there is a process involved in *doing instead of stagnating.*

A Special Note About Failure

The major complaint I hear from kids, especially teenagers, with ADD is that everyone focuses on the failures, and they already know about the failures. The worst things a parent can say to a kid who screwed up is: "Look at what damage you have done. Do you see what you have done? You have wrecked your mother's car." Of course he sees what he has done. He desperately needs you to tell him what to do next. He is a child, after all.

Instead of waiting for the next teacher visit or counseling session, begin working now with your child on the three-step action plan. Choose one activity and focus on how it feels.

Keep Moving Ahead

Just as children dream up monsters under the bed where only dust bunnies dwell, the fears we create through inner dialogue are almost always worse than the true challenges we face. I want your child to be the hero of her life. And I want you and her other family members to be the cheerleaders. In facing challenges and achieving goals—even small ones—your child will begin to escape the limitations of the ADD diagnosis.

This, now, is your quest. Use this opportunity. Don't run from it. Help your child find the path that carries her above and beyond this challenge.

My high school football coach used to say, "Always be moving in a positive direction. Even if you are pushed back a time or two, always move toward the goal, even if it's an inch at a time." This advice may be applied to my plan as well. A diagnosis of ADD can stall a family's progress. That is understandable. It is important, then, to get moving as soon as possible in a positive direction, even if the goals seem simple.

FIVE

Taking Control
of the Medication Madness

arry was seven years old when his parents, Mark and Judy Williams, were first called to the school by the social worker because he was not performing to the established academic standard. This meeting became the first of many in which the school authorities continued to recruit Larry's parents into discipline strategies that they hoped would teach him the value of cooperative behavior. The diagnosis of attention deficit disorder was mentioned, but the problems seemed to relate to the behavioral difficulties he was having rather than a medical issue.

One morning in March, the social worker said that the school would require Larry to be evaluated by a medical doctor for a drug called Ritalin that could counter the "disease" called ADD. She went on to say that refusing to take Larry to this doctor might provoke a charge of child neglect by the Child Protective Services because of lack of proper medical care. The Williamses were mortified by the threat of facing a court trial for the custody of their son, and they wondered why such pressure was brought down on them to submit to the diagnosis-and-medication regimen.

The medical test was a basic physical, with no cognitive or neurological assessment. Regardless of what these tests might have shown, Larry was medicated with Ritalin. For seven years Larry was maintained on various dosages and supplementary medications whenever his behavior appeared to become more distracted, and for seven years Larry hated every minute of it. He disliked the way he felt, but the threat of losing him to the authorities kept the Williamses vigilant.

During his fourteenth year, Larry died because of "long-term use of methylphenidate (Ritalin)," according to the chief pathologist at the hospital where he was taken and where the autopsy was performed. The signs of small vessel damage and hyperextension of the heart were obviously the results of Ritalin, and no other factors influenced the course of this fatality.

I've treated hundreds of children with ADD, and the typical story I hear from their mothers goes like this: "The kindergarten teacher diagnosed him with ADD because he was so hard to control, so I began staying in the classroom with him. Our plan worked, at least most of the time. But when my son entered first grade with the ADD diagnosis on his record, the principal insisted that I place him on some kind of medical management. Otherwise, he threatened to put him in special education classes from then on. When I offered to sit with him in the classroom, the principal tuned me out. For the next twelve years, I watched my child live under medication."

Medical students are often warned that "sometimes the treatment can be worse than the disease." I sincerely believe that is often the case when children with ADD are given medication to control their symptoms.

ADD medications are most often prescribed by family physicians—not by a pediatric psychiatrist—which makes me very suspicious. How much understanding do such physicians have of these very potent drugs? My personal and professional opinion is that they should be used very cautiously and only on a short-term basis with specific goals in mind. Most experienced school counselors concede that such medication loses most of its effectiveness by the teenage years anyway, so medications are not a long-term solution for ADD.

There are better and healthier options for treating your child's ADD, beginning with a strong family environment and a focus on healthy behaviors and goals, as we have discussed already, and including a range of approaches to stimulate the brain and focus the child's attention naturally, which will be discussed in subsequent chapters. I base my understanding of medication on years of experience in working with children and on years of working and researching ADD. Although I have had training in psychopharmacology, I always seek recommendations from referring physicians in matters related to medication. I also want to be very clear that I do not have any direct responsibilities for issuing prescriptions or for making the necessary laboratory assessments critical to any drug protocol, especially with children. However, I consult with a group of medical experts when devising medication strategies.

Let us be fair with doctors. There is an old saying credited to Abraham Maslow, a famous psychologist: "If the only tool that you have is a hammer, everything looks like a nail." Physicians nowadays are asked to evaluate and treat hundreds of childhood problems, and most feel that the only tools they have are drugs. Doctors also rarely observe the daily behavior of the child who is being treated. They usually have to rely on the observations and opinions of parents and teachers—not only as a basis for diagnosis but also for evaluating the results. Too often the only feedback the doctor receives on a medication is that the parent no longer brings the child in to see him. If the physician doesn't hear anything more, he assumes the medication worked properly. But in truth, it could be that the parents simply looked elsewhere for help, or gave up.

The Circular Firing Squad

Too often when a child has ADD, everyone responsible for helping him is shooting in the dark. Doctors often don't get good follow-up information. Parents get frustrated and make decisions without adequate professional input. Instead of circling the wagons against ADD, we form a circular firing squad and shoot at one another.

Typically, parents, physicians, and teachers find themselves at odds over a child's treatment. Parents are often bewildered about what to do to help and protect their child. School administrators, understandably, are most concerned about the learning environment for all of their students. Too often, busy physicians treat the symptoms, not the child.

That is madness. But it is understandable madness and it is prevalent. We are a pill-popping, quick-fix society. School administrators are under pressure themselves to get classrooms under control. Few physicians are trained adequately to deal with ADD children. I have attended medical conferences on ADD in which the doctors on the dais obviously had no clue about the long-term adverse effects of medicating children. It is a very serious business, especially when dealing with any drugs that affect a child's neurological system.

Most drug studies are based on research conducted on adults. Until recently, no studies systematically examined the long-term effects of drugs used on children, such as methylphenidate (Ritalin) and amphetamines (Dexedrine and Adderall). Some of the side effects of these drugs can be profound. They can be a greater threat to a child's health than most if not all ADD symptoms. Certainly, they can cause psychosis, including manic and schizophrenic episodes. Of 192 children diagnosed with ADD at a Canadian clinic, 98 were managed by drugs, mostly methylphenidate. (See the report by E. Cherland and R. Fitzpatrick in the *Canadian Journal of Psychiatry,* October 1999.) Of those treated with drugs, 9 percent developed psychosis, which went away only after removal of the drug. How many of the unmedicated children developed psychotic symptoms? Zero!

Since scientists cannot experiment on children, at least since World War II, rats stand in as subjects, and some generalizations can be made regarding drugs and developmental issues. Dr. William Carlezon of McLean Hospital and Harvard Medical School showed, in a controlled study, that rats that received Ritalin at an early age were more prone to develop the psychological state of learned helplessness and less likely to eat in their adolescent years, especially healthy foods, than rats without the drug.

Unfortunately some physicians typically do not stop medicating when psychotic symptoms appear. Instead, they may slap on another diagnosis, of depression or antisocial personality, and then treat this diagnosis by adding antidepressives, mood stabilizers, or neuroleptics (commonly used for epilepsy) to the treatment mix. It is not unusual for me to see children taking as many as five different medications, all based on adult prescriptions because their physicians are trying to counter the side effects from earlier prescriptions. Meds upon meds is madness upon madness.

Taking the issue of prescribing adult psychotropic medication to children at another level, the FDA has cautioned physicians in prescribing Paxil, an antidepressive medication, for anyone younger than eighteen because of the high risk of actually inducing suicidal ideation. The British Medicines and Healthcare Products Regulatory Agency included Celexa, Effexor, Lexapro, and Zoloft as being too risky for kids, and it banned Paxil in June 2003. At the heart of this controversy, children as young as four are being administered antidepressives.

The side effects are not restricted to psychiatric problems. Stimulants excite the whole body, not only the brain. Stimulating medications also affect the cardiovascular system. Matthew Smith, a fourteen-year-old student diagnosed with attention deficit disorder, was treated with Ritalin. After he died, on March 21, 2000, his heart was found to weigh 402 grams (compared to the average 350 grams for a grown man's heart).

One of the side effects of Ritalin is that it boosts the activity of the heart and cardiovascular systems so that they develop beyond what is considered normal. Accepted medical procedure is to constantly monitor the heart and cardiovascular systems by conducting echocardiogram readings to provide for early detection of the dangerous state that an enlarging heart can create. In Matthew's case, this was never done, and his parents were never told of the availability of this critical measure. In this vacuum of information, Matthew died.

When the blood pressure reaches abnormally high levels in overactive children, a potent antihypertensive, clonidine—an adult drug—may be prescribed for children already on Ritalin. This combination plays havoc with the body's attempt to balance the antagonistic reactions from the different drugs. Children have also suffered spasms and convulsions, and there is some danger of liver damage from medications used to treat ADD and side effects. Sleep and appetite problems resulting from medication are also of concern.

Side Effects to Consider

Parents need to understand the potential dangers of drugs used to treat ADD. Although only 50 percent of children with ADD can be helped through drug therapy, the ones who respond to drug treatment face the following possible side effects:

- nervousness (amphetamines, 5.5%; methylphenidate, 5.7%)
- insomnia (amphetamines, 5.5%; methylphenidate, 5.7%)
- confusion (amphetamines, 8–12%; methylphenidate, 2–10%)
- depression (amphetamines, 39%; methylphenidate, 8.7%)
- agitation (amphetamines, 10%+; methylphenidate, 3.3–10%+)
- irritability (amphetamines, 17–29%; methylphenidate, 11–19%)
- stunted growth and development (methylphenidate, 25%+)

Other side effects, in a lower rate of incidence, include

- exacerbation of behavior symptoms (hyperactivity)
- hypersensitivity reactions (allergy-type reactions to environmental agents)
- anorexia (eating disorder)
- nausea
- dizziness
- heart palpitations (heart rate fluctuations)
- headaches

- dyskinesia (movement-of-the-body problems)
- drowsiness
- hypertension (high blood pressure)
- tachycardia (rapid, racing heartbeat)
- angina (heart pain)
- arrhythmia (heart rate changes)
- abdominal pain
- lowered threshold for seizures

Dangerous Buildup

Consider too that every drug builds toxicity. Toxicity is related to the inflammationlike reaction of the body to a substance that is not natural, and can act like a poison to the system. No synthetic compound (which all drugs are) has the identical molecular structure of a natural substance. Since no one can patent a natural substance, the drugs we take are chemically engineered alternatives. The hormone replacement synthetics that women took for menopause symptoms, for example, were not the natural hormones of progesterone or estrogen. There were severe consequences in the aftermath of administering these replacements.

It is also true that the body builds a tolerance to every drug, and over time, the efficacy of the drug will diminish. This combination of toxicity, overreaction (allergic reactions), and diminished effect can cause many health problems.

The data for drugs used to treat ADD are scary. The excellent research—reviewed by Peter Breggin in *The Ritalin Fact Book*—has shown how toxicity buildup from the use of stimulants can do significant damage to the brain if the stimulant is taken over an extended time period. (Granted, laboratory work with animals using adult and higher dosages increases the likelihood of negative effects, but many of these toxic effects have been seen in humans as well.) Research has indicated the following negative effects:

- reduced blood flow
- reduced oxygen supply

- reduced oxygen utilization
- persistent biochemical imbalance
- persistent loss of receptors for neurotransmitters
- persistent sensitization to stimulants
- permanent distortion of brain cell structure and function
- brain cell death and tissue shrinkage

Is Ritalin a Gateway Drug?

If side effects are not enough to cause deep concern for any parent, there is the additional danger of mentally conditioning a young person to think that taking a pill should be the first option for every problem. Drug enforcement groups around the world have categorized the brain-stimulating drugs Ritalin, Adderall, and Dexedrine as Schedule II drugs that cause addiction and abuse.

Studies have shown that normal animals can easily become addicted to methylphenidate and amphetamine. Animals addicted to cocaine will turn to amphetamine or methylphenidate as a substitute for cocaine. Similarly, humans addicted to methylphenidate and amphetamines are known to cross-addict to cocaine. In a lengthy overview of brain function—"Is Methylphenidate Like Cocaine?" (*Archives of General Psychiatry,* June 1995)—the authors concluded that Ritalin and cocaine have identical effects on the brain. Does that surprise you? It shouldn't. In treating a child's behavioral problems with drugs, our message to the child isn't much different from that of the street-corner pusher: "The answer to all your problems is right here in this little packet. Take a hit and everything will be all right."

Am I exaggerating? I'm afraid not. I have seen the reactions of children who are administered these drugs. They quickly learn that their minds are altered by popping a pill, and since this is so easily accomplished, they never learn basic anxiety management skills. Instead of learning to cope with the normal hassles of growing up, they become reliant on the quick, temporary fix.

Consider Alternatives Before You Medicate

Before you wash the entire contents of your medicine cabinet down the drain, let me say that there is some good news in all of this information. The good part is that the brain of those with attention deficit disorder can be stimulated. These brains are not fixed organic units without choice—they will react to stimulation. The child's brain is responsive and subject to possible intervention from a huge variety of sources besides medication. Electromagnetic stimulation has been researched for years and implemented for Parkinson's and depression. Physical exercise is stimulating. Music serves as a major source for stimulation.

I admit that drugs are not my first choice of treatment, but there are two points to consider.

First, certain drugs are useful and have helped many of us live better lives, especially in emergencies—but they are generally not meant for long-term treatment. We have developed a peerless medical care system based on very good science, but its focus is critical care: what to do when an emergency comes, such as when someone gets shot. But treating ADD children is a long-term proposition. This problem area lies in the arena of chronic disease, which is not well understood.

Second, hyperactive behavior has many sources, and these origins are sometimes far beyond the reach of the medicine bottle. Thorough and specific assessments need to be made in each case. I oppose the typical shotgun approach to medical treatment for ADD, in which one drug is supposed to cure all symptoms.

As I've noted, there are dangerous side effects for many medications used to treat ADD. Parents should educate themselves and demand answers from their physicians about the potential side effects of drugs prescribed for their children. Don't let the medical professionals brush you off. Demand answers.

Find a physician who is willing to be a member of your child's support team. Push that doctor to test for specific problems. Then, with that information, you can discuss possibilities, which might or might not include a drug. If there is a medication recommended, get to know exactly what that drug is supposed to do, and what monitoring is required for all health conditions related to the administration of that drug. Above all, decide if it is working in the way that you want it to work.

If the goal of treatment is to help your child focus in his schoolwork and settle down in class, but the prescribed drug simply makes him dopey and docile, then that drug is not working the way you want it to.

In the audit below are fifteen areas of concern for you and your physician to consider when treating your child's ADD. Each has a specific recommended medication regimen; however, each child is unique, so not everyone responds the same way to every drug. A person's internal biology may change according to age, the time of the day, his current emotional state, and factors of physiology. Just as some of us are morning people and some are night people, we know that twelve-year-olds are definitely different from fifteen-year-olds. Girls are different from boys in their response to medications.

Keep this in mind as you demand explanations about the effects of medications from your team doctor. Ask for specific information about your child's behaviors and how they will be affected.

Medication Audit

Most of the audits in this book are designed to help you individually, but this one is different. This audit is based upon the doctor's expertise. Your doctor will make recommendations for choosing tests and assessment methods. Your job is to ask questions and understand the treatment strategy under consideration.

Since most physicians are not usually trained to examine your child's psychological state, I would recommend that a clinical or counseling psychologist be considered as a part of the team. He or she should have a broad knowledge of tests in this arena, and can assist both you and the physician in gathering information on your child's psychological profile.

I would recommend testing in the following areas of assessment for attention deficit disorder:

- *memory, immediate:* the ability to recite information within a short period of time (one second)
- *memory, recent:* the ability to reflect and hold memory over the recent hour even when other topics are discussed or problems addressed
- *memory, remote:* the ability to remember topics from the distant past
- *continuous concentration:* the ability to hold attention over a twenty-minute period
- *two- to three-step instructions:* the ability to remember at least two or three pieces of information and to then perform some operation with this information—such as arithmetic manipulation of the facts or reversing the order of a sequence
- *spatial reasoning:* understanding the relationships of distance and form
- *visual memory:* the ability to see items and remember them
- *embedded cues:* the ability to see details within a distracting picture
- *pacing:* the ability to achieve and maintain a pace or rhythm
- *social sequencing:* the ability to understand the social context of events and the basic dynamics between people
- *logic:* the ability to use a form of deductive or inductive reasoning
- *learning patterns:* the learning patterns the individual usually adopts (visual, experiential, kinesthetic, and so forth)
- *frustration tolerance:* the ability to tolerate ambiguity and to solve problems over time
- *visual learning pattern:* the pattern in which the per-

son solves spatial problems (trial and error, learning from mistakes, recognizing need for support)
- *verbal abstractions:* the creative associations between topics and objects

Medicate to Help, Not to Control

ADD children, like most of us, become depressed and anxious when they can't perform to their own expectations. They get stressed when they realize they are not catching on as fast as their classmates. They may act out in anger. Drugs are not going to remedy their problems. They want to do better, not just feel better.

The only valid reason for any medication is to enhance the child's abilities to learn and grow. Medicine should not be regarded as the way to modify behavior to suit a teacher's need for order in the classroom. Medication should be used to *enhance* the child's abilities, not to simply control behavior.

The bottom line is simple: use medication for the enhancement of cognitive functions, and equip the child with approaches and techniques for successful life skills through education and counseling.

The Basis of ADD Drug Treatment

Attention deficit disorder is thought to be the result of a complex brain dysfunction, and most medications used to treat it are designed around that theory. The brain is like any other organ. It has to be in balance for optimal performance. If it is operating too fast or if its many functions are not engaged at the proper speed, then the individual shows symptoms of things like schizophrenia. The use of stimulants to speed up the brain works for many children because the drugs operate as a powerful energizer.

The good news for these young people and their parents is that their brains can be stimulated in healthier ways. People with ADD have functional brains that simply cannot shift into the proper brain pattern when it is time to focus the mind and quiet the body.

The brain is actually a massive collective of more than 100 million brain cells. At least another billion cells play a supporting role in supplementing its diverse activities. Each cell has ten thousand or more points of connection to other cells. The brain is a complex organ that we've just begun to understand.

The brain looks like a loaf of bread that is split down the center with a slit that runs up at an angle, creating two similar-looking halves.

The Brain

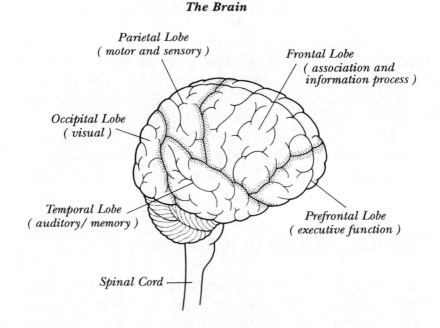

Parietal Lobe
(motor and sensory)

Frontal Lobe
(association and
information process)

Occipital Lobe
(visual)

Temporal Lobe
(auditory/ memory)

Prefrontal Lobe
(executive function)

Spinal Cord

The names assigned to these areas are based on dissection findings. They serve to define some of the functions of the brain.

- The *frontal lobe* usually carries the responsibility for processing information and managing how we categorize or make associations.
- The *parietal lobe* is involved with the motor functions

(moving our body parts around) and sensory functions (receiving feedback from these movements).

- The *occipital lobe* is the visual cortex and is involved with the processing of sight.
- The *temporal lobe* is generally where we learn and interpret language, and it is also in this area that we organize and maintain our memories.

Two Brain Constellations with Reference to ADD

If we focus on the brain as the source of most ADD symptoms, there are two constellations, not one, of symptoms that appear to be associated with the disorder. This separation of roles might clarify the needs for an individualized diagnosis of ADD, based on differential issues of abilities.

BRAIN CONSTELLATION #1

The major cluster of symptoms related to attention and distraction appears to be triggered in the *prefrontal and frontal cortex,* located just underneath the forehead. This is considered the most evolved of all the brain centers. It is the "boss's office" of the brain, which watches, supervises, guides, and focuses our behavior. It contains executive functions, such as time management, judgment, impulse control, planning, organization, and critical thinking. You can see that if this area is functioning at a low speed, there are going to be a lot of problems at home and at school, especially when it comes to learning something new.

The medications Adderall, Ritalin, and Dexedrine work by enhancing the production of the neurotransmitter *dopamine* in the prefrontal cortex area, which stimulates its functioning. One of the immediate responses from those who take these drugs is an improvement in handwriting and in the ability to record thoughts on paper. Overall motor coordination is also quickly improved.

BRAIN CONSTELLATION #2

Since the *temporal lobe* is responsible for memory, this area is directly involved with the functions related to the ADD problems of retention, learning, and mood stability. Other problems can also be evident with temporal lobe impairment, including a heightened sense of smell or various odd tastes in the mouth.

Impulsiveness, disorganization, and short attention span are some of the chief obstacles to school achievement. These characteristics can be linked to temporal lobe disorders. Interestingly enough, stimulants such as Ritalin appear to be ineffective in attempting to stabilize some of the temporal lobe conditions. Anticonvulsant medications such as Neurontin, Depakote, and Tegretol are often successful in stabilizing the temporal lobe activity. Many physicians add Adderall to these anticonvulsants to extend attention span (prefrontal function) once the temporal lobe is stabilized.

There are many complexities involved in managing various brain problems through use of these high-powered chemicals. In order to fully appreciate this approach, you would almost need instruction from a full-time neurologist who conducts SPET (serial peri-ictal single-photon-emission tomography) scans of the brain on a regular basis.

SPET and EEG scans purport to give more reliable clues about how the brain is functioning than does the simpler observational approach, which is pretty much like shooting in the dark. By directly observing the brain in operation and administering treatments, the physician can determine the effects on that particular region of the brain. You must know where you are aiming and you must be able to observe whether or not the effect of the medication is enhancing the function that the child really needs.

The Mind-Body Approach: An Action Plan

Drugs have a narrow window of effectiveness. If they work, you can see the rewards, but you can't see the side effects quickly.

Even though the patient and his family may celebrate their effectiveness on the good days, there is no guarantee that the side effects of the medications won't be worse than the ADD symptoms themselves. Are the risks worth it? In the vast majority of cases, I don't think so, and certainly not for the long term.

I prefer a mind-body approach to treatment that combines the power and immediate response of the most appropriate drugs with the best aspects of psychology and learning theory. By combining these approaches, we eliminate the more questionable and dangerous drugs along with their negative side effects and toxicity issues. We can also set up concrete goals and accountability for effective measurement.

Those who advocate drug treatments talk in mystical terms of drugs "serving as teacher" to the patient. I'm more concerned that drugs will become the master of young people, enslaving them to addiction. I prefer *training* the body and mind to be part of their own healing through a method with the daunting name of *psychoneuroimmunology,* or what I refer to as *psychoneurology* for short.

Commonly known by the abbreviation PNI, this method was developed by Dr. Robert Ader, a psychological scientist at the University of Rochester. Dr. Ader was studying whether lab animals could be trained to react negatively to the taste of a substance when he discovered that their immune systems had learned to respond to the substance and had become conditioned during the testing. In other words, the rats' white blood cells were reacting to a sugary nontoxic substance as if it were a poison. The implications were amazing because it meant that a single cell can be taught to behave just like Pavlov's dogs. (You may remember how his dogs, conditioned to salivate when they heard a bell ring, demonstrated how humans have associative learning.)

Through Dr. Ader's work, psychologists learned that the immune system could be taught. Methods were developed to use a conditioning substance to stimulate immune activity. We saw that we could fool immune cells so that they would become engaged and mobilized. This method of engaging the immune system through outside stimulus or inner beliefs came to be known as psychoneuroimmunity.

PNI has been applied to a number of human conditions to enhance or reduce the immune response. It has been used in treating lupus, skin grafts, cancer, the side effects of chemotherapy, multiple sclerosis, and many other diseases and conditions. In my discussions with Dr. Ader and other behavioral scientists, I learned that it is feasible to train any organ or cell. The method involves finding a suitable stimulus with a predictable effect, then associating that stimulus with another stimulus, so that the response to either stimulus is the same. This is very important for brain functions because we know the brain has a tremendous capacity to learn. The process of brain relearning or remapping is called *neuroplasticity,* and has been utilized in many ways in rehabilitation of brain damage and in overcoming brain dysfunction such as dyslexia.

In one method, psychologists can use drugs in combination with the body and mind to control physiological systems. We first identify a drug to treat the patient's symptoms. We give it to the patient along with a substance (such as chocolate or peppermint or chicken broth) that has a unique odor or taste. The idea is that the patient's body and mind will associate the smell and taste of the substance with the action of the drug. After a brief number of conditioning trials, the body and brain respond to the smell and taste of the substance as if it were the drug, and the desired conditioning will occur.

This may sound a little far-fetched at first, but we've long observed that the mind can have a powerful impact on the body. Just thinking about your favorite candy makes your mouth water, doesn't it? Simply visualizing someone physically attractive can stir other bodily responses. Similarly, in experiments where alcoholics were given a substance that smelled, tasted, and looked like whiskey, they became intoxicated even though there was not a drop of alcohol in it. In certain voodoo practices, people have died as a result of being convinced that someone had poisoned them.

The mind-body triggers and responses show how *perception and imagery* can be used to influence physical responses in all parts of the body, even down to individual immune cells. I've found that using mental imagery to create physical responses in

ADD children can have enormous benefits without the potentially dangerous side effects of long-term drug treatment.

The influence of the mind on our body's immune system has been well documented. Any medical student will tell you that she has experienced symptoms of diseases she's had to study in med school. Patients given placebos often report feeling better even though they've been given nothing stronger than a sugar pill. These insights are not limited to people with medical knowledge.

Norman Cousins's experiences in healing from a deadly form of collagen disease—which he writes about in his classic *Anatomy of an Illness*—are often cited as another example of how the brain and body work toward the natural state of wellness.

> The greatest force in the human body is the natural drive of the body to heal itself—but that force is not independent of the belief system, which can translate expectations into physiological change. Nothing is more wondrous about the fifteen billion neurons in the human brain than their ability to convert thoughts, hopes, ideas, and attitudes into chemical substances. Everything begins, therefore, with belief. What we believe is the most powerful option of all.

Assessment and Trials

For training children to be part of their own healing with limited use of drugs, I developed a procedure that I followed in treating Kay, a sweet, brown-eyed nine-year-old. She was a very shy girl who was falling behind in her school assignments because she did not appear to understand her work. She would often gaze out the window as the teacher was talking to her, and although she was not aggressive, she was talkative. The assessment revealed that she had attention deficit issues with specific problems in concentration, likely a prefrontal lobe problem.

The physician wanted to give Ritalin to Kay, but we decided to implement a psychoneurological plan in which we would condition her brain with a substance and use Ritalin to link to the conditioned response. Here are the steps we followed:

1. The team doctor was recommending a medication, and she identified exactly what the medication would do for the specific brain function. The drug was to stimulate the prefrontal lobe for increased attention span. The doctor described in detail what the medication looked like and even drew pictures of friendly circles (with smiles) that went to the brain part and played a rough game of football. The cheerleaders were there too, depicted as other cells that were watching the game.

2. The plan was discussed with Kay and she embraced the idea quickly. However, instead of the football players being the drug, Kay switched the imagery so that the cheerleaders were the real powers. They instilled hope and inspiration for the players to win. (This was a smart kid.)

3. The next task before administration of the drug was to find a substance that had a unique smell and taste that Kay had never experienced. Actually it was Kay's grandmother who concocted a recipe, a "secret healing formula." It had a lot of onions, lemons, and garlic in chicken broth (at least I think it was chicken broth) and several other powders. I added some vitamin B12, B6 (brewer's yeast), and ginseng for good measure.

   By the time all of the cooks finished, the concoction was certainly smelly enough and distinctively flavored. I was the first to taste it. Then Kay tasted it too. She made a face and swallowed with a little gulp. She was brave and did not complain.

4. The medication and the concocted substance were administered at the same time in full view of the doctor, who cheerfully encouraged Kay. Kay drew pic-

tures of her squadron of cheerleaders on her pad and made up a cheer for us to chant along with her.

5. As would be predicted by the use of medication alone, Kay was feeling much more attentive and the teacher was very positive about the day's work. Her attention span was measured with a paper and pencil test and she did very well. In fact she performed better than average.

6. After six administrations of the drug and recipe, Kay was administered the recipe alone and we waited to see if it had an effect similar to the medication's. Maybe it was the method or the placebo effect; Kay reported success, and her academic performances continued to be excellent. She was evaluated after another six administrations of the recipe without the medication and showed good results. In fact, Kay began to do better, and this might have been related to her hopes and anticipation of better control.

7. Kay was eager to drop the medicine. She remained attentive for the rest of the year without the drugs. She later admitted that she wanted desperately to show that her grandmother's recipe had a powerful healing effect, so she was very motivated, which may have affected the results. Maybe the vitamins helped too.

Self-motivation Is Critical

I have tested this method with twenty children for whom the psychoneurological approach worked with remarkable success; there were six cases that were utter failures. In all of the successful ones, I admit, the motivations of the patient were very similar to Kay's. There were strong underlying reasons to believe that this process would work, and the brew, along with the powerful imagery stories in which the family would participate, contributed to positive results. I enjoyed working and participating with these individuals because they brought a high level of creativity and enthusiasm to this unique healing process.

On the other hand, I did not enjoy working with the failures—not because they were failures, but because they chose not to put much effort into the program, and there were other issues that were going on between the child and the parents. I could not say whether or not this type of program would work in situations where there is no real motivation or where there is not a willingness to try something that relies on openness, support, and shared belief. I suppose that the axiom is true that many things will work with motivated people, but nothing will work when there are issues that take precedence over health.

Action Plan for the PNI Medical Treatment

If your child's doctor recommends a medication, consult with her to identify exactly what the medication will do for the specific brain function. If, for example, the purpose of the drug is to stimulate the prefrontal lobe for increased attention span, then teach your child to visualize what that would look like if he could see the drug enter the body and communicate its mission with the brain.

To do this, I have children visualize firefighters (representing the drug they've been using to control ADD) waking up a family (representing the brain) with fire hoses. Or I've had them visualize alarm clocks (the drug) waking up a sleepy child (the brain).

1. Go to your child and openly discuss these ideas. Create an image for the medicine doing its job on the brain and how it feels as it is working. Try to give the child a sense of empowerment and excitement over taking control of his own treatment through this process.
2. The next task before administration of the drug is to find a substance that has a unique smell and taste

your child has never experienced before. This might take some time, but the success of this exercise depends on the strongest smell and taste possible, such as cod liver oil or strong licorice. I often use chocolate-covered coffee beans. This may sound like cheating, since these candies offer a stimulant in the caffeine, but I believe that the learning association is enhanced, and kids love these things.

Note: Related brain research has found that patients with memory problems lack a receptor that binds acetylcholine, and when nicotine (in the form of patches) is introduced as a substitute, memory ability is significantly improved. This phenomenon has been researched in older adults at Duke University (H. K. White, *Psychopharmacology,* 2003), and I am certainly not recommending that you get your kid hooked on nicotine; however, under the care of an expert, the patch might prove to be a powerful stimulator in this area of the brain.

3. After the substance is chosen, arrange for the medication and substance to be administered at the same time. As soon as the child has taken both, go through the imagery exercise so the child visualizes the drug taking effect. Do this every time the drug is administered.

4. Continue the dual administration with the imagery exercises until you see the first signs of some improvement in the target symptom. Based on my experience, this will happen within five to six administrations. If attention span increase was the target, you may use a psychological test to measure the results for what would be considered average, or it might be a behavioral task that you measure.

5. After that, stop using the drug. Begin using the placebo substance only, while continuing to use the imagery exercise. Determine if the targeted behavior is maintained or improved with only the placebo used

as the medicine. You may want to adjust the special recipe with another one if it gets too boring or it needs a little spice.

Medication is a controversial issue—especially for parents—and there is much confusion surrounding the choice of whether or not to medicate the ADD child. The decisions that parents make for their children often have lasting effects. I have offered you a plan based on the science of psychoneuroimmunology. This approach calls for teamwork between the child, the family, and the physician. It relies on a plan developed by all parties. And it requires an understanding of the purpose of the medications to be used. The target behavior must be objectively measured, and there has to be support for the child's use of imagery to enhance the healing benefits of the process. All involved must embrace the healing ritual and commit their time and support to the success of the approach. If all of these things come together, I believe that you will be very surprised at the results.

I have seen children who were undergoing medical procedures in the pediatric ward respond to adult dosages of morphine as if it were water when they became upset. This tells me very clearly that there is more to a drug than just the drug's chemistry. Under acute stress, our physiology does not work in the same way as it might when we feel safe, when we have some emotional connection to the outcome, and when we have some real investment in success.

The bottom line is that your child must *participate* fully to get the desired results. Whatever the elements of the healing process you decide on, your child's body and brain will react with a receptivity that will vary according to attitude and emotional state. Make friends with the healing process that you choose, and the results will be different, and better.

SIX

Stress: An Enemy or a Friend

When I was beginning my graduate studies in psychology, I worked part-time at the Child Guidance Center in Lubbock, Texas. The mission of the center was to help troubled young people from the area's secondary schools cope with their problems. We didn't know much about attention deficit disorder in those days, though we sensed that much of the hyperactivity we were seeing had a neurological basis.

Since I had some teaching experience and I was trained to work with learning disabilities, I was put in charge of the boys' program. I had read the few books on hyperactivity and learning problems then available, so I decided to employ *play therapy,* in accordance with a popular theory that suggested children needed expression for their psychological stress. I believed then, because of my training, that a child's negative behaviors were the result of underlying psychological conflict. In play therapy, the therapist observed the play activities of children and determined the underlying psychological needs that were being expressed. The goal was to identify the children's personal sources of turmoil for therapeutic intervention.

Suppose a child, Johnny, was observed beating the stuffing out of a teddy bear. The therapist might invite Johnny to talk about it by saying: "Do you want to say something about how mad you are?" The hope would be that Johnny would respond by express-

ing why he is angry, such as: "I am mad, mad, mad at my mother."
The therapist would then work to help the child gain insights into
the sources and reasons for his anger at his mother.

That was the way it was supposed to happen, according to the
textbooks of the day. Unfortunately, the kids hadn't read those textbooks. At least the kids at the Child Guidance Center hadn't. Instead of offering great insightful resolutions, the boys under my
guidance destroyed the playroom and tried to beat the stuffing out
of one another too. They punched holes in the walls. They smashed
the lights. They bloodied one another's noses. Play therapy was a
disaster.

After those exhausting, failed attempts at progressive treatment
for the hyperactive children, I'd drag myself into the office of the
medical director who ran it, Dr. Mary Bublis, who'd shrug and tell
me: "Do the best you can."

My best efforts weren't doing the children any good at all. I was
frustrated. In search of more understanding and knowledge, I
went to a conference. I can't recall what the topic was, but I left
the conference an enlightened young man, thanks to the intriguing older gentleman sitting next to me. He looked like an ancient
wizard. He had long white hair. His skin had deep furrows and a
network of crevices. I assumed he was a retired doctor, but I did
not need to check his credentials.

During a break, we chatted. He explained that he often attended conferences just to hear the latest information in psychology, to "keep the mind sharp." We went for coffee in a nearby
restaurant. I was amazed at his wisdom and insight into topics that
I was studying at the time. Four hours later we finally left the coffee shop. I didn't learn anything of value from the conference. But
I will never forget the observations and advice I received from "the
wizard," who told me his name was Jon, though I never saw him
again.

During our chat, I told him of my frustration with my boys at
the guidance center. He chuckled and offered guidance. He
seemed to have an intuitive feel for these troubled children. One
of the things he said opened my mind. He offered that it could be
that the boys' problems in learning were derived from their hy-

peractivity itself, not from any psychological conflicts. He suggested that they might not have enough conflict or stress, so they were trying to create more. "If you didn't provide them with some challenges or present them with some conflicts, they would go out and create some for themselves," he said.

His view is widely shared today by those who study and treat children with ADD. Jon's suggestion for treating the children presaged the modern treatment philosophy. He said that our efforts to give the children "space" so they could work out their frustrations in a clinically controlled setting were only adding to their lack of stimulation. He said that their brains were not being challenged enough. But he cautioned that they needed to be challenged in very specific ways. The treatment approach he outlined had been used for generations with such children but abandoned for what were then thought to be more enlightened approaches—which were not working.

Maybe my frustrations made me more open to considering the "old way," or maybe it was the fact that Jon was a charismatic conversationalist. Whatever the reason, I thought his suggested approach had great promise. Jon instructed me to take the boys on an overnight camping trip. He suggested that I keep them busy building a fire, keeping it going, and singing and dancing. He even had a particular dance in mind, one that was more like walking and moving to the rhythm of a beating drum. I was the designated drummer. The song he gave me was a six-word sentence to be repeated for the duration of the dance. Looking back, it seems strange that I took this stranger's advice so seriously, but his intelligence and insight were persuasive.

When I returned to work and shared Jon's treatment suggestions with my boss, Dr. Bublis was not as enthusiastic. But she gave me permission to try it. After obtaining parental consent for the outing, we took the boys to a secluded camping spot on a nearby ranch. As dusk descended, I talked to them about how much fun we were going to have. Jon had correctly noted that these hyperactive children (who today would most likely be diagnosed with ADD) were easily bored.

I held their attention by telling them a campfire tale entitled

"The Spirit of José." The story is about how José became a "warrior of the Spirit," and I told the boys that they could do the same by doing a special warrior dance in which they would learn the secrets of "the walk."

By completing the dance and learning these secrets, they would then be able to walk for very long distances—just like the ancient warriors. I cautioned them that this step would be difficult because only true warriors passed this first test.

I told the boys that it was very important for all of them to pass and for them to support one another. This message was important. Developing a sense of teamwork was a key part of the treatment—the sort of teamwork a family can use in helping an ADD child.

That night I beat a drum to a rhythm that synchronized to the rate of a beating heart. The boys sang a song to the rhythm of the drumbeat. The lyrics were: "I am one with the Spirit." The boys were instructed to keep dancing until I instructed them to stop, and to listen for the secrets that would come from the Spirit. As you might imagine, they grew exhausted in a short time. But they'd taken my message about teamwork to heart. They offered support and encouragement to one another, and to their credit, they danced until the first gray streaks of dawn appeared in the sky.

I grew weary too. But I kept beating on that drum all night. Fortunately, I had a colleague along to keep me awake. As the sun rose, I asked the boys to tell me what secrets the Spirit had given to them. The answers were surprisingly profound for a group of young and restless males. One of the boys described the experience in which a man came to him dressed in a shaggy robe and told him that he would play a very important part in history, but that he needed to learn to look within himself more for truth instead of believing others. Mike was a changed kid. His life began to be a mission instead of a rebellion without a cause.

Another boy had a visitor in his mind as well, but his caller was a wolf. The wolf imparted the message that he would never be alone again, as long as he trusted the Spirit Wolf. His experience not only told me the basis for his troubles but also supplied the answer—a personal friend with power and love. Back at school he began to show more confidence in his meetings and he was significantly more joyful.

I told the boys that the secrets they'd discovered were very special gifts. We made plans to construct symbolic shields for each of them to portray the unity and strength they'd established during our night of dancing to the drums. That morning, we cooked breakfast. The boys were thoughtful and calm as we ate. When their parents arrived, they remarked that they'd never seen them so subdued.

Ingredients of Change

The campout was a success. Each boy received something from the experience that served to stabilize his behavior and increase his self-esteem. The reports from the teachers and parents were universally excellent, and we recommended successful discharges for all of them within the month, but each one of them returned from time to time to give gratitude for that night and to share the new experiences of their lives.

It seemed we'd found a method to help control the hyperactivity of these troubled boys. In search of a scientific explanation for the effectiveness of the campout experience, I analyzed what we'd done that night. The various elements of the drumming, the fire, and the dance all worked together. The hypnotic flames of the fire provided a central focus for the boys, who were easily distracted. The combination of the dance and rhythm of the drumbeat seemed to create a positive flow for their abundant reservoirs of energy. Dancing together gave them a sense of group empowerment and direction.

Over the years that followed, I continued to examine the forces and effects of "the wizard's" campout treatment for hyperactivity. Over the years, I have come to call this process *the good stress challenge*. Three factors appear to influence this effective and innovative approach:

- the good stress of the challenge
- the liberating experience of physical exertion
- the repetition in the song, which puts the participants in a near trance that relaxes them and inspires creative thinking

The Good Stress Challenge Audit

The following statements are indicators to determine if your child could benefit from a good stress challenge. Indicate whether each statement is true: *frequently* (3), *occasionally* (2), *infrequently* (1), or *never* (0).

	Frequently	Occasionally	Infrequently	Never
1. Your child is bored with life.	3	2	1	0
2. Your child is depressed because she feels as if she's on a treadmill with no goal or direction.	3	2	1	0
3. Your child is tired most of the time.	3	2	1	0
4. Your child often expresses that he would do almost anything to break the monotony in his life.	3	2	1	0
5. Your child gets frustrated when she doesn't feel that she is making progress.	3	2	1	0
6. Your child seldom feels good about himself.	3	2	1	0
7. Your child seldom looks for things that make her feel proud about what was accomplished.	3	2	1	0
8. Your child usually looks back over the past and feels like a failure.	3	2	1	0
9. Your child seems to have pain symptoms that migrate from one area of the body to another.	3	2	1	0
10. Your child wishes he were more productive.	3	2	1	0
11. Your child expresses that she feels better and more powerful when she gets angry.	3	2	1	0
12. Your child would probably do something that is dangerous or even stupid just to change a bad mood.	3	2	1	0

Scoring

Total the numbers you have checked for each item. Compare your scores to the interpretations below.

0-8: A score in this range would indicate good expectations of achieving some realistic goals. The child has enough interests to keep his mind active. If you asked him, he would likely mention several stresses he experiences in the form of challenges, although they might be described as "good," such as tests and examinations.

9-19: A score in this range would indicate that some goal-setting approaches would be helpful for mood states, and exercise would be beneficial. Your child may suffer some anxiety about success, and assurance would be helpful. Determine realistic levels of achievement.

20-27: A score in this range would be indicative of a need to be challenged for a specific goal, which would be important for attention deficit disorder. Structured activities, such as the campout described, and short-term athletic or card games are also good starters.

28-36: A score in this range would be a clear indication to begin a good stress challenge program, although this program would need to be designed for your child's individual needs. Assigning a buddy or partner in introducing good stress activities is usually a very good step, and finding a leader especially interested in your child can be a blessing.

The Challenge

The challenge is the goal you set for yourself or your child. Because of the link between biological and psychological actions, I recommend a physical goal. The challenge for my boys was to stay on their feet all night and chant. But you want to plan an activity that can be done daily, instead of only at special times. Your child might choose to perfect a yoga workout, complete a ten-mile run, establish a weight-lifting regimen, or undertake some sort of Outward Bound challenge, depending on preferences and means. Whatever challenge is selected, make sure it requires strenuous effort in order to produce the special brain hormones that are necessary to bring about a shift in mind states.

There must be a conscious effort to shift the brain into a higher state through a motivated set of activities that will create an exhaustion of the normal levels. Those dancing, chanting boys were very much interested in sitting down once the oxygen was depleted from their muscles, but it was important for them to continue with their activities so that there would be shift in their biochemical and hormonal actions. Runners will recognize what we are talking about here as an *endorphin high*.

The Exercises

It is also important to understand that, unless exercise can be stimulating, it may not be helpful at all. In fact, exercise can be harmful. Before you turn me in to the health police, let me assure you that I am among the 5 million psychologists who recommend exercise highly. In the medical textbook I wrote on alternative medicine *(Complementary and Alternative Medicine),* I noted that exercise is a superior treatment for depression, anxiety, hypertension, memory problems, agitation, chronic pain, and many other diagnoses.

Many studies show that exercise can be beneficial, but the after-effects can be problematic. In a recent study, researchers examined whether participating in sports was healthy. They measured immunity functions in football teams. The results indicated that if the football team was winning and optimistic, the players had very positive immunity indicators, and were sick with flu and colds significantly less than average. However, if the football team was experiencing losses and the players were pessimistic about the performance of their team, their immunity functions were lowered, and they experienced twice as many colds and incidents of flu as did the players on teams with positive records.

It all comes down to the meaningfulness of the exercises. Some time ago I was having a discussion with the successful owner of a chain of health spas. I was working a stress management program into his wellness classes. We discussed a marketing plan to attract more patrons into his spas. After I presented my ideas, he smiled and said, "These are good ideas, but there are some things you don't understand about this business. Many of my members just don't want to come all the time."

I was dumbfounded, but he went on to explain, "This is my business, and it goes like this. Let's say a woman comes in right after Christmas and she is feeling guilty about the weight she has gained. Although she is middle-aged, she wants to see herself as she looked and felt as a teenager. She buys a four-year contract for the use of the gym. She shows up for the first few visits because she is still excited, especially since she sees the twenty-two-year-olds dancing and exercising all around her—and she thinks that they all got that way because of the gym. She comes back a third time, realizing that they are young and she is not, but now that she has paid her money, she is going to get all that she paid for. She may show up a month later with renewed enthusiasm—for a day or so. We will probably never see her again until she's feeling the post-Christmas guilt, or maybe in June, when she figures she will work on her presummer disappointment in her swimsuit size."

I was taken aback at this revelation. I left with new insights into the health spa business and its understanding of the motivations of the American public. There is no question: exercise can be difficult to stick with on a regular basis. I could now see that it is very hard for most people to actually maintain a regular effort, even if the goal is very desirable. The delay of gratification is a real obstacle, and even though the woman we talked about wanted the body of a teenager, she found that exercise is work. For the young girls there, it was fun; but when someone tells you to exercise and have fun, it doesn't always compute. It is work—too much work for many people.

Exercise can be challenging and even provocative. It also can be counterproductive to a person with ADD if it just brings more boredom and rebellion. You have to find a form of exercise that excites your child. Running is not a passion for everyone, and neither is volleyball or bench-pressing weights for an hour a day. But if you are dealing with an ADD child, it's worth taking a close look at how exercise might fit into your child's health equation. I have prepared an exercise audit so that you can make some objective decisions about what kind of exercise might provide your child with the most motivation and stimulation.

Exercise Satisfaction Audit

What kind of exercise would be most satisfying for your child? In order to determine the best type of exercise program that would not only benefit her the most but also give the most pleasure, take a minute and administer this assessment. Have your child mark her opinion about these interests on the following items by circling one of four responses: *agree very much* (4), *agree mostly* (3), *disagree mostly* (2), *disagree very much* (1).

	Agree Very Much	Agree Mostly	Disagree Mostly	Disagree Very Much
1. I do keep my lifestyle orderly and routine.	4	3	2	1
2. I think that I am a competitive person and I like that part of me.	4	3	2	1
3. I go out of my way to be with other people.	4	3	2	1
4. I am stressed most of the time by expectations made of me.	4	3	2	1

	Agree Very Much	Agree Mostly	Disagree Mostly	Disagree Very Much
5. I find that I will put things off easily that I really do not want to do.	4	3	2	1
6. I like to do things quickly and accomplish tasks in short order.	4	3	2	1
7. I need support from others to do difficult tasks.	4	3	2	1
8. I like to set priorities for the most important tasks.	4	3	2	1
9. Sometimes I need structure to start a project.	4	3	2	1
10. I like to see progress in whatever I do.	4	3	2	1
11. I find it easier to complete projects if I am with a group of people.	4	3	2	1
12. I would describe myself as an extroverted person.	4	3	2	1
13. I really enjoy teamwork and working together for a common goal.	4	3	2	1
14. I do not like exercising for long periods at a time.	4	3	2	1
15. I would rather work out with another person than work out by myself.	4	3	2	1
16. I do not feel that I have completed a good workout unless I have exerted 100 percent of my effort.	4	3	2	1
17. I find group activities a lot more fun than doing things by myself.	4	3	2	1
18. I like to do exercises that make my muscles bigger.	4	3	2	1
19. I like a sport activity in which I am being challenged by another person.	4	3	2	1
20. I do like exercises that last a short time.	4	3	2	1

Scoring

Add the scores for only the odd-numbered statements and write the total in the place below. Then, add the scores for the even-numbered items and write the total in the space below.

Sum for odd-numbered statements   _____
Sum for even-numbered statements   _____

ODD-NUMBERED ITEMS: GROUP ACTIVITIES VS. SOLITARY ACTIVITIES

33-40: Your child is more comfortable working out in a group than doing solitary exercises, and usually finds shared participation with others helpful to her own motivation. The support of friends helps her in following through with an exercise routine. You should help your child plan an exercise program with group participation.

24-32: Your child enjoys group exercises mostly, but his most important pleasure comes when there is mutual support and co-operation, as opposed to competition. Your child tends not to want to "beat" another person in a game, but would rather enjoy some activity mutually.

18-23: Your child desires to plan an individual exercise program with a personal agenda and sense of order. He tends to find pleasure in activities that may have other participants, but where each member of the group has personal goals.

10-17: Your child's most enjoyable exercises are those she does by herself without the distracting frustration of working with others. Your child likes to focus on internal goals, rather than external expectations. Some of these goals may not just be targeted on strengthening body or building endurance, but be done for relaxation and to help in achieving an overall sense of harmony.

EVEN-NUMBERED ITEMS:
EXTERNAL OBJECTIVES SATISFACTION
VS. INTERNAL OBJECTIVES SATISFACTION

33-40: Short-term goals and immediate satisfaction are the motivating incentives for your exercise programs. Your child likes to *get things done* and move on through a daily schedule. For your child, a successful exercise program will be specific to goals set for himself, and the accomplishment of these goals is deliberate and focused. Make sure that the plan is achievable, with short-term goals that are realistic.

24-32: Your child enjoys *getting somewhere* and making some progress when she exercises. It helps to select exercises that have quantifiable measures, such as walking or jogging a measurable distance with a goal of extending that distance or increasing the pace. Weight lifting works well because the weight can be adjusted upward or the number of repetitions can gradually be increased as determinates of progress. Almost any exercise can be quantifiable, and your child can remain motivated by establishing an expanding set of measurements that you personally hold out as challenges for success.

17-23: Your child is more motivated by the consistency and discipline of exercising rather than making progress on a short-term basis. For example, he would be more motivated to walk or jog one or two miles each day and feel some internal success and pride, rather than use speed, endurance, or distance as external measures of success. The feat of personal and disciplined accomplishment is more important than achieving quantifiable improvements.

10-16: Your child is a person who is more internally motivated by her body needs. Success comes from how her body feels rather than through some objective, external measure. Exercises such as walking, jogging, or swimming can make a child feel good inside and will provide a sense of harmony and balance.

Exercise Selection for Maximum Satisfaction

The final step is to combine the "group activities vs. solitary activities" dimension with the "external objectives satisfaction vs. internal objectives satisfaction" dimension into one blended choice. On the square below, find the scores cross-referenced according to the odd- and even-numbered item sums. Within each of the boxes are examples of exercises where you will likely find the greatest satisfaction according to your child's exercise assessment. Remember these are only examples, and personal selections may be more relevant to lifestyle, experiences, and specific interests.

CHOICES OF EXERCISES ACCORDING TO PERSONAL NEEDS ASSESSMENT

	Group Activities (odd 24–40)	Solitary Activities (odd 10–23)
External Objectives (even 24–40)	tennis, group running, soccer, baseball, basketball, rock climbing, volleyball, racquetball, group exercise, dancing	weight training, solo running, speed running, endurance, competitive swimming
Internal Objectives (even 10–23)	cross-country group running, aerobic dance, tai chi (group), martial arts, group walking and hiking	stationary bike, treadmill, strength training, stair climb, yoga, solo running and walking

Songs

I discovered in my analysis of songs and chants that the type of song chosen was not as important as the breathing patterns that emerged as part of the vocal effort used to sing the song. If the individuals used a particular type of chant, they would adopt a breathing pattern known to have a powerful effect on their body chemistry. In fact, researchers at Harvard Medical School demonstrated the effectiveness of breathing patterns for the relaxation response with great success, but I was more interested in the control of ADD.

The underlying principle was based upon the rhythmic cadence that occurred during the breath cycles, so that if the person counted during his exhalations and inhalations, instead of repeating a lyric, the results were the same. For example, if the repeated numbers went something like "1-2-3 and 4-5-6, 1-2-3 and 4-5-6, 1-2-3 and 4-5-6," there was a noticeable and favorable difference in both behavioral and cognitive functioning. Kids could study better. They received higher grades on tests because of better memory functions, and there was a discernable increase in their self-esteem.

I continued to search for more understanding about how the major organs and systems influence and direct many of the specific brain functions. I discovered that each beat of the human heart produces strong electrical stimulation, and with each stroke it performs the vital function of supplying the brain with oxygen. Using the technology of biofeedback, we conducted some experiments in which we trained our patients to increase their heart rates while we monitored their brain patterns. Sure enough, there was a direct relationship between heart rate and brain pattern measurements.

To clarify our findings, we devised an exercise where the patients would breathe to the pattern of the heart, rather than follow an outside cadence. The plan was to have the child locate the heart pulse somewhere on the body (the wrist, the neck, the chest) and focus the breathing patterns on the timing of her heart. For example, if the out-breath was concluded in three beats of the heart, the in-breath would be timed accordingly. It did not make any difference how many heartbeats were used, as long as the timing was consistent. As these two functions became coordinated, the child could speed up or lower the heart rate by adjusting the breathing pattern.

Basically, this technique is like having your own internal

biofeedback, and it gives the child a sense of self-control. I had the kids put their hands over their hearts or find some other way to monitor their pulses. Several of them found pulse meters. The purpose of the game was for them to learn to focus on their breathing. This technique can be used in most situations, but is especially helpful in stressful or threatening circumstances.

This procedure was very effective in creating a total body relaxation response in a matter of just a few minutes. The kids liked it because the pattern was based on internal mechanisms they could relate to, and they did not have to remember the words and pacing of a mantra—and they could actually feel the change. Sometimes they would then begin to sing to their own body rhythm unconsciously, and the tunes were magical.

The children began describing this training as "tuning in to our body music," and that is exactly what was happening. Just think of the many sports teams and individuals who sing while working out, and many workers still sing or hum along as they do their work. All of this research began to bring a better understanding of music and health, and it indeed does seem to come from very old and very wise medicine.

Action Plan for the Positive Stress Challenge

It is not necessary to have an exact plan to begin, because most of the critical components will evolve naturally. As the challenges are accepted and success is seen, there will be a natural tendency to want to achieve additional goals because of the increased sense of accomplishment. The exercises will become more individualized according to what your child enjoys and the results he experiences. The breathing and songs will evolve as the child learns to listen to his own body music.

The critical thing is to get started. Being the slowest member of the football team when I was fifteen, I was "encouraged" to go out for track. The first day the track coach looked at me and said, "You are going to run with the cross-country team. They run about five miles, so take off. If you can't keep up, walk fast."

My reaction was, *I will be running until midnight!* I thought of myself as a football player, not a long-distance runner. I did what I was told and decided that I would run the whole distance. And I discovered that I was a much better runner than I thought I could be. I did not become the fastest cross-country runner, but I was successful in my mind because I met the challenge and succeeded. From that point on, I found joy in running.

Stress accompanies any fresh challenge. But stress is not bad if you can learn to use it to your benefit. Consider how you feel when you are presented with a task that you know is not a real challenge to your true abilities. You may feel angry that someone has so little faith in the capacities that you know you have. I remember when an ex-girlfriend congratulated me so effusively at my high school graduation that I felt insulted. I wondered if she thought that this was a major achievement for me and that I could do no better than just skim along to the point of getting out of school.

Imagine how it feels when a teacher lowers the expectations in reading lessons for the child with ADD. The message is clear: "You are too disabled to perform normal reading tasks." That is not the right challenge. That is definitely not the right message.

Positive stresses must encourage optimism, and at the same time they have to be demanding and represent a real accomplishment. These positive stresses, if properly chosen, can promote hope and encouragement for anyone who says, "I can and I will take on that challenge."

Lou was a small-framed boy in the seventh grade, and his size was only an additional detriment to the symptoms of ADD. He felt like an outcast. Not only did he feel inadequate to perform at the same level as his peers, but he had no unique talents or skills to identify himself as an individual, much less as a special person. He felt that he was invisible, and maybe he was. His classmates hardly knew his name.

I took a special interest in this boy because I knew that regardless of how much he could achieve, he would never find the self-assurance to see any progress. He needed to know he could achieve some success. So, as odd as it may seem, I sent him to the boxing coach as a candidate for the Golden Gloves competition. Boxing is done in weight divisions, so I figured the kid had a chance because he'd be pitted against someone of similar stature. He certainly had enough pent-up anger to learn to channel in a positive manner. I was not interested in him learning to be aggressive and violent, but I wanted him to find something in which he could have pride.

With reassurance from me and some counseling for his mother, Lou took on the challenge. He discovered that he could do ten push-ups, then fifteen, and then twenty-five! His progress was impressive and he called me regularly to report it with enthusiasm. As he began to muscle up he also directed more energy toward his schoolwork and improved his concentration. The boxing coach was one of those brilliant people who knew how to bring out the best in a kid. He felt Lou had real potential as a boxer. And he was right. In only his second year of competition, Lou won the state championship in his weight class.

I can't say for certain that Lou's success in improving his schoolwork came from his athletic training. The real factor was his dedication to his own success.

SEVEN

Detoxifying the Diet and the Environment

The first time I saw a fourth-grader named Ken as a patient, I sent him home. He was out of control. It was late Monday morning when he and his mother came to my office. I could hear his mother pleading with him before they reached the waiting room. Ken kept running up and down the staircase and leaning dangerously out over the railing at the top. When I walked into the waiting room, I found him tossing magazines up into the air and trying to catch them.

I knew that he was so wound up I'd never be able to test him that day. His mother had brought Ken's school reports and achievement test results, so I did have some basis for quickly reviewing his history. Trying to determine why he was so hyper that morning, I asked his mother what he'd had for breakfast. Just as I'd expected, he'd loaded up on sugars. He'd had orange juice, Coca-Cola, some milk, grapefruit, and a breakfast bar. I asked his mother to bring Ken back in three days but only after preparing him a very different breakfast. I recommended that she begin giving him breakfasts consisting of peanut butter over a rice cake, with some chocolate-flavored soy milk.

Thursday morning arrived. In contrast to the prior appointment, all was still in the waiting room. In fact, I had no idea Ken and his mother were there. Ken was curious as a kitten but he was much more subdued. He looked around quietly and asked a few calm questions. His mother was grateful for his behavior, although she seemed mystified. She said, "I don't know why he is so good today. Maybe this will be one of his good days."

The testing was uneventful and although Ken had some strengths and weaknesses, none of them were outside the range of normal performance. The school reports displayed a different story. They depicted him as barely above the line of mental retardation, with few skills except writing his name correctly. The reports were mostly about the teacher's frustrations with him. She couldn't keep him in his seat during class. His records showed that he did have a curiosity and interest in his subjects but little self-control and very little ability to concentrate for more than fifteen or twenty minutes. Then he'd be hanging from the light fixtures again. He was at his worst midmorning and midafternoon.

Intrigued by what I observed, I arranged for this child to serve as a research subject of an ADD study at the Clinical Ecology Research Division of the psychology department at the University of North Texas, where I was a consultant. There he was taken to a sterile room free of polluted air or substances. He was allowed to play with toys in the company of a research assistant while we observed him out of sight. He was also given a variety of foods during the morning to see if they affected his behavior.

Because he had not eaten breakfast that morning, Ken was hungry. We did not feed him until we'd observed and rated his behavior for a period. We noted his attention span by observing how long he'd spend in a particular activity such as building blocks or listening to a story. His behavior at that point appeared to be normal. After thirty minutes we fed him a breakfast similar to what he'd been eating before I'd suggested a change. Within five minutes, the Mr. Hyde facet of his behavior emerged. The toys became weapons and the research assistant became their target. After thirty minutes, the boy's behavior fit that of a psychotic. He was irrational, paranoid, and totally out of control. Ken's mother had been watching this process with me on the video monitor. She whispered: "That's my Ken."

But it wasn't Ken. The hyperactive, paranoid behavior was the result of the boy's physical reactions to the food he was consuming. His behavior was no different from that of dozens of other people we'd tested who'd proven to be highly sensitive to certain foods. Ken's problems were not mental. They were biological and chemical. He was overdosed on sugars, which caused his brain tissues to swell in an inflammatory and allergic response.

Ken's hyperactive, psychotic behavior was caused by two factors. First, his body's alarm system was triggered by the very smell of the food he was eating. As soon as its presence was detected, his brain responded and his body went into high alert. His heart started beating faster, and the instinctive fight-or-flee sense of panic set in. Second, the inflammation hit the boy's brain tissues, short-circuiting neural networks and triggering what appeared to be bizarre behavior.

Ken was tested with many foods while in the protective environment of the clinic. Those that triggered the psychotic symptoms were eliminated from his diet. We also devised therapies to help him work better in the classroom, but it was really the change in diet that put this bright child where he belonged—on the honor roll.

Environmental Triggers

Attention deficit disorder has many causes. I've learned to examine not only the patient, but his environment as well. Very often, the symptoms that bring a person to me are caused by environmental toxins and allergic responses. We live in a sea of toxicity. Our bodies are biochemical organisms. Like machines, they run according to the types of fuel we put into them and the environment around them. Our immune systems are challenged by materials unknown to those of our parents and ancestors. Children are particularly sensitive. They are like the canaries used in the early days of mining. When the air quality in the mines approached dangerous levels, the small birds would die, alerting the miners. The health problems of our children, I believe, are early indicators of the toxic environment we have created.

When I started testing all the children for heavy metals, I found that most of them had abnormally high levels of lead in their systems. That explains a lot to me and helps me in treating their symptoms. So I'm very serious when I advise that before you go to the expense of medical and psychiatric testing of your troubled child, you would do well to review the following list of toxicity responses to determine up front whether your youngster's behavior may be the result of a reaction to food products, or even chemicals hidden in carpeting, paints, or household products.

Your child may not be the only family member suffering if toxins exist in the home or in the foods you consume. Frequent colds, headaches, and digestive problems are familiar signs of potential toxins. The child's ADD symptoms may be only the most noticeable alerts to the presence of toxins or allergic reactions.

Auditing for Symptoms of Toxins in Your Child's Diet and Environment

It may take real detective work to determine the exact source of a reaction related to cognitive issues. Common sources include formaldehyde in new rugs or sheets, and even the perfume in shaving lotion. This is a checklist of symptoms caused by toxicity in the environment or by reactions to foods. To begin your search, check off symptoms that appear frequently at certain times of the day, such as after a meal, after the child arrives home from school, after he plays in the yard, or when it is time to go to bed. This time frame may be a real clue to factors related to symptoms.

Symptom	Present
• runny nose	( )
• hypersensitive skin	( )
• itchy eyes	( )
• stuffy nose, sneezing	( )
• rapid pulse	( )
• marked behavior change	( )
• increased anxiety	( )
• red ears or cheeks	( )

Symptom	Present
• mood swings	( )
• stomachache	( )
• gas and bloating	( )
• constipation or diarrhea	( )
• dark circles under the eyes	( )
• red eyes	( )
• rash	( )
• headaches	( )
• diminished reading ability	( )
• diminished memory capacity	( )
• diminished concentration	( )
• diminished arithmetic skills	( )
• diminished control over emotions	( )
• diminished visual acuity	( )
• sleep problems	( )
• diminished appetite	( )
• behavior stimulated by tobacco smoke	( )
• sugar craving	( )
• symptoms worse on damp days	( )

By the way they dress, you can usually sense from kids with ADD a number of symptoms related to environmental issues. Because their immune systems are so sensitized, they are overreactive to many conditions in the environment. For example, their skin is usually sensitive to their clothes; they may wear their T-shirts inside out because the seams or labels are scratching them.

If you checked one of the signs above, you probably have checked five or six, because children tend to have overlapping symptoms, and you should probably conduct a more precise assessment of possible environmental stimulations. It is easy enough to check out the possibility that your child's symptoms are related to food or the more common environmental toxins such as those found in certain paints, carpets, and clothing. Simply isolate the child from the suspected material for at least seventy-two hours. Then submit the child to the material and observe whether the symptoms reappear.

A Dirty World

We live in a very dirty world. Toxins exist all around us. Our bodies have adapted to some, but new forms appear all the time and every individual's immune system has its own vulnerabilities. In the last fifty years, we've introduced all kinds of new toxins into the environment. Sewage pollutes our lakes and seas. Factory and vehicle emissions poison the air. Homes and buildings often have built-in toxins. We do too. Each of us carries some level of pesticides embedded in our body fat. If enough accumulates, we could die from them. Of all our organs, the brain is most sensitive to pollutants and toxins. Consider what a few ounces of alcohol do to impair thinking. It is only logical that environmental pollutants would also have a powerful effect.

In 1997, an unusually high number of residents in the Chesapeake Bay area were found to be experiencing memory loss and learning problems. Scientists discovered that their symptoms were linked to a huge fish kill in Chesapeake Bay. The fish died because an opportunistic bacteria, *Pfiesteria piscicida,* multiplied in the nitrate-rich waters. The humans who'd eaten fish or drunk river water were affected with symptoms of memory loss and learning difficulties. The sources of the nitrates were traced to the manure of chickens, hogs, and cattle flushed into feeder streams and holding basins by heavy rains. This is one small example of a giant problem.

Children around the world have been victims of lead poisoning, which can cause a wide range of learning disabilities. Lead is found in the air, in water, in the interior paints of older homes, even in the dirt of playgrounds in many urban areas. Leaky underground gasoline storage tanks are a huge source. When water is purified it turns acidic and can leech out lead from the fittings. In 1998 the *San Francisco Chronicle* reported that two water filtration systems exceeded the state level of allowable lead content by sixty to seventy times. One of the substitutes used for lead in gasoline was methyl tertiary butyl ether, or MTBE, which, it was discovered, accumulates in water and poses its own problems.

Polybrominated diphenyl ether (PBDE) is hardly a household name, but it is in every household, as a fire retardant in your furniture. It is credited for saving three hundred or more lives a year; however, you can't get rid of it. Swedish scientists reported that PBDEs were present in mother's milk over the past quarter century, and the level has risen consistently. Because we can't get rid of this stuff, it builds up in our systems and becomes toxic. The data are clear that concentrations can create major imbalances of the thyroid, which in turn affects growth and development, especially neurological growth.

As if our protective agents are becoming our problems, government researchers found evidence that vaccinations given to our children contain a mercury preservative, thimerosal, and have caused problems in 140,000 U.S. children. The disorders specifically related to neurological developmental issues, such as autism and language delays.

Heavy Metal Toxins and Pesticides

Detoxification of heavy metals and pesticides is a very intensive process, requiring a family's concentrated effort. I worked with a five-year-old boy named Drew, whose story is typical. Drew did not suffer from the restlessness and lack of sleep most often found in ADD children, but he was diagnosed with other symptoms. He was talking excessively. He was always jumping from balconies and other high places. He couldn't play any games for more than a few minutes. Yet he had an engaging personality and a very high level of intelligence. He was a fascinating child who could hold his own in conversation with any adult.

As with many of the ADD-diagnosed children I have seen over the last five years, Drew tested for lead levels four times higher than normal. His parents found that although their house was relatively new, the construction crew had used several lead pipes for the plumbing. His family got rid of those pipes, but once lead is in the human system, it can create neurological and liver disease at any time.

Drew's father was a physician who reacted quickly to our findings. The method he chose for his son was a detoxification process he devised, and I have used this process as well, using high magnetized water intake and a supplement called DMSA (meso-2,3-dimercaptosuccinic acid). Being a bright child, Drew understood the challenges and agreed to participate. It helped that he was kept advised of his body's lead levels during the detoxification process. It took two months, which is actually surprisingly fast. Drew's father explained that small healthy bodies respond to the treatment better than large older ones.

In the two years since his treatment, Drew has become the little boy his parents and teachers had hoped for. He is well mannered and calm, and fascinated with computers. He is also amazingly articulate, funny, and wise. I wish all ADD cases were so easy to resolve.

It is frightening how environmental agents can affect our bodies and minds. Pesticides that kill insects and other pests paralyze their neural systems. The same things happen to us, though the pesticide manufacturers assure us that since we are much bigger, they should not bother us. But bugs do not have fat, and we do. We store pesticides in our body fat. As the pesticide levels build, our health is endangered. Stress can release those pesticides built up in our systems and cause havoc with our neurological systems.

Our most basic needs for survival are air and water. To protect our water supplies, we use chemicals like chloride as purifiers. It is used to keep bad things from growing in the water, but if too much chlorine treatment is used, it can have a negative impact on those who drink it.

It is a delicate balance. Chlorine treatment is necessary to kill bacteria in water. After all, hundreds of animals and insects die and decay in our lakes and even our water towers. Birds are among the most common, and they carry a variety of diseases and germs. The fact that our water has become increasingly polluted has created a billion-dollar business in filtered water. Filtered water has the advantage of having the harmful particles taken out, but it also has the good things taken out, such as minerals and nutrients. Distilled water is the least healthy because it has no ingredients for the optimal health of our bodies and minds.

Bottled water sold in the United States is not necessarily cleaner or safer than most tap water, according to a four-year study. The National Resources Defense Council tested a thousand bottles of 103 brands and found one-third were contaminated. They found organic chemicals, bacteria, and arsenic. Our regulations are inadequate, obviously. At the national level, the Food and Drug Administration is responsible for bottled water safety, but the FDA's rules exempt water that is packaged and sold within the same state, which accounts for 60 to 70 percent. Roughly 20 percent of states have no regulations. The FDA exempts carbonated water and seltzer. Even when bottled water is covered by the FDA's rules, it is subject to less rigorous testing and purity standards than those applied to city water.

According to the Environmental Working Group, using analyses compiled from USDA and FDA pesticide data from 1992 to 1997, there are significant health risks associated with foods that are contaminated. The following table illustrates their findings:

MOST CONTAMINATED FOODS

Rank	Food
1	apples
2	spinach
3	peaches
4	pears
5	strawberries
6	grapes (from Chile)
7	potatoes
8	red raspberries
9	celery
10	green beans

The fact is that there are many things in the environment that can contribute to your child's ADD symptoms. Those include

- newly painted surfaces
- perfumes (women's or men's)
- chlorinated swimming pools
- gasoline or petroleum products
- pesticides
- cut grasses or harvested crops
- household chemicals, such as cleaners
- gas stoves

Food As Cause

For most children with ADD with whom I have worked, my treatment plan included a nutritional component. A healthy diet with optimized nutrients is vital for anyone's brain to function at its highest capacity. It is clear that we function based on what we eat, so a child will be more efficient if he or she has a balanced food plan. However, some food can be poison to some children. I think sensitivities to foods must be evaluated because of the high incidence of allergic reactions that cause ADD symptoms.

The food substances that cause the most problems are commonly found. (Numbers with an asterisk are derived from J. Egger in *Lancet,* March 1985.)

- Artificial colors and preservatives are usually the leaders (79 percent)* on various lists of culprits for creating ADD symptoms. These include red and yellow food coloring agents used in cherries and other fruits. The preservative substances that cause symptoms include sodium, formaldehyde (big in Mexican beer), pickles, and brine (such as salt).
- Processed milk and milk products were also listed in the top foods (64 percent)* for triggering ADD symptoms.

- Wheat products were also a major contender (49 percent),* but only breads and cereals that are not whole grain.
- Although sugar was in the lower levels of causative agents (16 percent)* in the study, I have seen many children affected powerfully by sugars. My guess is that it causes more problems than the study found.
- Interestingly, oranges and grapefruits are implicated in most studies (57 percent).* I suspect that individuals who drink large amounts of those juices develop a resistance to them.
- Eggs are another interesting food that has been implicated, but eggs are seldom eaten raw. I wonder if it is the preparation of these foods that triggers ADD symptoms. A boiled egg is a different food from a fried one.
- Monosodium glutamate (MSG), a taste enhancer frequently used in Chinese restaurants, was implicated in most of the studies; however, few mentions were made because of the low use.

These are the major foods that have been investigated and found to have negative impacts on children's health. But there are many other substances that have the power to cause reactions. I know of one individual who developed hives as a reaction to honey, and another whose throat would close to the point of strangulation when he tasted mustard.

Diet Adjustments Work

The great news is that substituting healthier foods can immediately reduce ADD symptoms in many cases. There are a number of excellent studies that have demonstrated 50 to 70 percent resolution of hyperactive behavior and increased concentration spans with alternative menus. This is a treatment that most families can handle easily.

In my experience, one of the biggest food culprits in triggering ADD symptoms is the food on school menus. When we investigated what was being served for breakfast in schools with learning disabilities students, we were amazed to find that most of the outrageous behaviors could be attributed to food the children had eaten. Doughnuts, sweet rolls, sweetened orange juice, and even processed milk can trigger antisocial behavior.

In a series of investigations at the University of North Texas Research Lab for Clinical Ecology, we found that learning disabled students showed remarkably better behavior after our recommendations for diet changes were implemented in the school lunch programs. If you suggest this, you may meet with resistance from school administrators, but if you show them the research—feel free to use this book—they should be willing to at least try adjusting their menus. After all, disruptive behavior is their problem too. Hospitals have their problems in this regard as well. I've often advised families to take their own foods to hospitalized children because institutional food can trigger adverse physical and behavioral reactions.

Chemicals that affect the brain are everywhere. I remember only too well when Mark, a lively eight-year-old, was taken to the hospital for symptoms of psychosis. The parents discussed the situation with the doctor who specialized in environmental medicine. He asked me to investigate the progression of the boy's psychosis. I observed the quick relief of his hallucinations within twenty-four hours of his admittance, but I went further into his neural and cognitive functioning. We kept him for observation for four days, and each day brought more improvement. The medical experts weren't doing anything but feeding him healthy food.

However, within a week of his return home, the same bizarre behavior returned. Finally the answer emerged, and there is a good ending. It turns out that Mark was an avid builder of model airplanes and he had been eating the dried glue off his fingers and smelling the fumes for at least four weeks. Although I doubt that he would have developed a habit, model airplane glue can be a powerful brain state alteration agent, even to the point of becoming an addiction.

Action Plan for Eliminating Toxins

Treating ADD with diet changes and internal cleansing is increasingly popular because it is drug free and often very effective. There are growing fields of health care that specialize in cleansing the body of environmental agents. Naturopathic physicians are gaining wider acceptance. But don't be disappointed if they are not totally successful. There may be other contributing factors for your child's ADD symptoms.

Clearly, foods and pollutants are conspirators in activating ADD symptoms. Parents can minimize the effects of these pollutants with this step-by-step plan. This process is based on the reduction of toxicity in the child's body, but the stage should be set by a concerted effort to eliminate such substances from the environment. Check the plumbing, your water supply, your household cleaning materials, and find alternative methods of pest control to pesticides.

Step One: Stimulate the Body's Natural Cleansing Enzymes

The body is designed to drain away toxins naturally, so rather than fight this process, the ideal approach is to stimulate it. Some food toxins are water soluble and can be eliminated naturally through the body's own cleansing and waste system. The axiom that the more water you put in, the more you get out, works well, so the strategy is to introduce as much water as appropriate for a diuretic effect. Green tea and melons have been used to help this process along.

Step Two: Exercise

Aerobic exercises can enhance the release of toxins in many ways. Regular exercise promotes the transfer of gases in the lungs, which means that a person who exercises can breathe in oxygen and other important elements of the air, while eliminating toxins by exhaling. By breathing efficiently, immunity levels are heightened and white blood cells become more efficient in "eating up" the pollutants.

Our bodies can become overwhelmed by toxins and allergy agents; our tissues and organs can become like a sewer system where everything stands stagnant. Exercise works to drain the system of those unwanted toxins. The lungs and heart perform heroically to eliminate the pollutants. Muscles contract and squeeze out unwanted by-products included in lactic acid. Skin pores open and release poisons too.

Step Three: Conversion to Water-Soluble Toxins and Release

This next step is not required and you may want to consult someone who has expertise and experience in this process because it is uncomfortable and has some risk. When fat-soluble toxins are being converted and released, they can pose a danger. At this point, a person can become ill unless he takes protective measures by ingesting strong antioxidants such as vitamin C, vitamin E, vitamin A, and coenzyme Q10, with loads of water.

Leads and pesticides generally are not so easy to shed because they often get absorbed in the fat and are released very slowly. You can't sweat them out in the sauna. But if you want to help the body transform some of the fat-soluble substances to water-soluble ones, there are a number of natural supplements that have been shown to stimulate the natural enzymes (cytochrome P450) for this purpose. The favorites reported to me are vitamin B6, DIM (found in cauliflower, brussels sprouts, and broccoli), and forskolin. The enzymes pancreatin, papain, bromelain, trypsin, chymotrypsin, and rutosid have been recommended, and have actually been combined by a German company as a very popular substance called Wobenzym N, which has produced some strong results in this regard. These substances can be bought at most natural foods stores.

This phase may not be the best idea for a vacation. The person may experience stiffness in the joints and nausea. These symptoms are a sign that the purge is working, but if they continue for more than a few days, let your body catch up with the antioxidants. As the toxins are released into water-soluble status, they will be released by the body through the liver and kidneys.

Step Four: Opening the Gates of Detoxification

Whether or not your child went through step three, the body will start a major program to get rid of the bad guys, and this is where you open the gates of detoxification. It may help also to get your sweat glands in high gear. I recommend saunas, massages, spas, hot mud baths, hot wraps with herbs (making you look and feel like a human burrito), and even long walks. The concept is to increase the flow of water-soluble toxins out of the system.

As the toxic fluid leaves your child's body it needs to be replenished with good water and a lot of it. Several glasses a day is not too much at this point; a little lemon juice will help. Green tea is another excellent supplement, as well as Gatorade and other sports drinks that stabilize electrolytes.

At the beginning of this chapter, I wrote of Ken and the success we had when we changed his nutritional plan. The behavioral patterns of many other children and adults have been positively affected by similar changes in diet. But keep in mind that it is critical that the patient's family be supportive and involved.

Food Trials

Each child is different, so every diet has to be adjusted carefully. This also means that the lifestyle of the family may be affected. Invariably, someone will note that the new milk tastes funny or that the menu has some strange food.

Open communication and discussion is vital to the success of a diet adjustment for ADD children. Discuss the ideas and logic as the diet changes are administered. Encourage feedback from the child with ADD so you can quickly determine which diet changes are having the greatest impact on her behavior.

A Challenge

It is probable that the world did not suddenly become polluted and the cause of a disorder by which we will certainly be doomed. It is clear from medical anthropology that humankind has been moving from one area to the next to escape its own environmental sewage for generations, indeed, from the beginning. Perhaps because of a sense of desperation, or even greed, we use up the resources in abundance, leaving our children to suffer the consequences.

For the first time in human history, humans have not had to live on the edge of survival for food, and consequently, we are on the verge of an epidemic of obesity. Interestingly, we may be the first humans to have to make choices for the best food and to live in the healthiest environment. Parents will be the first to make those choices, especially if their child has ADD. Parents are being challenged for the safety of their children as never before. In the days when bears and lions were threats to children, the dangers were more obvious than the secret potions in the pesticides under our sinks and the manufactured food we have learned to take on faith. Instead of making our own food (who remembers how to make butter or a meat loaf?), we have learned that those heat-'em-up dinners taste pretty darn good. I am not condemning the food industry, but I am asking, do you really know what your child is doing under your supervision?

We, as parents, are going to have to add another task to our job description—looking at what our kids are consuming or being exposed to. I am not talking about the basic five food groups. If you suspect your child has ADD or you have been dealing with the symptoms, you need to investigate the possible toxins she has been subjected to. Look for contaminated water and problematic food, and check for heavy metal absorption.

But perhaps most important is to begin a steady schedule of cleansing. All of us need some ongoing routine so we can help our bodies get rid of the built-up toxins. Just like teaching your child to brush her teeth, wouldn't it be a good idea to go on a periodic fast together, like a juice fast, or simply drink water for the day? These procedures have been taught by spiritual sects for as long as we know. Maybe they knew something we need to remember.

EIGHT

The Hero's Nutritional Plan

Pete, age nine, is one of the most energetic boys I have worked with. This kid never walked anywhere. He ran. Unfortunately, his high level of energy was causing him problems. Just two months into the start of the school year, he'd earned a reputation for being rebellious and defiant. Pete seemed to enjoy the company of other children but he hated playing structured games. He had an experienced teacher but she was tested by his hyperactivity. He couldn't sit still and he was always blurting out comments.

Pete's parents brought him to see me after he was diagnosed with attention deficit disorder. His teacher would not allow him back in her classroom unless he was placed on Ritalin. Thankfully, the family's physician referred Pete to me instead.

Interestingly, in the previous school year Pete hadn't been nearly as wild in class. His teacher in that class had spent more time building a one-on-one relationship with him, and Pete had tried hard to control his impulsive behavior.

His was an intriguing case, though not untypical in many ways for an ADD child. I interviewed his family as a group. Pete was there, and his sister Sara, who was two years older, and his mother and father. During the hour-and-a-half discussion, Pete was a model boy. He played with the Tinker Toys I'd given him while we talked about his behavior. His mother said his birth was without complications, though it did cause some conflict with his older sister, who felt displaced from the mother's attention and began to throw tantrums. Nancy wisely taught Sara how to bottle feed Pete, and that helped the situation.

He was a restless baby, often sleeping for less than two hours at a time. As he grew, his play habits showed a limited attention span. He'd move from one toy to another constantly. Pete was also slow to walk and to talk. As often happens, his older sister, who'd come to view herself as Pete's caretaker, translated his baby talk babble and served as his interpreter until he reached kindergarten age. Once he'd learned to walk, he was constantly on the move. He'd run off so many times that his parents kept a beeper on him. People in the neighborhood referred to him as "the beeping kid."

There were troublesome aspects of the family's lifestyle. Pete's diet was loaded with sugar. He'd spoon it into his mouth from a bowl when his parents weren't looking. His favorite meal was rolls with butter and apple juice. His mother gave him that as a reward for good behavior. She noted also that Pete often became lethargic and irritable in midmorning and midafternoon, "like a tired baby who doesn't want to go to sleep."

Pete's father, Milton, maintained that he'd had similar problems as a child yet he'd grown up OK. He was defending his son's behavior as normal, and also indicating that he'd probably suffered from the same poor nutritional habits. It was evident that there was likely a genetic link.

Pete's test results were exactly as I had expected based on the clues I'd been given. He had average to above-average scores for his native abilities, such as abstract reasoning and general knowledge; those areas that require rote memory, especially coupled with long-term memory—such as the alphabet and addition and subtraction—were problems. Tests for young children aren't always reliable, but it was very clear that Pete had difficulty concentrating on tasks. Yet I did not see signs of learning disabilities, such as letter reversals or spatial errors in his drawings, which are usual for his low maturity level.

From a psychological perspective, Pete experienced low self-esteem and he was fearful of what might happen to him because of all the attention being paid to his problems. He worried about his parents and sister dying and leaving him alone. He had developed an elaborate fantasy world, which is not unusual for his age, with a sophisticated set of characters with whom he felt secure. He admitted that when he became bored or frustrated, he'd create imaginary adventures with his fictional friends. This was not particularly helpful for his achievement in school, but it did give him a sense of control that offered him some security and self-confidence.

I told Pete's family and physician that he did have symptoms of attention deficit disorder and that he needed therapies to help develop his learning skills. But Pete was capable of good behavior and he'd done well on many of the tests. So I did not recommend medication unless we needed it as a backup to other approaches.

My recommended program included a complete nutritional program (including allergy testing), family therapy to strengthen family communication and parenting skills (see Chapter Fourteen), biofeedback to help Pete learn control of his stress reactions (see Chapter Ten), and a physical challenge component to focus his energy and build his self-esteem.

The treatment program worked well in Pete's case, especially the nutritional component. Pete wasn't really happy about being weaned from his processed sugars and starches in candy, of course, but he admitted that he felt better throughout the day. He no longer went into the dumps at midmorning and midafternoon. And he did better in school. With those successes, he also relied less on his imaginary world.

Pete was not cured of ADD. He still had symptoms. But they were manageable with the program we worked out. Pete took pride in the fact that he'd learned to control his behavior. He described it like being a diabetic; only he had it better—no shots.

Changing a child's diet can help in many cases. I've seen the results with my patients, and other physicians and psychologists report similar successes. This is not cutting-edge science. The earliest forefathers of modern medicine, Asclepius and Hippocrates, wrote of the curative properties of certain foods—and the fact that others could cause allergic reactions.

Not all families, or family members, welcome diet changes that restrict sugars and starches. Brothers and sisters may rebel at losing their Ding Dongs because of a sibling's ADD therapy. In such cases, if they are young enough, I remind them that the Power Rangers take care of their bodies by avoiding french fries and burritos. "If you want to look like a hero, you have to eat like a hero," I tell them. "If you want to look like a loser, you can eat like a loser."

A healthy diet is important for all children and adults but it is critical in the treatment of those with ADD to maximize their concentration, learning capacity, and self-control. The following audit may be helpful in focusing on exactly what dietary elements might be contributing to your child's symptoms.

Audit for Diet-related Symptoms of ADD

Go through the checklist to assess those ADD symptoms that might be diet related. Since metabolism is often a heredity factor, this study might be helpful in starting a family project to establish support and enthusiasm for a healthier diet.

Behavior	Frequency of Occurrence		
	Often	Sometimes	Never
1. Craving for food with high sugar	( )	( )	( )
2. Having very deep lows in energy	( )	( )	( )
3. Lacking in concentration	( )	( )	( )
4. Unable to entertain oneself with an activity for long periods	( )	( )	( )
5. Disorganized in work matters	( )	( )	( )
6. Confused in receiving information	( )	( )	( )
7. Quickly fatigues mentally	( )	( )	( )
8. Restlessness and boredom with high needs for stimulation	( )	( )	( )
9. Wide variation in memory capacities	( )	( )	( )
10. Highly sensitive to criticism	( )	( )	( )
11. Refers to need for food to restore energy	( )	( )	( )
12. Consumes food rapidly	( )	( )	( )

Behavior	Frequency of Occurrence		
	Often	Sometimes	Never
13. Drinks large amounts of fruit or sweet drinks	( )	( )	( )
14. Avoids competitive intellectual games	( )	( )	( )
15. Obsessed with high action drama	( )	( )	( )

Scoring

For each "Often" you marked, give a score of 2, and for every "Sometimes," a score of 1. Sum up your scores for a raw score in a range of 0–30. You will note that these descriptions are similar to the items on a list of attention deficit disorder symptoms; however, this list relates specifically to metabolism issues. Consider the interpretation of the final score.

- For final scores in the range of **0–5,** the individual may not have a metabolism issue that relates to ADD.
- For final scores in the range of **6–15,** the individual has ADD-type symptoms that are related to metabolism issues and ADD symptoms.
- For final scores of **16–22,** there are significant issues of metabolism and ADD symptoms, and a diet is recommended.
- For final scores of **23–30,** a nutritional assessment would be recommended, especially in regard to foods that may have allergic properties for the individual and may be promoting ADD symptoms.

Metabolism and ADD

The genetic link in ADD has been discussed and documented for some time, but a characteristic associated with a gene has to be elicited and provoked by the environment to manifest itself. (For example, a genetic characteristic such as running speed may never show itself unless the person is exposed to the appropriate exercises and opportunities for that trait.) Often characteristics become manifest by food, especially those foods that create stress in the system.

Proper nutrition is important for everyone but it is more important for a person with attention deficit disorder. You don't create ADD with nutrition, but you can make it better or worse with what you eat.

Parents often feel guilty or defensive when I raise questions about their child's diet. My mention of bottled formula and its lack of fatty acids often provokes people to anxiety. It's not that any one dietary thing causes ADD, but it can intensify the symptoms. Certain bottle milk and manufactured baby foods do not always have enough fatty acids for the development of the infant's brain, eyes, and heart. If Pete's brain did not have the genetic disposition toward ADD, this might have been a factor in his slow development.

No one knows the cause of attention deficit disorder. The prevailing theory holds that it is a complex brain developmental issue. Brain scans tend to confirm that the brains of ADD children are smaller than average (3 percent), according to Dr. F. Xavier Castellanos of New York University. SPECT studies by Daniel Amen depict specific zones of the brain that correlate to ADD symptoms. My own studies with EEG have been very consistent with the brain development concept.

Another theory holds that the smaller brain is the result of a developmental problem in the *metabolism* of the child. That means the brain is not receiving enough nutrients so it functions at a lower level. This theory would mean that even normal people would develop ADD cognitive symptoms if their diets were poor.

Even those with healthy diets can lack essential minerals and vitamins. Researchers have shown also that defects in the stomach walls can result in the loss of the nutrients we consume. This can contribute to a number of medical problems, including cardiovascular disease, cancer, and dementia.

Abnormal metabolisms are among the most important factors to consider in children with ADD, regardless of the cause. Proper nutrition is vital. There are four critical food components (fatty acids, sugars, minerals, and vitamins) that are most vital for these children.

Essential Fatty Acids (EFAs)

Our bodies are composed of billions of cells. Each cell is sur-rounded by a waterproof membrane composed of different types of fatty acids that separate the watery contents of the cell from the watery fluid outside the cell. These fatty acids are essential for two reasons. First, they affect the properties of the cell membrane and the ability of the molecules to bind to receptors in the membrane. This is critical to developing bridges across cells so as to promote ef-fective body coordination. Second, and probably most pertinent to the brain, these essential fatty acids produce a series of hormones, including *prostaglandins*. Prostaglandins promote communication between cells, especially those in the brain and the retina of the eye. When fatty acids are lacking, the typical symptoms are thirst, scaly skin, frequent urination, and learning problems. The most ef-fective essential fatty acids for brain health and function are found in fish, particularly fatty fish such as tuna and salmon, and veg-etable oils like flaxseed oil.

Sugar

When you take in natural sugar, it goes to the bloodstream and waits to be transported by the insulin from the pancreas. It is stored in the cells as *glycogen*. Your muscles, liver, and fatty tissues can store this glycogen for later, but your brain cannot. When a normal person takes in sugar, it enters the bloodstream and be-comes blood glucose. Remember, the brain doesn't store glyco-gen. But in normal people, the adrenal glands produce stimulants, called *epinephrine* and *norepinephrine*. These chemicals step up the glucose to the brain, making it more active and functional.

ADD kids don't produce the same level of stimulants as normal kids. That's why their brains go into a sleep mode. To counter that, children with ADD instinctively increase their physical activity to stimulate themselves and jump-start brain activity. You thought they were acting crazy and being irresponsible? In truth, they are trying to do the opposite. They become frantic in their efforts to stimulate themselves, so they do what appear to be crazy things, like walking on ledges, climbing towers, and running amok. High-risk behaviors cause fear and anxiety that stimulate the brain. ADD children need natural sources of carbohydrates, especially if they are experiencing stress, but that does not mean candy bars and Cokes. Natural complex carbs are found in whole grains (brown rice, oats, whole grain breads), whole fruits, and vegetables—starchy (yams, legumes) and nonstarchy (basically all other veggies).

Minerals

The brain depends on minerals that make up only 0.5 percent of the brain's weight yet serve important functions for balancing and enhancing every neuron. Calcium and magnesium are essential to the neural network. Calcium acts as a traffic cop in nerve cells, directing the uptake and release of neurotransmitters. Consequently, it interacts with the balance of the sodium and potassium across the cell membrane and regulates the speed of transmission for every nerve cell in your body.

Foods high in calcium include yogurt, cow milk, soy milk (preferred), rice milk (actually the sweetest of all the milks), cottage cheese, canned sardines with the bones crushed with the meat, beans, lentils, and chickpeas.

Magnesium also serves as a dance partner to calcium and other minerals. It magnifies their effects and enables calcium to do its job. In two recent studies coauthored by T. Kozielec in *Magnesium Research* (1997), 94 percent of ADD children showed low magnesium. More important, when fifty ADD children were administered 200 milligrams a day, their hyperactivity significantly decreased. Another study found low magnesium levels in 95 percent of children with ADD. In a follow-up, researchers administered magnesium to half the children with ADD in their study. The group that received the magnesium showed improvement in their behavior. The others showed no change. Among the magnesium-rich foods are nuts, seeds, whole grains (including breads), and hard water.

Zinc also is important to the health of ADD children, and all of us. I use a simple taste test for zinc deficiency. I ask a child to taste a liquid formula called Zinc Tally, and if she cannot taste it, she is zinc deficit. This assessment can be done by you, and it is immediate. Virtually every person I have seen for ADD therapy has proven positive. Most zinc is concentrated in the brain membranes and acts like a soldier to guard the nerve cells from free-radical attack. However, it also serves as an electric contact for neurotransmission, helping convert serotonin into melatonin, which is the chief regulator of rhythms. Zinc is abundant in proteins, such as meat, poultry, fish, and shellfish.

Vitamins

Vitamin C plays a major role in the body's healing process. It strengthens the walls of blood vessels and acts like a glue to fortify them from invaders like cold germs and cancer cells. The brain contains more vitamin C than any other organ in the body, with the exception of the adrenal gland. It is critical in the production of norepinephrine, dopamine, and serotonin, all considered major players in cognitive functioning and emotional stability.

If vitamin C is a known hero in the immune system, vitamin B6 is a multiple-threat secret weapon. It enhances the effects of minerals and vitamins. It helps combat virtually every disease. I recommend it in nearly every diet therapy. It is one of the most studied vitamins, and a lack of it is believed to contribute to a wide range of health and mental problems including seizures, autism, depression, headaches, chronic pain, memory, agitated behavior, anxiety, and sleep difficulties.

There are a host of fruits that offer vitamin C; however, instead of devoting the rest of the chapter to a list, I will mention the most potent that can be recognized in the United States:

- grapefruit
- guava
- kiwi
- mango
- orange
- papaya
- persimmon
- rose hip

As you might expect, ADD children often have low levels of vitamin B6. When those levels are raised, their hyperactivity is reduced. I've often said that if anything has the power to do good, it also has the power to do bad. But there are no downsides to B6 as far as scientists can tell. I also recommend its big brother, B12. It increases energy, lessens anxiety, and boosts learning and concentration. It is an excellent treatment for children with ADD.

Foods high in vitamin B6 include fortified cereals, bananas, garbanzo beans, baked potato (skin and flesh), chicken breast (without skin), oatmeal (fortified), and pork loin (lean only). On a lower level, but still noteworthy for kids, are sunflower seeds, wheat bran, peanut butter, and walnuts.

Sources of vitamin B12 include mostly high-protein foods, such as beef, fish, eggs, milk, soy cheese, rice cheese, tofu, fish, and beans.

OTHER SUPPLEMENTS SPECIFIC TO ADD

Supplement	How It Works	Dosage for Children
Multivitamin and mineral supplement (children's formulation)	Assists in maintaining the normal function of neurotransmitters; helps prevent nutrient shortfalls	Follow manufacturer's dosage instructions on the label
DHA from fish oil	An essential fatty acid that plays an important role in brain health	500–1000 mg daily

OTHER SUPPLEMENTS SPECIFIC TO ADD *(continued)*

Supplement	How It Works	Dosage for Children
DMAE	A natural substance found in fish that helps build and restore acetylcholine, a brain chemical involved in concentration	50 mg in the morning; 50 mg in the evening. Gradually build to 250 mg twice a day.
Phosphatidylserine	A special type of lipid involved in brain function and metabolism	100 mg daily
Glutamine	An amino acid (protein) that may stimulate mental alertness	250–500 mg daily
Theanine	An amino acid extracted from tea and certain species of mushrooms that has a calming effect on the nervous system without creating sedation	100–200 mg daily
Pycnogenol or grape seed extract	Two forms of herbal therapy that have been used to treat ADD and ADHD; both substances help increase blood flow to the brain and protect brain cells from damage.	Follow manufacturer's dosage instructions on the label. (Therapeutic dosages range from 25 to 100 mg a day.)
Probiotics	Helps restore healthy bacteria in the intestinal tract. Healthy bacteria is destroyed by the overuse of antibiotics, creating imbalances believed to be a risk factor for ADHD in children.	Discuss appropriate dosage with your pediatrician.

Those are some of the most helpful diet supplements I've found for children with the ADD diagnosis. There are others that have been shown to benefit ADD children. Some that are often mentioned in the literature are iron, manganese, copper, cobalt, selenium, and chromium.

Note: Always check with your doctor before giving supplements to your children, particularly if they are taking medication. Some supplements will interact adversely with medication.

The Next Step Toward a Nutritional Metabolism Plan

Trying to control an ADD child's eating habits is like attempting to herd cats. These children have powerful cravings and they are easily influenced by the equally powerful and pervasive advertising of the fast food industry. Given all the influences working on today's kids, it is hardly a surprise that they prefer french fries and greasy burgers to lettuce and tofu.

The U.S. Department of Agriculture assessed dietary practices among 3,300 children and adolescents in 1991. Only 1 percent (higher than I expected) met all the national recommendations for daily servings of the five food groups. Sixteen percent did not meet *any* of these requirements, and—I know this comes as a big shock—nearly half of the calories they consumed came from fat and sugar.

Trying to count calories or preparing precise meals of half a cup of this and two ounces of that will drive you nuts. You might as well try to teach pigs to sing. As my grandmother used to say, "They won't ever learn, and all you will do is annoy them."

The Hero's Diet Plan

Over the years, I've developed a commonsense nutritional plan for ADD children that doesn't include high-priced foods or supplements and doesn't require a culinary arts degree to prepare. There is one requirement for this nutritional plan to work. The entire family needs to go on it. No exceptions unless there is a medical reason. It is hard enough to change a child's food habits without having a brother or sister (or father or mother) eating his favorite fast foods in front of him. It is also important to show family support and solidarity. And good nutrition is good for everyone.

I named this the Hero's Nutritional Plan because these are truly the meals of champions. Remember how Popeye ate his spinach? Real-life heroes, such as athletes and astronauts, eat healthy foods too.

Step One: Eat Naturally

Our bodies were not designed to handle processed and greasy foods. Put the fryer and the microwave in storage. I recommend eating most foods in their most raw and natural states. Those that need to be cooked for safety reasons (such as killing bacteria and bugs) should be boiled or grilled over a low flame to reach at least water's boiling point (212°F). For example, chicken eggs may have salmonella and meat can have parasites, which will be killed at that temperature.

To get your children to eat raw vegetables and other healthy raw foods like raisins, put a little peanut butter or honey on them. Here is my recommended natural food plan:

FOOD GROUP RECOMMENDATIONS FOR CHILDREN WITH ADD

Food Group	Minimum Number of Daily Servings	Examples of Daily Serving Sizes
Lean proteins (meat, poultry, fish, eggs, protein alternates such as legumes or tofu)	2	2 oz. of meat, poultry, or fish; 1 egg; ½ cup of protein alternates
Fruits and vegetables	5	½ piece to 1 piece of fruit; ½ cup chopped fresh fruit; ½ cup water- or juice-packed fruit; ½ cup frozen unsweetened fruit; ½ cup juice; several cut-up pieces of raw vegetables; ½ cup cooked vegetables; ¼ cup legumes (beans or lentils)

Food Group	Minimum Number of Daily Servings	Examples of Daily Serving Sizes
Milk substitutes (rice milk)	3	½ cup milk substitute; ½ cup yogurt; ½ oz. cheese; ¼ cup cottage cheese; ½ cup sugar-free ice cream or ice milk
Whole grains (breads and cereals)	4	½ to 1 slice bread; ¼ to ½ cup cooked cereal; ½ cup dry cereal; ¼ cup pasta, noodles, or rice; 2 to 3 crackers
Fats	Use sparingly	½ teaspoon vegetable oil, salad dressing, mayonnaise, natural peanut butter, margarine, or butter (flaxseed oil is a recommended fat because it is a good source of brain-protective fats); 1 tablespoon or one child's handful of nuts or seeds

SAMPLE THREE-DAY MENU

DAY 1

Breakfast
½ cup cooked oatmeal
1 cup rice milk
1 banana

Snack
baby carrots
crackers (2) with natural peanut butter

Lunch
tuna sandwich (2 oz. tuna mixed with a little mayonnaise on two
    slices of whole grain bread)
½ cup vegetable soup

Snack
½ cup sugar-free yogurt with ½ piece of fresh pear

Dinner
2 oz. chicken
½ cup green beans
¼ to ½ cup mashed sweet potatoes
½ cup sugar-free ice cream

DAY 2

Breakfast
"pig in a poke" (Cut a small hole out of the middle of a slice of
    whole-grain bread; place in small frying pan coated with veg-
    etable spray. Break an egg into the hole and cook on low to
    medium heat until the egg is fully cooked and the bread is
    toasty.)
½ cup of cut-up cantaloupe

Snack
granola bar
½ cup milk or rice milk

Lunch
small lean hamburger patty on a whole grain bun with lettuce
¼ cup to ½ cup cole slaw
½ cup milk or rice milk

Snack
½ cup pineapple chunks or two rings of pineapple, juice-packed
small handful of nuts (such as Brazil nuts)

Dinner
2 oz. roasted turkey
¼ cup to ½ cup mashed potatoes
½ cup green peas
½ cup sugar-free ice cream

DAY 3

Breakfast
fruit shake (½ cup sugar-free yogurt or ½ cup sugar-free ice
    cream blended with ½ cup milk or rice milk and ½ cup of
    frozen berries or other fruit)
1 slice whole grain toast with ½ teaspoon butter or margarine

Snack
banana
½ cup yogurt, milk, or rice milk

Lunch
healthy fast food lunch (grilled chicken sandwich with small side
    salad and reduced-fat salad dressing)

Snack
whole grain crackers with cottage cheese or cheese slices

Dinner
½ cup pasta with spaghetti sauce and 2 oz. lean ground beef
½ cup cooked zucchini
½ cup sugar-free yogurt with ½ cup fruit cocktail (water- or juice-
    packed)

Step Two: Supplementing Essential Fatty Acids

Essential fatty acids are usually consumed in the many forms of
fat. There are good fats and bad fats. The bad fats are classified as
saturated fats, which congeal at cool temperatures, like butter or
beef fat. The good fats stay in a liquid state all the time, such as

oils that come from deepwater fish (herring and cod), and olive, flaxseed, and canola oils.

Cow's milk contains several problematic ingredients, including bad fats. I recommend soy milk and rice milk as substitutes for dairy. You can even make nut milk from mixing ground nuts with boiling water in a blender or food processor. Actually this milk is often preferred by children for its nutty flavor.

Step Three: Reduce Sugars

Simple sugars are processed rapidly by the body, causing rapid highs and lows in energy. But there are bad sugars and better sugars. Those with high glycemic levels are more destructive to emotional and cognitive functions because of the tendency to flood the body with glucose.

EXAMPLES OF GLYCEMIC LEVELS OF FOODS

Foods	Rating
glucose	100
carrots	92
honey	87
molasses	85
brown rice syrup	80
whole wheat bread	72
brown rice	66
sucrose (table sugar)	59
spaghetti	50
oatmeal	49
whole wheat or rice spaghetti	42
oranges	40
yogurt and ice cream	36

Foods	Rating
maltodextrin	25–30
fructose	20
soybeans	15
peanuts	13
popcorn	12
water	0

Adapted from Jenkins, Wolever, et al., "Glycemic Index of Foods: Physiological Basics for Carbohydrate Exchange," *American Journal of Clinical Nutrition* 32 (1988), 362–66.

A general rule for carbohydrates is to substitute starches for the simple sugars. Simple sugars include white sugar, brown sugar, honey, corn syrup, and cane sugar. Starches, such as pastas and potatoes, are complex sugars that are broken down more slowly, creating a more stable supply of glucose and supplying a more appropriate level of stimulation. Fruits contain carbohydrates and fiber and are excellent sources for minerals and vitamins, which have many positive attributes for the body. But they also contain a high concentration of simple sugars. Applying the high response/high-yield principle, I would recommend substituting fruits that have high fiber, such as tomato and pineapple juice.

Step Four: Minerals and Vitamins

The best method for getting minerals and vitamins is through food. The body can more easily digest it and adjust the levels more easily. Moreover, the body will often reject many vitamins and simply excrete them. People who take megavitamins have the most expensive urine in the world.

Tracking a child's vitamin intake in food can be difficult. It is also true that many foods are no longer as nutritional as they once were because of the way they are grown commercially. Today's commercially grown apples are not the same fruit grown on backyard trees. Here are the recommended daily requirements for children with ADD. Do whatever you can to ensure that your child gets what he needs.

vitamin C	500–1000 mg
vitamin B6	50 mg
vitamin B12	50 mcg (I like desiccated liver for this substance)
Zinc	15 mg
calcium	260 mg (in combination as dolomite)
magnesium	160 mg (in combination as dolomite)

Dolomite is a natural substance that has calcium and magnesium in it, and is incredibly cheap. For generations, Native Americans sought out the dolomite in west Texas dirt when they became ill. There are dozens of other vitamins and minerals recommended for general health, including iron, manganese, copper, cobalt, selenium, and chromium.

I would recommend looking at the dietary reference intakes (DRIs) of the Institute of Medicine of the National Academy of Sciences. Keep in mind that these values are set as the minimal values for deficiencies that are inherent in malnutrition rather than being relevant for prevention or specific to ADD symptoms.

Vitamins and other supplements are not cures for ADD symptoms but they can help manage or reduce them. I consider proper nutrition a cornerstone in treating all health problems. Every year we get more scientific proof to support what our mothers and their mothers have told us for years: we are what we eat, or what we don't eat. That is why the first step in treating your child's ADD symptoms should be the creation of a healthy diet.

The science of nutrition is still in its infant stage, and there is more hyperbole than facts. Optimal nutrition depends on each indivdual's chemistry, metabolism, psychological status, environment, and a hundred other dimensions that are difficult to quantify. I am learning something new every day, and this chapter serves as more of a primer than an encyclopedia. Food preparation varies with culture, expertise, effort, and even the frustration or joy of the cook. If you are interested in pursuing this direction, my favorite references are *The A.D.D. Nutrition Solution* by Marcia Zimmerman and *Healing the Hyperactive Brain* by Michael Lyon, M.D. I have found the following Web sites to be especially helpful:

- www.ADDtoC3Kids.com
- www.dietspace.com
- www.feingold.org
- www.thenutritionsolution.com

In my clinical experience the nutritional approach to ADD is both a rewarding as well as a frustrating path. It becomes rewarding when your child begins to understand that it is her responsibility to control her ADD symptoms through natural means. This is a major step toward global healthy control because it is well documented that lifestyle is the most important feature of wellness. However, children tend to grow up at different rates, and their food requirements change as well, making meals an everyday challenge. It is difficult to assess exact responses to nutritional components. This is like trying to measure a child's height while she is bouncing on a trampoline. It can never be a perfect calculation.

Nevertheless, we require nutrition to function, and if you cannot predict consequences, that should not discourage you from learning about what makes your child tick. This specific approach will do just that, and maybe that is the real treasure.

NINE

Healing Sleep

Jack, ten years old, was sitting sullenly between his shell-shocked parents in my office waiting room when I walked out to get him for our first session. His teacher referred him to me because she suspected he had ADD.

When I introduced myself, Jack's mother immediately dumped ten pounds of school reports in my hands. She didn't say a word but her eyes begged for help. I'd talked to her on the telephone a few days before so I knew that she was desperate. Jack's behavioral problems were escalating rapidly.

Jack didn't look up at me. He seemed to be asleep, or on the verge of it. He was so lethargic I might have thought he was drugged if I hadn't known that his parents had avoided that.

I excused myself for a few minutes to review his school records, leaving the sad family to wait in silence. I saw from the reports that Jack was capable of being a well-behaved, good student. He had the ability, but Jack's moods swung wildly from the near comatose state I'd just seen in the waiting room to frantic, out-of-control rages.

The records showed he was irritable and impulsive most mornings at school. As the school day wore on, he was almost impossible to control. When he wasn't bouncing off the wall, he was sleeping in class. By the end of the school day, he would settle down and appear willing to learn, though it was too late for that. His best periods for focus and concentration were in the after-school hours. At those times, he participated in sports and in computer games, showing skill in both.

Because he could be charming and obviously had the ability to do well in class, Jack was at first labeled "manipulative and spoiled" by teachers frustrated with his performance. At least two psychologists even considered that he might have an "antisocial personality." Nobody had figured out how to correct his behavior.

After reading over the first three years of his school records, I had to admit that he was acting in an antisocial manner. I asked Jack to talk with me privately so I could hear his view of things. During our talk, I noticed a clue often overlooked in diagnosing ADD symptoms in young people. The assessment proved significant and, in the end, provided a rewarding therapy for him and his family, not to mention his teachers.

The fatigue and irritability displayed between his episodes of destructive energy indicated to me that Jack's behavior might be related to sleeping problems. My suspicions were confirmed on the office questionnaire his mother filled out. She noted that he slept poorly. He complained that he could not breathe and had to change positions frequently to get enough air.

After his physician examined him and found no physical obstructions or evidence of sleep apnea, additional investigation revealed that Jack was extremely sensitive to dust and goose down. Guess what kind of pillow Jack had slept with for years: a goose down pillow that he'd had since childhood.

It took several weeks to find a substitute pillow acceptable to Jack, who was pretty picky about his pillows. To further help his breathing while sleeping, I also suggested that he use a nasal dilator, one of those adhesive strips for his nose, such as Emmitt Smith of the Dallas Cowboys wears. Once we'd made those changes, Jack underwent a striking transformation.

Would you believe he not only became an excellent student but he also won the state spelling bee? And yes, he was wearing his Emmitt Smith strip when he did it! After that, those strips were all the rage among the spelling bee crowd.

Weary World

Concentration and mood stability are both related to the quality of sleep and rest a person gets, so it only makes sense that ADD symptoms can be triggered by a lack of quality snooze time. About 80 million Americans are chronically sleep deprived, often because for many people there just doesn't seem to be time to sleep. No longer do we get to sleep when the sun goes down so we can arise with the rooster's crow. High levels of caffeine in soft drinks, alcohol, and common medications like Ritalin and Dexedrine contribute to the causes of sleeplessness. HBO, MTV, and ESPN are also factors for many young people.

Each of us has a personal twenty-four-hour rhythm of mental activity called a *circadian rhythm.* Most people follow the same pattern, but it is not difficult to get out of sync. Most ADD children have messed-up sleep patterns. There are usually five stages of sleep, but a person has to reach the second and third stages to reap the benefits of true mental rest, and then the fourth and fifth for relief of physical tension. The dreaming phase apparently helps both forms of internal rehabilitation.

If your child does not sleep well, the symptoms of ADD will likely appear in some form. And if a child already has an ADD-related neurological problem, the lack of sleep will compound his challenges significantly.

Audit for Sleep Disturbance Symptoms

The following audit is best measured by someone who can observe your child's behavior most of the night, which of course will mean that the observer too will be sleep deprived. This is just a way to observe whether your child has symptoms of sleep disturbance. If he does, you may want to consider taking him to a sleep disorder clinic for treatment.

Check off symptoms observed during the sleeping hours as well as in the waking periods.

1. Your child has a very difficult time getting to sleep on a routine basis.   ( )
2. Your child seems to fight the bed, twisting and turning all through the night.   ( )
3. Your child expresses the need to spend the night with you or another person on a consistent basis, showing fear about sleeping alone.   ( )
4. Your child fights and fusses whenever bedtime approaches.   ( )
5. Your child is a fragile sleeper and wakes up several times a night.   ( )
6. Your child has been wetting the bed on a consistent basis (nocturnal enuresis).   ( )
7. Your child talks in her sleep (somniloquy) frequently.   ( )
8. Your child walks in his sleep (somnambulism) frequently.   ( )
9. Your child has frequent nightmares or unusually vivid dreams.   ( )
10. Your child worries about not being able to sleep and obsesses about getting a good night's sleep (sleep anxiety).   ( )
11. Your child snores consistently.   ( )
12. Your child often seems to stop breathing for a short period of time. (This is most obvious as a trait in a snoring pattern when the snoring stops with the nonbreathing period, and suddenly restarts with repositioning the body.)   ( )
13. While sleeping, your child's legs and arms seem to be jerking, oftentimes waking her up (this is called periodic limb movement—PLM).   ( )
14. Your child has trouble sleeping when fatigued or taken out of his usual routine.   ( )
15. Your child talks of feeling sadness and depression.   ( )
16. Your child is grieving.   ( )
17. Your child is constantly worried.   ( )
18. Your child is suffering from an allergic condition.   ( )
19. Your child has difficulty in having routine sleeping periods because of family schedules or family crisis.   ( )
20. Bedtime has become arguing time.   ( )

Scoring

If you checked off enough of these symptoms to detect a pattern, it is likely your child has a sleep problem, and the probability of it being a factor in ADD is close to 100 percent. It may not be the sole issue, but sleep problems will be important in the management of ADD, regardless of the degree of cause.

Action Plan for Better Sleep

Unfortunately there are few experts on the sleep issues of children. Even sleep clinics have little to offer except in the diagnosis and care of apnea, which is usually an adult problem. There is not really a medical specialty designated for the diagnosis and treatment of childhood sleep disturbances, beyond the pediatrician's or psychologist's wise advice, in most areas of the country. If nothing like that exists in your area, the action plan that follows may be helpful. It is based on three scenarios:

- breathing problems
- neurological problems
- behavioral issues

Breathing Problems

The most severe concern for a child with sleep problems is obstructive sleep apnea (OSA), which means that the child stops breathing for short periods of time. This can lead to brain damage and heart problems from lack of oxygen. The most common sign is snoring, but this may not be present. And not all kids who snore have apnea. Most of the time, snoring occurs when a person falls asleep, and his jaw relaxes, and the tongue and tissue collapse into the breathing passage. Many times this condition has a physical cause, such as a throat passage blockage that might require surgery. Overweight children often have this problem due to enlarged fat deposits in the throat. Bottom line: if the symptoms of an irregular breath rhythm are present, check it out with your physician.

Breathing problems during sleep can also occur for other reasons. Your child may have an allergy that manifests itself in the night hours and closes the breathing passage. This is very common. These closings may not be severe enough to cause brain and heart damage, but the lack of normal breathing will disrupt your child's sleep so that it won't refresh him as it should.

I have seen many approaches work for families, short of medicine and surgery. A cheap and quick fix can be the nasal dilator—breath strip—which simply spreads the nostrils out for better air passage. There is another device that clips directly on the septum (the divider between your nostrils) and purports to open up the passages as well.

There are some excellent throat sprays, especially those with herbal mixtures, that apparently help the tissues to maintain their integrity. Some sprays include a multivitamin dosage (B2, B6, C, and E) with a supplement of almond oil, olive oil, sunflower oil, and eucalyptus oil. I don't know for certain if these nutrients do any good, but I have seen a number of people swear by the products. These can be found at most drugstores or at Internet Web sites (browse for "snoring"). There are also mixtures for specific allergies.

Chin straps also have helped relieve the breathing problems of sleep-deprived people I've known. This prevents a sleeping person's mouth from gaping open so that tissues and tongue sag and block the air passages. A chin strap keeps the mouth closed and the passages clear. It may make your child dream of being a football player, but there are worse things, right? Again, these are easily found in most drugstores or on the Internet.

Neurological Problems

A wide range of symptoms fall into this category. Bed-wetting is a big one. More than a third of the children with ADD suffer from this problem. Most outgrow it by age ten, but some persist into their teenage and adult years. Many ADD children also walk or talk in their sleep. Some do all of the above.

One of the fascinating aspects of sleep dynamics is how our bodies are protected from our physical reactions to our dreams by a neurochemical named *acetylcholine,* which paralyzes our muscles while we sleep. Most of us may have violent dreams, but we don't yell or walk out the door—because of this protective chemical. However, when people have less than normal amounts of this chemical, they will act out their dreams. These are the people you have to watch carefully or they'll disappear out the bedroom window.

Most children who wet the bed do so because they are actually dreaming of urinating. It would make sense that as they begin to mature, changes in their neurochemistry will help stop the sleepwalking, speaking-in-sleep, and bed-wetting episodes. By the way, this developmental time line does have a genetic factor; parents of ADD kids who wet the bed were usually bed wetters themselves.

If your child is having these problems, you should explain that bed-wetting is not a fault in self-control, nor is it psychological. Blaming the child for bed-wetting is unfair and it won't help. But it is not a difficult problem to manage. You can work with your pediatrician or look for suggestions on various Web sites. I have had success using what I call *bladder stretching*. When your child has a small bladder capacity, the urge to urinate occurs more often. By building greater bladder capacity, the child won't feel the need to go so often.

You won't find it on any of the hottest exercise or yoga videos, but I've found a simple bladder-stretching exercise that seems to help significantly. Each day, the child is encouraged to drink as much liquid as possible, usually multiple glasses of water. Then the parent encourages the child to keep holding the urine beyond the first sensations of urgency. When a child does this, the bladder size increases and the sphincter muscles increase in strength and tone. Now, you don't want to torture your child or force him to hold it until he loses control, of course. I also wouldn't advise doing this in a car during a long trip. I've found that it helps to instruct the child to think of this as a "stretching" exercise and to make sure that there is always a bathroom, or at least a place in the woods, where he can relieve himself when necessary.

Behavioral Issues

BRAIN HYPERACTIVITY, OR "WINDMILLING"

Although bed-wetting is a problem for more than a third of ADD children, the chief complaint I hear is that when they go to sleep, their minds start racing. This is also known by the colorful name of *brain windmilling*.

In describing this sensation, children complain that they just cannot stop their minds from thinking, which turns into worrying. They think about problem solving, about what their friends are doing, and a million other issues, so that the sleep state seems never to come. And when it does, it is usually about thirty minutes before the alarm goes off.

Most people have this problem at one time or another. I've found it occurs mostly in April, when taxes are due, or about the time a parent realizes that a child is getting near college age. Stress and sleep are a poor mix. It's nature's mean trick that sleep is one of the best cures for stress, but stress often makes sleep difficult. Sleep is a vital restorative process physically and psychologically. But natural sleep is the best form. Sleep medications are extremely problematic because of the possibility of addiction. There are other ways to induce sleep. One of them is based on the same home remedy often suggested for comforting a puppy freshly weaned by its mother—a ticking clock.

Regardless of what you have heard, a completely silent, dark room is not the most conducive environment in which a child can sleep. In fact, it is plain scary. A soft light can be reassuring. Depending on the safety measures used, and making sure to use lead-free ingredients, burning candles can have an amazing impact on the anxiety levels of children. Those fake log setups with the backdrop of colored flames have also shown to be helpful. I have never used those flickering electric candles, but they might work as well. Holding a security object like a blanket or soft animal can help a child to feel secure. Aromas are very powerful in helping the brain settle down, and there are a number of commercial products that use scents such as rose or jasmine that purport to aid in relaxation. However, I think that something with the aroma of the parents (or even the dog) works best, such as a used towel. I completed a research project once that showed that the scent of relaxation is transmitted through the sweat glands, and I base my recommendations on that study as well as my own observations.

Just as frightened puppies with windmilling dog brains associate the ticktock of the clock with the heartbeat of their absent mothers, our brains respond to acoustic sounds. Researchers have found that recorded low-volume drumbeats matching the frequency of the heart during sleep cycles help induce sleep for patients struggling with racing thoughts. I've found in my own clinical research that this works best when patients are allowed to choose the most comfortable rhythm pace. Sleep lab researchers monitored EEG measurements of patients' brain waves when the drumbeats were played and saw that the waves lowered to match the drumbeats, inducing sleep within ten minutes in most cases. This works even with babies enduring painful medical procedures and with patients complaining of chronic pain. Most sleep as long as the drumbeats are played.

I've used this simple treatment countless times to help sleep-deprived ADD children. There are other sleep-inducing sounds that work. Recordings of ocean waves and a subtle beat on a gong are effective. There are commercial tapes of sleep-wave sounds that are more subliminal than audible but I have not researched their effectiveness. Some people respond well to classical or New Age music when trying to sleep. Kenny G knocks me out, literally. Other folks say childhood lullabies work well for them, perhaps because of the memories attached to them.

If you've ever fallen asleep during a massage you know that tactile rhythms work too. Of course, you've got to find someone willing to rub your back throughout the night, which might be a challenge. Some children and even some adults find rocking back and forth in a chair or in bed helps counter the racing mind, putting them into deep sleep. Anything that slows the brain patterns can work. It is really a form of self-hypnosis.

ANXIETY REDUCTION AND SLEEP

When we are afraid, our minds go on alert, and that inhibits sleep. The body chemistry churns up the adrenal flow, and the messages to all systems are either fight or flee. Sleep isn't even on the program. When anxiety includes a fear of going to sleep—which is often the case with children—the challenge is even greater.

A good, nonscary bedtime story can work wonders in these cases. Often, age-old parenting practices are based on more than simple tradition. Chicken soup has been found to boost the immune system, and telling bedtime stories can work well in bringing sleep to a fearful child. The parent's voice is a source of comfort to most children. They've heard it since their earliest times inside the womb.

I don't recommend anything from the brothers Grimm, or tales of Frankenstein. There are stories specifically designed to induce relaxation and sleep. There are three steps to these stories: breathing patterning, release of tension through the body, and embracing the sleep state.

When you help your child reach a relaxed, meditative state, the benefits of sleep are multiplied greatly. Don't ever put a wound-up child to bed in hopes that he or she will just wear out and go to sleep. That won't help the child get high-quality rest. Experts in sleep therapy make these recommendations:

- Establish a set bedtime every night.
- Avoid resorting to naps or sleeping in to catch up on sleep.
- Eat lightly before bedtime. Excellent choices of last snacks contain tryptophan—bananas, mild cheese, chamomile tea, and the old favorite, milk.
- Avoid heavy exercises late in the evening.
- Avoid arguing in the late evening.
- Complete all homework assignments before getting ready for bed.

Family therapy might be extremely beneficial as a means to enhance the sleeping benefit for a child, especially if there are family conflicts and crises that get dealt with when the child is in bed. Whether or not you believe it, children can hear bickering and hostility while asleep.

BREATHING PATTERNS

Breathing patterns during states of anxiety and stress are unbalanced. You breathe in much more deeply in such situations because the body and brain are demanding more oxygen as part of the instinctive fight-or-flee response, which requires an alert mind for problem solving and revved-up muscles in case the problem can be solved only by getting the heck out of there. Some people hyperventilate (thus the origin of the phrase "Boy, are you hyper!") when they get stressed because they take in so much oxygen the body can't handle it.

The good news is that people can learn to control their breathing to calm their minds and their bodies. Many people instinctively do this by taking deeper in- and out-breaths when they are having trouble getting to sleep. The more relaxing breathing pattern will generally move them into a sleep state fairly quickly, even faster than counting sheep.

In most situations the regulation of the breath is all that is needed for release of stress because the mind and body cannot hold tension while holding the relaxed breathing pattern. But a little support and coaching can help. I use this story to help my young patients understand the value of rest and relaxation:

> There was a very smart boy named Tom who was having a tough time in school. He felt that he could never get caught up with his schoolwork, and he was getting very anxious and stressed. In fact, he got so stressed that he could not sleep.
>
> Then he discovered something very important. He

found that he could release his worrying and get a good night's rest, which helped him do well the next day in school. Do you know how he did it?

He learned to count his breaths, so that he breathed out the same as he breathed in, making him feel a lot better.

Let's see how that works for you. I will count as you breathe in: 1-2-3-4-5-6-7. OK, now breathe out: 1-2-3-4-5-6-7. Now breathe in: 1-2-3 . . . Oh, you ran out of space, didn't you? That is OK. It takes some practice, so I will just count and see as you adjust to the counting. In: 1-2-3-4-5. Out: 1-2-3-4-5. In: 1-2-3-4-5 . . . 1-2-3-4-5 . . . 1-2-3-4-5 . . . 1-2-3-4-5 . . .

I suggest that the parent count for the child for at least ten minutes to get his breathing rhythms evenly paced. It takes patience, but the child will begin to feel a release after two or three minutes and soon he or she will begin to nod off. Once again, it beats taking a sleeping pill.

RELEASE OF TENSION THROUGH THE BODY

Many adults and children go through the day unaware of the tension and stress bottled up inside them. The body stores stress in specific regions of the body, depending on our personalities. Some people develop tension headaches. Others get stomachaches. These tension centers create an imbalance that interferes with sleep. One way to relieve that tension is to take an imaginary journey through the body. Start from either end, the head or the feet, and progress to the other end, following a thought process like that in this script:

Tom got in a very comfortable position and closed his eyes. He breathed in a relaxed rhythm, letting all of his tensions and worries go out with each breath.

Beginning at the end of his toes, he relaxed each part

of the body step by step, moving up his feet to his an-kles, still breathing out the tension. He begins to feel warmth in his feet as the muscles relax and more blood flows through them.

Slowly he focuses on his ankles, lower legs, and calves, relaxing those big muscles, breathing out the stress in them. Then he relaxes his upper legs and thigh muscles, allowing the tension to melt away.

The flow continues up the body from the pelvis to the belly and chest. He is feeling more and more re-laxed. Then the flow goes to the back, up the spine, across the shoulders to the top of his neck. Tom is breathing and relaxing all of those muscles.

Now the flow goes down each arm and into the hands, relaxing all the muscles. Tom is letting go of any-thing in his hands or in his mind, breathing out stress.

And finally, the head. Tom relaxes his jaw muscles, then his eyes, and every hair at the top of his head, breathing and relaxing more and more.

If you use this script with your ADD child, remember that the relaxing tone of your voice and your own easy breathing are as important as the words you say. If the parent is relaxed, the child will follow.

Embracing the Sleep State

Like many adults, children have irrational fears, such as dying in their sleep or being left alone. If those fears are on their minds, they become fearful of going to sleep. You can comfort a child by telling him that sleep is a safe haven where your love will protect him. Affirming words and prayers can also be helpful.

An audiocassette or CD repeating the message of relaxation and security at low volume can be reassuring source, particularly if you find soothing music. Or you can record a relaxing message for the child and play it on a recorder. Here is one I have used with patients:

> Tom was relaxed and began to feel safer and safer, more and more comfortable. He began to release all concerns and problems of the world. He settled into the safety and comfort of his bed, knowing that there is no need to hold on or worry, letting go.

Depression

Depression is one of the worst enemies of sleep, and often physicians miss the signs of true depression when examining children. When a child is depressed the cause can be inhibited neurotransmitters, which interfere with sleep in addition to causing feelings of sadness and obsessions with loss. Grieving from the loss of a pet, a friend, or a teacher can also cause this sort of childhood depression. The usual symptoms are irritability, sluggishness, hyperactivity, and inattention.

The best action plan for depression, especially for a child, is exercise. Take care, because children tend to go all out until they burn out, which may hinder the quality of sleep. It is best to establish an exercise routine through tai chi, or yoga, or a set running distance, so that the child can learn to monitor his body while exercising. The more strenuous workouts should be done in the morning or no later than midafternoon so the child doesn't become overtired. But there should be some form of milder exercise routine an hour or two before sleep. This exercise program should consist mostly of stretching the muscles and limbering the joints. Walking twenty minutes will offer excellent results if it is done in a framework of relaxation and not competition. One of the best parts of walking is that it gives parents and children the opportunity to talk about feelings and issues. I believe it is also important to touch on spiritual bases prior to sleep as a way of putting the mind at peace. Prayer can serve to give a child assurance and hope, regardless of your faith, and it affords the parent valuable opportunities to instill values.

Finally, tell your child a story at bedtime to put him in a positive and relaxed state of mind. I do recommend tales of protective heroes and good Samaritans. Or the imagery can simply be a visional experience, such as the one described below:

> Relax and let all of your cares dissolve with each breath, knowing that if they are really important, they will be waiting when you wake up. Just relax and see anything that is holding on to your attention let go and disappear. And what will probably appear in its place will be something very wonderful and happy. Let these things happen. Just let them go as you let your hands relax, your legs relax. Yes, let them go, and let appear before you wonderful gifts.

Supplements for Better Sleep

Sleep medication for children is usually a disturbing proposition. There have been no clinical trials to determine correct dosages for children, and they have poor effects anyway. Most of the time these medications have the reverse impact, making the child hyperactive. However, there are some food supplements that appear to be effective because of the imbalances in various vitamin and mineral levels related to hyperactivity. For example, there have been cases in which calcium levels were markedly lower than expected and the children had muscle restlessness, which was relieved with a low administration of calcium and magnesium.

Listed below are some supplements that may be very helpful for sleep issues. You should consult with a nutritionist or homeopathic doctor before implementing a supplement program.

Vitamins and Minerals

- calcium and magnesium: These regulate relaxation, especially with muscle tension and physical restlessness. Dose (twice a day): calcium, 500 mg; magnesium, 250 mg.
- B complex: B vitamins are depleted under stress; they may be stimulating in certain individuals, so take them in the morning.
- 5-HTP: This form of tryptophan now available is particularly helpful for difficulty staying asleep; 5-HTP increases serotonin levels. Dose: 50 mg before bed. 5-HTP will help within one week if it will be helpful at all. Dietary sources of tryptophan include turkey, eggs, fish, dairy products, bananas, and walnuts. (Tryptophan as a supplement was removed from the market after a contaminant caused severe side effects.)
- melatonin: Manufactured in the pineal gland, from tryptophan, this is responsible for appropriate circadian rhythms and is used to prevent jet lag. Dose: 1 to 3 mg before bed. Note that a lower dose may be effective when a higher dose is not.
- niacinamide: A muscle relaxant with gentle, tranquilizing effects. Dose: 70 to 280 mg daily, either in divided doses during the day or at bedtime.

Herbs

Herbs may be used in the form of dried extracts (capsules, powders, teas), glycerites (glycerine extracts), or tinctures (alcohol extracts). Unless otherwise indicated, teas should be made with one teaspoon of herb per cup of hot water. Steep covered five to ten minutes for leaf or flowers, and ten to twenty minutes for roots.

Drink two to four cups a day. Tinctures may be used singly or in combination as noted. The herbs are listed in order of increasing strength; use the gentlest herb that is effective.

- chamomile *(Chamomilla recutita):* This mild sedative calms gastric upset. One cup of chamomile tea before bed is often all that is needed for mild insomnia. In a few patients, chamomile may cause gastric upset.
- lemon balm *(Melissa officinalis)* alone, or in combination with catnip *(Nepeta cataria):* For nervous sleeping disorders and mild digestive complaints, take one cup of tea or thirty to sixty drops tincture one to three times a day.
- passionflower *(Passiflora incarnata):* The aerial parts of passionflower are a very effective herbal remedy for insomnia; take 2 to 4 ml one half hour before bedtime.
- valerian *(Valeriana officinalis):* A sedative, anodyne, bitter. Side effects of too high a dose can include nausea and grogginess. It is traditionally used in combination with passionflower and hops *(Humulus lupulus)* for treatment of acute stress. Persons with depression should avoid hops. Dose: equal parts herb in one cup, one to three times a day, or tincture of thirty to sixty drops, one to three times a day.
- St. John's wort *(Hypericum perforatum):* For insomnia with anxious depression. Dose: fifteen to sixty drops (½ to 2 ml) three times a day, or 250 mg three times a day of herb or herb extract for depression. Side effects may include skin rash, photosensitivity, and gastric upset. It may take four to six weeks to become effective.
- Jamaica dogwood *(Piscidia piscipula):* Jamaican dogwood is a powerful remedy for insomnia, particularly when the sleeplessness is due to nervous tension and pain. Take 1 to 2 ml just before bedtime. Jamaican dogwood is arguably the strongest herbal anodyne

for sleeplessness. Jamaican dogwood combines well with passionflower, valerian, kava, and St. John's wort.

- Essential oils (three to five drops added to a bath) may be effective as part of a bedtime ritual. Commonly used herbs are lavender *(Lavandula angustifolia),* rosemary *(Rosmarinus officinalis),* and chamomile *(Chamomilla recutita).*

Homeopathic Suggestions for Acute Symptoms

- *Arsenicum album* is for insomnia caused by anxiety (especially about health), especially in perfectionists who develop panic attacks.
- *Nux vomica* is for insomnia from overuse of stimulants, caffeine, drugs, or tobacco, especially in competitive, aggressive people.
- *Coffea cruda* is for insomnia from a racing mind, especially if the stress is adjusting to a positive event.
- *Ignatia amara* is for insomnia (or excessive sleeping) after grief.

Exploring Options for Optimal Sleep

I hope this chapter has made you more aware of the role sleep plays in ADD and has provided some action plans for implementing approaches to help in this arena. This is not an all-or-nothing chapter in which you are expected to do everything and more. But this is the time to assess whether or not a sleep issue is interfering with your child's progress and if the resources available can change the course.

Help is a phone call away. You may want to contact the National Sleep Foundation (202-785-2300) or the American Sleep Disorders Association (507-287-6006) for more information or referrals. It is possible that your child's ADD stems from sleep disorders, especially if the symptoms have appeared recently. This may sound too easy, but it costs little to check it out.

Regardless of the cause of ADD, the management of objective and effective restoration is critical. A child's tolerance and endurance is limited, and some provision has already been made for that component—sleep. All the medicine and counseling in the world cannot cure the effects of too little restoration through the sleep cycles. That is the natural cycle of healing.

TEN

Train the Brain
Biofeedback Approaches

Howard was a feisty ten-year-old whose fourth-grade teacher described him as her worst nightmare. That is a hurtful thing for a parent to hear. Too often, though, unenlightened educators are unable to see past ADD symptoms and into the heart of the child.

This boy was quick-witted and energetic, with a personality that reminded me of a younger version of zany comedian Robin Williams. His teachers said that Howard was too smart for his own good. Again, it was a classic case of being critical instead of helpful. Howard was a cutup who didn't know when to cut it out. He couldn't stay focused in class and he wouldn't allow anyone else to focus either. The teacher was understandably frustrated because Howard was also a charmer. At least twice a week, he'd be sent to the principal's office for creating chaos in the classroom with his funny remarks. The problem was that the principal thought he was hilarious too.

Howard's mother brought him into my office in search of a way to rein in her son's personality. She was afraid his comedic talents were going to ruin his chance for an education. And this was a very bright kid. She'd heard that I used "some kind of electrotherapy to calm kids down." I think she was hoping I'd give him a quick zap and send him back to school ready for the Ivy League. Howard seemed up for the experience. He obviously thought it would give him a lot of new material for his classroom comic routines.

He entered my office wide-eyed and with a mischievous smile, like a Marx brother ready to romp. "Can I see the brain-zapping gizmo that is going to make me into a vegetable?" We had a good laugh at that. The kid had charisma, no doubt about it. He was also extremely articulate and agile minded. I wasn't going to sneak up on him with any therapies. I'd have to lay it out and get him to buy in.

I didn't try to rein Howard in. Instead, I worked within his comfort zone. I joked with him, telling him I'd gotten out of the Frankenstein stuff but that I had some fun methods that might help him get along better in school. Because he loved action movies, especially the Ninja films, I asked him what he knew about martial arts. He said he copied the moves he saw on the screen but he hadn't ever taken lessons. He was eager to learn more. Once I had him focused, I explained that the first lesson in any martial art was the skill of centering to bring the body and mind into balance. He grasped the concept immediately in that context.

I then told him that his challenge was that nobody wanted him to lose his spark and enthusiasm. They just wanted him to use his talents and energies, including his humor, for good rather than for mischief. Just like a good Ninja warrior. And to do that, he needed to learn the martial arts skills of focus and concentration.

By that point, Howard was motivated. To begin, I asked him to focus on the second hand of a watch. He tried, but it was a struggle. That simple test helped him see what his challenge was, yet it wasn't a put-down. Nobody was calling him names. I offered him some martial arts focusing tools. One of them was chewing gum, which is helpful for many ADD kids. The chewing action and the joint stimulation apparently calm the agitation of many children and aid in concentration. I also had him listen to soothing music with drum rhythms as a means of quieting the distracting rapid thoughts that are typical of ADD kids. After using those methods, we went back to the second hand of the watch, and slowly, we extended his focus time to fifteen seconds, then thirty seconds, then sixty seconds.

Howard found the music especially helpful. Since he couldn't wear a headset in class, I taught him how to use the memory of the music to help him concentrate. At the end of the session he had extended his concentration to three minutes. It was a small amount of time, but it marked a big step. I did give him homework, which was to keep trying to extend his concentration time with the aid of an inexpensive watch I gave him.

Biofeedback Is Fun

When we met again, I told Howard we were moving into the high-tech phase of his martial arts training. I hooked him up to a biofeedback monitor that uses computer software to measure a subject's body temperature as he is tested. Stress responses often restrict blood vessels, causing the body temperature to drop because of lowered blood flow. The skin temperature will go up when the blood vessels relax because of the increase in blood volume.

Study after study has shown that the symptoms of attention deficit disorder can be controlled through biofeedback. This approach is not an absolute cure for every aspect of ADD. However, it has worked well in helping a child learn to control disruptive racing thoughts and impulsive behaviors that impair the ability to focus and concentrate.

Biofeedback offers therapies that help ADD children learn to control basic stress reactions, such as heart rate and cardiovascular reactivity. It works best with people willing and eager to take responsibility for their own actions. It can make a huge difference not only in a child's learning ability but also in his self-esteem.

My passion for treating ADD kids really began when I discovered the power of biofeedback. I consider it to be one of the most important breakthroughs for people suffering from neurological problems. I admit that this tool appealed to me because using it is so much fun. It allows patients and their parents to participate in their own treatment and I think that is a great thing too. In the case of ADD kids, it turns treatment into a series of games, which is so much better than treating them with drugs.

Biofeedback treatments were first developed in the early 1970s and they have advanced greatly since then. The old machines took up an entire room and they were so sensitive that a fire truck going down the street would throw off readings. We had to put up foil wallpaper and turn off the lights in those days. And patients often wondered if they'd wandered into a horror movie.

In biofeedback, computer images and sounds provide images of what is going on inside the patient's body. There are five major biofeedback technologies used by mental health professionals for ADD:

- Thermal monitoring (using temperature biofeedback)
- Pulse monitoring (pulse meters or EMG)
- Electroencephalogram (EEG)
- Galvanic skin response (GSR)
- Respiratory patterning

Thermal and pulse monitoring reflect how your cardiovascular system is responding, and the electroencephalogram shows how your brain is functioning. The galvanic skin response, often used in lie-detection devices, reflects overall emotional responses on the skin. Respiratory patterning has been used to help people alter how they breathe and to monitor destructive patterns.

Thermal Biofeedback

This is the least intimidating and easiest method to learn, so it is often the first I try with a patient. It also works well with children, who enjoy the games it employs, which is another reason why I began my treatment of Howard with it. I've taught children as young as four to use this approach.

As I noted, thermal biofeedback monitors a very basic human response. When most people get anxious, their hands and feet get cooler because the body restricts the blood vessels as a response to stress and anxiety. This restriction causes less warm blood to flow and the temperature of the skin to lower. The average human peripheral (finger) temperature is approximately 90°F, but I have seen temperatures in obviously stressed people drop to 70 degrees—less than room temperature. Dead people can be warmer than that, but they aren't much fun when it comes to biofeedback games.

Getting back to the living, when people relax, the upper levels of healthy body temperature are around 97 degrees. Some research has showed that when the temperature is higher than 94 degrees, the parasympathetic system begins to kick in and you have heightened immunity responses and more healing energy—also known as *chi* in Asian cultures. Buddhist masters, known for their control over their bodies and minds, have allegedly demonstrated their powers by raising their body temperatures to a level so high it melts the snow around them.

Howard wasn't ready for that yet. So we started his biofeedback training with a computerized biofeedback basketball game that responded to Howard's body temperatures. In this game, the players on Howard's side would continue to make goals as long as he remained relaxed, which maintained his normal, warm body temperature—measured through a device on his finger. But if Howard got anxious and caused his body temperature to drop as the blood vessels constricted, the other team would make goals.

This game was a real challenge for Howard. He could stay in a relaxed state for only about ten seconds when we began. As soon as he became distracted and agitated, the other team would pour in the points. Still, it was a challenge he enjoyed, and as he mastered it, he began learning how to relax and control himself, which resulted in increased focus and concentration.

At first, of course, we didn't talk about how this related to his behavior and performance in school, but when I helped him see the connection later, he admitted that his tendency to act out in school was related to feelings of anxiety.

Neurobiofeedback

After four successful sessions with thermal biofeedback, I told Howard that he'd finally graduated to the "brain zapper." It's slightly more scientific name is the *electroencephalogram,* or EEG. It is also known as a brain wave monitor, measuring neuro-biofeedback. The principles of the EEG are very similar to thermal biofeedback. Brain waves can be measured by attaching three or more electrodes to the skin on the head. Thankfully, you don't have to screw them in. (That's so messy!) Instead, you use a thick goo that makes the electrodes stick to the scalp. The electrodes are also wired to a computer monitor. It works like a lie-detector machine except that it measures brain activity. It doesn't hurt and the patient doesn't have to lie down while some Dr. Frankenstein scares the bejesus (Howard's term) out of him.

There is no outside electrical charge involved. This isn't shock therapy. The brain generates its own electrical impulses, which are measured by the computer's acting like a voltage meter. It registers the electrical impulses put out by the brain.

In using neurobiofeedback, the child and I can see the brain patterns and brain functioning. More important, he can be taught to control those patterns. It is a great tool for gaining mastery of the ADD symptoms related to brain activity. Our brains have wonderful self-healing powers. They can reroute neuron networks around lesions or other troubled areas of the brain and restore normal function. This is called *neuroplasticity.* Even emotional responses long thought to be purely neurological dysfunctions, such as obsessive-compulsive disorders, can be changed without brain surgery through the use of neural biofeedback.

My fascination with the function of the brain began with my graduate studies at Texas Tech University. Later I became immersed in clinical studies during my internship at New York University Medical Center, Rusk Institute, where we helped people with malfunctioning brains restore them. We saw some incredible results. And we learned that even lab rats could change their brain functions through neural feedback.

This was an exciting discovery because it opened the possibility of treating ADD patients and others without using drugs. Around the same time, Elmer Green, a pioneer in biofeedback at the Menninger Foundation, released a study of how mystics from India had learned to use yoga to change their brain patterns and to control their autonomic systems—the functions of the body that act automatically, like breathing, circulation, and sweating.

In more recent years my students and I conducted experiments showing how internal control of brain waves, muscle groups, and cardiovascular changes could strengthen immunity and neurotransmitter activities. This is called *behavioral* medicine.

I've applied many of the things I've learned in my research to my treatment of ADD patients, including Howard, who proved to be a very good patient, in defiance of what his teacher had said about him. Within six weeks, he mastered the EEG by using biofeedback games. He taught himself how to raise his brain waves from sluggish Alphas to more energetic Betas. His success was notable in the classroom too, where his behavior improved significantly. He no longer created chaos every day and he started doing very well in his studies.

I am proud to report that Howard lost none of his charisma and delightful personality. I fully expect that we will be seeing him one day soon onstage or in the movies, entertaining us with his sparkling wit. Just the thought of Howard still makes me smile.

There are also a number of biofeedback techniques parents can try themselves. *Stress cards* are widely available. They have a disk or dot that changes with temperature, similar to the mood rings that periodically come back into vogue. As your child's moods change, the color on the card or in the ring changes too. This uses the principles of thermal biofeedback, although the ring color changes are often subtle and slower to change than the child's mood. I have often recommended them for practice, and they are very inexpensive.

Other Brain Training Methods

Neurobiofeedback, or neurotherapy, the monitoring and control of brain waves, offers great possibilities for treating attention deficit disorder. It allows a patient to train the brain. I have also had great success treating ADD children like Howard with the uses of respiratory patterning and pulse monitoring.

RESPIRATORY PATTERNING

Respiratory patterning is a very new technique and has been used primarily for respiratory problems, such as asthma, and some cardiovascular conditions. Basically the approach is to measure the contractions of the diaphragm in the breathing pattern and give feedback as to what would be considered a normal pattern.

PULSE MONITORING

Pulse monitoring is the most basic form of cardiovascular biofeedback. It focuses on the pace of your heart, so that you learn to speed your heart up or, more likely for health reasons, slow it down. This can be done with a simple pulse meter found at the local sports store.

These instruments also are a bit slow to respond but they work well enough to help train a child to adjust his heart rate. I gave one to an ADD patient, Sue, who came to me because she was having trouble in her favorite sport, baseball. She felt that her inability to focus was ruining her batting average.

I explained that concentration could be learned. I gave her a pulse rate device and showed her how to use it to slow her heart rate. I felt her anxiety and internal conversations were the real problem. She needed to learn how to calm herself. She returned in three days with a gleam in her eye. She had dropped her pulse rate from ninety beats a minutes to seventy-two!

Next, I taught her how to use the second hand on a watch to do the same thing. She mastered that in two days. The final lesson, I explained, was to use her mind to slow down the baseball as it came toward her from the pitcher's mound. I wanted her to be able to read the print on the ball or to count the stitches. It took her all of an hour to do that.

She was elated because the side benefit was that she began hitting the stuffing out of the ball. In the final five games of the year, her batting average was an astounding .800. Not bad for a kid who had batted zero in tryouts.

Anxiety confuses the brain and actually speeds up the perceived speed of things, probably because of the lack of coping skills and the fear of failure to manage the events that come to us. Sue learned a secret of life as well as a trick in hitting a baseball. When Sue graduated from high school several years ago, she sent me a package with my pulse rate device and a short note: "Thanks for helping me hit the ball every day of my life." Things like that can make even a grown man cry.

Biofeedback Audit

Not every child's symptoms can be relieved through biofeedback treatments. The following questions will help you assess whether or not this is an option you want to pursue.

Behavioral Items

	Yes	No
1. Does your child appear to become overstressed easily with decision-making tasks?	( )	( )
2. Does your child often retreat from or compensate for tasks that require intellectual skills?	( )	( )
3. Does your child have difficulties in relaxing, often constantly worrying about negative possibilities?	( )	( )
4. Does your child easily become frustrated when attempting to express his feelings, and either withdraw or threaten to become physically abusive?	( )	( )
5. Does your child lose focus of attention easily?	( )	( )
6. Does your child have difficulties sleeping?	( )	( )
7. Does your child forget things after a short time? Does he forget to turn off the water, forget where her homework is, forget what time it is, and so forth?	( )	( )

Cognitive Items

1. **Memory of Information Forward:** *Say,* "Repeat these numbers after I say them." *The numbers are to be presented at the rate of one per second.*

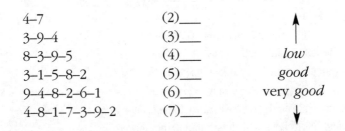

4–7	(2)___	
3–9–4	(3)___	
8–3–9–5	(4)___	
3–1–5–8–2	(5)___	*low*
9–4–8–2–6–1	(6)___	*good*
4–8–1–7–3–9–2	(7)___	*very good*
6–1–7–9–3–2–5–8	(8)___	

Score: Highest number correctly produced: _____

2. **Bits Backward:** *Say,* "Now repeat these numbers backward after I say them. For example, what would you say if I said, '5–3–8'?" *After the child demonstrates an understanding of the task, begin the sequencing. The numbers are to be presented at the rate of one per second.*

4–7	(2)___	
3–9–4	(3)___	
8–3–9–5	(4)___	*low*
3–1–5–8–2	(5)___	*good*
9–4–8–2–6–1	(6)___	*very good*
4–8–1–7–3–9–2	(7)___	

Score: Highest number correctly produced: _____

3. *Say,* "Spell the word *brother* backward."
4. *Ask,* "Who weighs more if John is lighter than Mark, but heavier than Sam?"

SCORING

If these items are marked as descriptive or indicative of poor performance, then those items could be considered as test items for follow-up later. However, if the child is marked for poor or low performance on three or more, neurotherapy biofeedback would be recommended.

The Model of Neurobiofeedback for ADD

Biofeedback technology can be very intimidating. Most of the equipment has been available only in the last twenty years, but like the electronic game in the closest mall, the fun is in the development of personal control through the machines. Nevertheless everyone wants to know what neurobiofeedback is.

Apart from using the electroencephalogram (EEG) as a biofeedback therapy, the EEG serves as a basis for diagnosing ADD because it is just another elaborate piece of equipment that shows a person what his brain is doing. By seeing it, he can figure out ways to modify it. I like to use the example of someone hooked up to an electrocardiogram, the EKG, which tells you how your heart is doing. The heart is like a generator that runs on a specific electrical wave form, just as the brain is another generator. But the heart is a little less mysterious than the brain. If you want to play around with the EKG, you can experiment by breathing in different patterns to see if the heart waves change. You can try different images, such as seeing a hunter aiming his gun at you, and see the EKG waves jump, or imagine sleeping by the ocean, and see the heart waves smooth out.

The brain is the same. If you are looking at the brain waves, you can experiment with ways of changing them so eventually you will learn how to control them. The brain waves can be very confusing if you look at them in their raw form. As explained in the first chapter, medical science has condensed brain waves into four general categories, Delta, Theta, Alpha, and Beta. A person diagnosed with ADD shows a high predominance in the Alpha and Theta ranges, and the inability to sustain Beta ranges in the higher magnitudes greater than Alpha, Theta, or Delta, so necessary for concentration and problem solving.

Electromagnetic waves are discussed in terms of hertz, or cycles per second. Delta waves form the general category for the

sleeping brain (0.5–3.9 hertz). Theta waves generally are correlated to a brain state of twilight sleep, hypnogogic states, or trance
(4.0–7.9 hertz). The Alpha range is considered a calm and relaxed
but focused state (8.0–12.9 hertz), while the Beta range is a problem-
solving or excited state (more than 13 hertz).

Brain Wave Categories

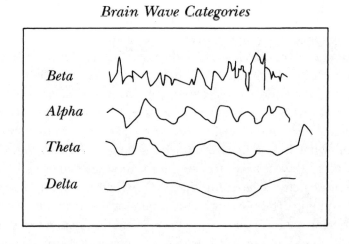

What the computer does is give a signal, such as a tone or a
light, when you are producing brain waves in the category you
want. If you want to produce a high percentage of Alpha waves
(the relaxation zone), more than 50 percent, and the computer
shows that you are averaging less than 25 percent, you won't hear
or see the signals, and you'll know that you need to change that
response in some way. When you begin to get the signals, you
know that you are on the right track and you increase what you
are doing, making the signal stronger and more predictable. This
is the feedback mechanism that can be so important, and you may
not actually understand the linkage of why it works. It just does.

This modality, often referred as *neurotherapy,* offers so much
potential to help overcome attention deficit disorder. If you were
producing only a minimal production of Beta waves, indicative of
an ADD brain, then you could begin to train your brain to function at higher frequencies with more appropriate methods than
drugs and sugar. I have had children accomplish this task with two

basic techniques, the use of imagery and breathing patterns. Using imagery, a child can fantasize a battle in which he is the hero and winning. Or the child can imagine running a race or competing in a contest, or even analyzing a puzzle.

Breathing patterns are also very powerful. Just as slower breathing patterns can calm a child and help him fall asleep, so can faster and deeper breathing patterns quicken the brain to achieve Beta ranges. These same applications have been applied to the control of epilepsy seizures in which the child learns to change his brain patterns to counteract the obstacle of brain barriers, such as scar tissue and tissue swelling related to stress or allergic response. If your child's brain does react with some sort of restrictions to food or environmental circumstances, causing poor blood circulation and the occurrence of ADD symptoms, then it would behoove him to learn these basic methods for control.

A New Frontier

Neurobiofeedback approaches are very exciting because they offer a relatively short-term solution for a lifelong problem. There are excellent professional biofeedback therapists with the right kind of equipment who can work with the full range of age groups and deal with specialized problems appropriate for this kind of approach. The two best resources for finding specialized therapists are the Biofeedback Certification Institute of America and the Association for Comprehensive NeuroTherapy.

Although these opportunities may or may not be available to you, I have found that there are a number of biofeedback techniques you can use in your own home, as discussed earlier in the chapter—for example, use pulse meters and even stress cards or mood rings to monitor thermal changes. I have often recommended them for practice, and they are very cheap—about one dollar at my last sortie into a store. You might get one free from your local psychologist or mental health center.

Neurobiofeedback is a new frontier, and although it was heretical only a generation ago to think that we could change our autonomic nervous system (blood pressure, heart rate, brain waves), we have made it commonplace today. Why should it be so problematic to change the physiology of ADD in our brains? It is certainly within our potential to heal ourselves of immunity deficits and neurotransmission imbalances, such as occur in many diagnoses of depression.

This step requires two decisions. One, you must decide if you and your child want to take the responsibility for learning this process; two, you have to take action. It does not happen by wanting it to happen. You have to begin the exploration and have the courage to learn from failure, because both a no and a yes are answers, and can serve as a basis for healing or learning to heal.

But the bottom line to success is whether you and your child want to engage in the joyful play that neurotherapy offers. It is a learning experience that can be practiced at home. Your child can show her innovations in body control. I have had several youngsters learn the biofeedback games so well that they had contests for the best control of their bodies. After all, it is a physical feat and one that could serve a child for the rest of her life.

ELEVEN

Healing Sounds

The most heartbreaking cases that come to me are those ADD children who've lost hope, or those children whose parents have lost hope for them. Lucy was one of these patients. The sixteen-year-old had been diagnosed with ADD ten years before I saw her. She had been through the wringer when it came to treatments. Medications were no longer effective for her because she'd been on them so long. There'd been at least four attempts to treat her with psychotherapy. They'd also put her on special diets and tried all kinds of vitamins.

Lucy had developed an attitude of resignation and was depressed. She had given up on her life and gave in to her flights of imagination. Instead of making an effort to concentrate when engaged in a conversation, she would talk about her associations to the content. For example, if you asked how she was feeling, instead of responding with some description of her condition, she might laugh and say, "Do you really expect me to answer that question because it is you, the *doctor,* who is asking it?" The circumventing of the topic was defensive on the one hand and indicative of her floating anxiety on the other.

Her mother was on the edge of desperation. She'd heard me give a talk on ADD and the importance of remaining positive and hopeful with children. But I could tell that the mother was losing faith in her daughter's physicians and the entire medical and psychological approach to ADD. Lucy was treatment savvy by this point, which often happens to ADD kids. She had misgivings about being psychoanalyzed by yet another psychologist. I told her only that I wanted to help her regain control of her life. I hooked up Lucy to the neurobiofeedback machine described in the previous chapter and explained to her how it worked. And then I went a step further.

I knew that Lucy's self-confidence was hurting because of her long-term struggles with ADD. She also had lost faith in physicians and psychologists. So I showed her a gizmo that I'd been working on with my adult son, basically a headset with controls. It was a new approach to ADD therapies, an acoustical acupuncture device. The basic purpose of the device was to emit sound frequencies specifically oriented to brain waves that are stimulated by the acupuncture points in the ear.

I explained that the gizmo just produced a set of sounds that might influence her brain directly, instead of her having to control them by will. As she fiddled with the knobs I showed her the differences in her brain patterns and I asked her to experiment with her gizmo while she attempted some simple mental puzzles. She became excited as she began to differentiate changes in her emotional state.

In a whisper she asked, "Can I get high with this thing?"

I shrugged at the question and said, "You can do anything you want because you are in control."

There are ADD patients who respond well to standard methods of treatment, and I'm always glad when that happens. There are also, however, patients whose symptoms simply defy those treatments. I never give up searching for new ways to help those patients. My willingness to remain open-minded about all forms of healing has benefited hundreds of young people. I don't care what the treatment is. If it doesn't have dangerous side effects or violate any law or code of medical ethics, I'm willing to consider it for the good of my patients.

Stimulating Sounds

My lifelong search for therapies to alleviate ADD symptoms took me into the realm of acupuncture years ago. The underlying premise of this ancient healing art is the belief that we have central energy points on our bodies that can stimulate our immune systems. It has been researched thoroughly in this country as a pain relief approach as well as a technique for relieving anxiety. The ancient theories hold that acupuncture brings all of the body systems back into harmony. Since the symptoms of ADD are believed to be the result of an imbalance in the metabolic or neurological systems, it makes sense that acupuncture might well restore balance harmony to those symptoms.

Theory is one thing, practical application is another. In 1979, Dr. Vert Mooney, head of orthopedic surgery at Southwestern Medical School, asked me to help him develop a pain clinic at the hospital for patients with chronic lower back pain. He explained that many patients with chronic lower back pain did not respond to the traditional surgical techniques employed. The underlying belief among surgeons was that there might be some psychological basis for their pain that could not be touched by the knife.

Dr. Mooney felt that these patients were falling through the cracks. There were no resources for them, no comprehensive programs. He felt that their pain was a combination of medical and psychological problems, so he asked me to put together a clinic to address both. I spent six months searching for ways to help these patients, using both medical and psychological approaches. Nothing seemed to be working.

I finally found a clue when I went through the psychoneurological assessments we'd done for each patient. I noticed that many of them, like many ADD patients, had terrific problems in concentration and memory retention. The logical explanation would be that the constant pain made it difficult for them to focus and retain information.

In search of answers, I decided to treat the ADD symptoms of each chronic back pain patient. One of the basic principles of treating people with learning disabilities like ADD is that their brains are not damaged; they are just not as developed as they should be. One of the methods for enhancing brain development is to use rhythmic exercises.

Music therapies, drumbeats, and other rhythmic acoustical and visual signals are known to relax the brain and bring clarity and focus to it. When I used these with the chronic back pain patients, we had some remarkable success in alleviating their symptoms. I also discovered specific frequencies that worked especially well.

A Healing Gizmo

In search of a tool that focused sound for the stimulation of acupuncture points in the body, I turned to my son, T. Frank Lawlis, who is an electronic engineer. I told him I was just looking for a return on my investment in his education. He gladly paid me back with a nifty little device similar to a Walkman cassette player.

Our gizmo has earphones and two knobs, one to control frequency, the other for volume. It works by stimulating acupuncture points in the ear with acoustical vibrations. The patient hears only a low hum and feels some vibration. My patients often note improvements in mood and concentration levels after just a few minutes of treatment.

Constant acoustical stimulation patterns the brain waves into consistent frequencies. By applying it to the acupuncture points in the ear, especially in those areas that stimulate the brain, it puts my patients' brain waves into the Theta range, which is the trance state you go into just before falling asleep.

People with attention deficit disorder have brains that function at a low range, and their hyperactive behaviors are actually instinctive efforts to stimulate it to higher frequencies. That's essentially the same thing my little gizmo was doing with the use of acoustical stimulation to the acupuncture points. I believe it is important to give my patients an active role in their own treatment. ADD patients often have low self-esteem and it is of particular benefit to engage them in the process of healing themselves. They can do that with our gizmo because the controls allow them to determine what frequencies work best in waking up their brains. In our tests, patients discovered they could focus better, lift themselves out of depression and pain, improve memory retention, and lower their anxieties.

I've even had considerable success restoring functions for patients who've been out of work because of head injuries, and with some Parkinson's patients who've been able to control tremors. I also used the gizmo to help relieve anxiety and stress symptoms among alcoholics and drug addicts.

Our gizmo had two controls for each ear. Patients were instructed to adjust the controls to their comfort levels. Most people quickly made adjustments to address their most troubling symptoms. They started with the lowest frequency for the dominant ear and slowly increased the frequency until there was a perceived change in that symptom. Each person then made adjustments that suited her.

When I gave the gizmo to Lucy, whose brain waves were being monitored, we saw an immediate effect. So did she. She loved it because it gave her control of her own therapy. For an hour, she played around with the knobs and frequencies. Together, we monitored her brain waves for each adjustment. She was literally squealing with delight in our biofeedback room.

Although I had only one model of the gizmo at that point, I let her take it home. (I am a softie.) When I saw her two weeks later, she had all kinds of stories to tell me about how well it had worked for her. She'd even tested it on her boyfriend, who'd been dealing with his own problems by using recreational drugs. It worked for him too, she said. At last report, Lucy was doing well in college and whenever she had trouble focusing, she'd plug into her gizmo.

It also worked very well for another patient. Al had been the victim of a rear-end car collision. He was a successful executive prior to the accident, but he'd been partially paralyzed and in constant pain for two years. His judgment and memory were severely impaired. His own board of directors was contemplating his removal from the company he'd founded. With the help of our gizmo, he alleviated his symptoms and returned to work successfully.

The Science of Gizmo

The acoustical device is based on four therapeutic concepts:

1. Brain wave functions are related to energy states of the body.
2. Harmonic stimulation can affect physiological systems.
3. The acoustical vibrations can stimulate acupuncture points related to the brain and other organs.
4. Personal control of a process has a positive psychological impact.

1. BRAIN WAVE FUNCTIONS

Remember the saying "Music has charms to sooth a savage breast"? Ancient healers used drumbeats in their healing rituals because they sensed what neurological research has since proven, that brain wave functions can be triggered by acoustical stimulation. Dr. Gerald Oster of Mt. Sinai Medical Center in New York did research on this beginning in the 1950s, showing the effects of sound waves on brain wave patterns.

When I studied music rhythms of the great composers and various cultures' music and drumming configurations, I found unique patterns consistent with different neurological states. I do not think that anyone can argue the fact that music can lift spirits as well as lower the energy level of an individual. Certainly most people I have observed respond to dancing music with positive feeling and movements.

2. HARMONIC STIMULATION

In order to handle the stimulated changes caused by the acoustical vibrations at the acupuncture areas, the nervous system is forced to reorganize itself at a higher level of functioning, evolving a new structure that can handle the input. As the brain continues to receive this input, the nervous system will continually reorganize itself in a series of quantum leaps—some at a micro level of functioning and some at a much more global level—until a new structure has been created that can easily handle this input. When a person is surrounded by highly energetic sounds, such as music, the whole body responds. The urge to dance is universal. It makes us feel free because the total response of mind and body forces us to stop worrying about business or what to fix for supper. The person discovers new energy when she can fully interact with the music and reaches a higher level of functioning.

3. ACUPUNCTURE STIMULATION

The healing effects of acupuncture are well documented. Acupuncture points work because one system of the body can affect others just as a change in breathing rate affects your heart rate. The principle is often referred to as the holistic response of the body and mind.

4. PERSONAL CONTROL

ADD patients desperately want to take control of their minds and bodies because they feel that their symptoms are controlling them. It is important, then, that any treatment or therapy you follow provide your child with a sense of control. The gizmo we designed enhances the sense of empowerment by giving the patient control, and it also allows each patient to tune the treatments according to his comfort levels.

Acoustical Healing for Your Child

The gizmo has become more sophisticated in its design and more powerful in its applications, becoming commercially known as the BAUD, or *bioacoustical utilization device,* and can be bought. Consult the Web site bioacoustical.com for information. It has been applied to other medical situations, such as addictions, food cravings, and depression.

Although our little invention works well, sound stimulation can come from many sources, including music played on your stereo or live drumbeats. Listening to a steady beat, even singing and dancing to a constant rhythm, can have beneficial effects for ADD patients. Naturally, some music is better than others. I would not recommend listening to Willie Nelson's "Half a Man" as therapeutic stimulation.

I have my patients bring in their personal music selections and monitor their EEG tracing for change in wave amplitude in Beta ranges. The large majority of these patients brought classical music. We've seen success with a wide variety of music hits, and the most successful I've found is Mozart, for some reason I cannot fathom.

Sound Therapy Audit

Many researchers believe that attention deficit disorder symptoms can be triggered by traumatic events, either physical or psychological in nature—even events that have been blacked out of a child's memory. To determine if this is the case with your child, administer the audit history:

1. At any time in your child's life was there a sudden change in behavior? For example, sometimes a child seems as if he is following a typical behavioral pattern, but within a few months, he turns into another personality.

2. At any time did your child experience a trauma, physical or psychological (such as grief, violence, conflict), and depressive symptoms followed?

3. Does your child appear to react to a frustrating situation by becoming depressed and angry, and often react impulsively?

4. Does your child have a low tolerance for pain, skin sensitivity, or frustration?

Cognitive Function

In a setting free of distractions and without high expectations for performance, administer the following tasks to your child:

1. **Cognitive Flexibility.** *Read out loud to your child:* "Assume that there are four pictures in front of you. The first picture is a man with a fishing rod, walking out the door. The second picture is the man meeting another man who appears friendly and is wearing a business suit and holding a briefcase. The third is a picture of the two men walking in different directions." *(These can actually be drawn and shown if desired. This is not a visual test.)* "What would be the next picture?" *(Correct answer: any appropriate response—one of the men fishing, both fishing, and so forth.) Accept the answer and ask:* "Give some more possible answers other than the one you came up with." *(Most people can come up with at least three more appropriate answers. Consider any less as "not successful.")*

2. **Embedded Audio Figures.** *Instruct your child, saying,* "Take this pencil and tap it every time you hear the letter *A* following the letter *E*. Now tell me what you are supposed to do." *If your child correctly articulates the instructions, begin. Administer the letters at a rate of two per second:*

   "A-T-P-L-E-A-R-A-C-T-I-A-E-A-A-C-X-W-A-P-K-A-L-Y-D-E-A-X-E-P-J-Y-E-A-E-A-E-P-F-Q-A-E-E-A-G-E-A-V-R-M-E-A-N-T-E-I-A-I-R-O-A-R-A-E-E-A-Q-O-A-E-A-P-A-E-Q-B-E-C-A-E-G-V-E-T-A-B-E-A-T-G-A-E-C-A-E-H-A."

SCORING

  4—no mistakes
  3—one or two mistakes
  1—three mistakes
  0—four or more mistakes

Discussion of Results

Although these audits are far from a clinical assessment, they are generally more insightful than what you might get from most professionals because you are observing firsthand what your child is doing and how he is coping. As you discover the kind of information and possible ADD limitations related to this approach, you can begin to create similar questions and assess the effectiveness of what you are doing.

If there were significant observations in the history and some flaws in the cognitive performances noted in this chapter audit, I would recommend the acoustical acupuncture approach. The most powerful aspect of this approach is the control it gives the patient.

The History Stuff and Real Science

I realize that I could write about this for hours, but I want to stop here with the whole engineering trip. I want you to understand the underlying reasons and purpose for what has gone into this device, not to sell you but perhaps to tell you that this is not voodoo magic.

This model of change is based on the work of scientist Ilya Prigogine, winner of the 1977 Nobel Prize for work on the growth and evolution of what scientists call *nonlinear open systems*. Scientists have applied Prigogine's work to everything from how a seed germinates to how a corporation expands, a highway system grows, a cell divides, and an audience breaks into applause. Neurophysiologically, this reorganization in the brain causes the creation of new neural pathways, resulting in communication between parts of the brain that previously were not communicating, or were communicating only a minor amount.

I believe that this phenomenon is due to the shift in microtubule patterns, as discussed by Roger Penrose in *Shadows of the Mind*. *Microtubules* are skeletons of the nerves, and it has been learned in the last ten years that these skeletons vibrate in patterns yielding 10 billion different models and are associated with specific emotional states. More important, these patterns have a contagious effect on other microtubules, causing emotional shifts. What this means is that much of our emotional information and reactions is based not on the linear transmissions of neurons, but on the sense of rhythm of our nerves. It may be true that we have "fibrations" that we generate as a function of our emotions.

This broader definition of vibrational energy would not only explain how a person can affect another person's emotional state by just being present, but also explain the impact of the tones produced by the stereoacoustical design. In this way, not only is neurological energy enhanced and predicted by shifting the brain frequencies, but the energy can also be filtered through emotional patterns for the most effective brain stimulation, diminishing anxiety and depressive barriers.

Stephane Conti of the Southwest Fisheries Science Center, in La Jolla, California, has measured the acoustical profile of the average human body, and from his results, our acoustical human form looks like a big, elongated chicken egg. In other words, we are interacting with the sounds around us beyond our skins, and interestingly, this is the identical shape the energy scientists speak of regarding our electromagnetic fields. Does it make sense that acoustics, in the form of energies, would alter our entire health status, especially the brain?

What Now? Action

Another hybrid concept that is available is the imagery-induced acoustical approach that has been used for ADD. Basically this approach employs a simple CD that offers musical harmonics known to stimulate the frontal and temporal lobes of the brain, along with vocal instructions on breathing patterns and suggested experiences. By learning the associations through the spoken instruction, children can practice this multiple sensory program when they can store it as a learning reflex. They can bring up the music in their heads, or listen only to parts of the music on their portable Walkmans, and begin to automatically attune their attention. These CDs are available through Mindbodyseries.com.

Whether you try the gizmo, get the CD, discover a specific music composition, or dance, the action steps are the same. I am serious about your finding some kind of similar approach. But the secret is not an external source that makes you well, it is the inward journey to make the judgments from the inside to the outside. Before anything can be helpful, even with medications or psychotherapy, you have to go inside yourself and assess the goodness or lack of health. It is the rhythm, the dance, that makes things become harmonic.

TWELVE

Body Electric

A friend of mine who has been a pediatrician for thirty-six years told me of an eleven-year-old patient, Ryan, who had been given medication to control his ADD symptoms, which included destructive behavior. But Ryan's medication made him depressed and overly docile. His parents commented that "this was nicer behavior, but this is not our Ryan."

My pediatrician friend took Ryan off his medications and tried something different, an approach that has yet to be widely accepted by medical scientists, but that has worked for his patients many times. As a result of this very benign method, Ryan's parents and teachers noted, he became more cooperative, easier to talk to, and less argumentative. He also learned to recognize when he was tired and ready for bed, and he responded to discipline better. In short, Ryan became more like a normal boy and, as his parents noted, more like himself.

My pediatrician friend accomplished this with the use of nothing other than a set of magnets.

Magnetic Concepts

There is nothing inherently good or bad about magnets, electro-magnetic waves, or electricity. The nervous system is built on the principles of electromagnetic transmission, and electricity has been used in medical treatments for some time. The pacemaker and magnetic resonance machines are only a couple of ways electricity can be helpful.

But there are concerns too about overexposure to electromagnetic waves. Like most adults, I've observed children sitting entranced in front of television sets and wondered about the effects it has on their minds and bodies. Color sets do put out small amounts of radiation. They also give off waves of light that are in the same frequency as Alpha waves. These subtle light waves, not to mention the numbing mediocrity of most television shows, can put a viewer in a trance state.

This is similar to the hypnotic trick of swinging a shiny object in front of a person and talking him into a deep relaxation. When we watch television for hours at a time, we are exposed to these color stimulations, small doses of radiation stimulation, not to mention far too many commercials for personal hygiene products.

In my experience, certain very sensitive children do seem to go into a low-functioning brain pattern while watching television for extended periods. That concerns me in particular for ADD children. I often recommend to parents that they limit the amount of time that they allow their ADD children to watch television or to play on the computer. It isn't always a popular bit of advice because those two activities have become such a part of our culture, for children and adults alike. A child's father once told me: "You were doctoring when you were talking about my son's brain waves being messed up, but now you're meddling when you're talking about my television watchin'."

As I told him, in many cases I've seen a child's ADD symptoms subside when he's cut back on TV and computer time. Television is not the only source of electromagnetic wave forms that could potentially influence your ADD child's behavior. Although there have been conflicting findings in other studies, one published in the *Journal of Oncology* revealed that users of mobile cell phones who spend more than an hour a day talking on the phone are almost a third more at risk of developing a rare form of brain tumor. The same scientists also found a cancer link with digital mobiles, old-style analogue mobiles, and digitally enhanced cordless phones.

The tumors in those cases were in the temporal lobes, the same part of the brain affected in some forms of ADD. I don't know for certain if there is a link, but I do know that ADD children are more sensitive to outside stimuli than most. How can you protect your child from the potential dangers of electromagnetic waves? I wouldn't advise anything as dramatic—or silly—as a tinfoil turban. But there are measures you can take to gauge whether your ADD child should limit his television and computer time.

The theory about potential ill effects holds that while electromagnetic forces can imbalance the brain's neurological processing system, sophisticated and noninvasive applications of electromagnetic stimulation have been highly useful in treating patients with abnormal brain functions.

Though some scientists and physicians remain skeptical, the use of magnets in mattresses, pillows, comforters, and shoe pads for electromagnetic therapy has gained popularity in recent years. Many people claim good results in alleviating pain, and from my observations and conversations, an increasing number of pediatricians are using them to treat the symptoms of children with attention deficit disorder.

Before you spend any money on magnetic devices, I'd suggest that you conduct the following *electromagnetic audit.* I hate to make recommendations of therapies that don't have scientific support. Yet many patients and physicians claim that these magnets have been helpful. I do not have any financial interest in any of the items, believe me. I just want you to know what treatment options are available. You will have to make up your own mind about their effectiveness.

Electromagnetic Audit

This is a brief audit to determine if electromagnetic therapies may benefit your child. Please check the appropriate response for you or your child.

1. **Concentration Rhythm Test.** *Explain to the child:* "I am going to tap out a rhythm with my pencil, then I want you to tap out the same rhythm." (*Rhythm—dump-dee-dump, dump-dee-dump, heart rhythm.*) "OK, you beat it." *If the participant has the right rhythm, continue.* I want you to continue to beat that rhythm. Now, do not pay any attention to me because I will be doing my thing, you do yours. OK?" *Allow to continue for twenty seconds, beating various rhythms and determining if the participant maintained his rhythm.*

> *Scoring:*
> **0**—no variation from rhythm
> **1**—some difficulty but consistent
> **2**—loses rhythm
> **3**—cannot keep any rhythm

2. **Social Sequencing Concentration.** "I am going to tell you a story and when I am finished I want you to tell me as much as you can remember." *Check off each chunk of text that is recalled verbatim, regardless of order.*

> John Samuels, / an immigrant / from Mexico, / came to Philadelphia / in September 1978 / and applied for American citizenship. / He was employed by the city / as a clerk / and after five years was promoted to assistant manager because of his hard work. / He won citizenship / in December 1984 / and sent for his parents. / They brought with them his lifelong sweetheart, / whom he married, following a short engagement. / The couple moved into an apartment on Twenty-first Street/ and his wife got a job as a clerk.

"Now tell me as much of the story as you can."

> *Scoring:*
> **0**—9 or more chunks remembered
> **1**—8 or 7
> **2**—6 or 5
> **3**—4 or less

3. Auditory Receptive Concentration. *Have the child read the following paragraph (if appropriate for reading level):*

> Lorri was a young twenty-two-year-old lady who had a job as a secretary at a law firm. She had many friends and loved to go out dancing, and she was very, very good at this activity. She would sing along to her favorite songs as she danced, her favorite song being "Runaround Sue." Her much-loved dance dress was bright red. The top part had sparkles and the bottom part was very full so that it went out when she swirled. Her best dance partner was a tall guy by the name of Frank, who had a tremendous personality and a big laugh. They would dance until the sun came up on many occasions. Lorri was offered a raise in salary if she would become the office manager, but she turned it down because it would interfere with her dancing, since she would have to work late at night. Lorri and Frank eventually got married, and later became dance instructors.

Now take the paragraph and ask the child how many details she remembers.

> *Scoring:*
> **0**—15 details and story line
> **1**—10 to 14 details and story line
> **2**—5 to 9 details and story line
> **3**—fewer than 5 details; loss of story line

4. Does the person have problems maintaining attention in listening to a presentation, such as a lesson in mathematics or even in a subject she particularly enjoys?

> *Scoring:*
> **0**—no problems
> **1**—occasionally
> **2**—most of the time
> **3**—constant problems

5. Does the person have difficulty maintaining a focus on what she is talking about, such as telling a story or talking about a given topic?

    Scoring:
    0—no problems
    1—occasionally
    2—most of the time
    3—constant problems

6. Does the individual catch on quickly to learning tasks that have details?

    Scoring:
    0—no problems
    1—occasionally
    2—most of the time
    3—constant problems

7. Does the individual have poor study discipline?

    Scoring:
    0—no problems
    1—occasionally
    2—most of the time
    3—constant problems

Overall Scoring

If the person scores a 2 or more on any of the items, this is a sign of significant problems in concentration and attention. This explains why the person has learning challenges. Sum up all the scores, for a range of 0 to 21, and compare the score to the general interpretations:

    If the score is **0 to 4,** the electromagnetic therapies might not be appropriate.

If the score is **5 to 15,** a trial of one magnetic product might be helpful.

If the score is **greater than 15,** two or more magnetic approaches might be helpful.

The Nature of Electromagnetic Medicine

The body's neurological system functions with nerve impulses that travel and communicate with one another along nerve cells that are like hoses or passageways. They have a series of side gates that open for the passage of various molecules. Each molecule carries either a positive or a negative electrical charge. Most of the molecules inside the nerve cell carry a negative charge, specifically chlorine (Cl), whereas the predominantly positive-charged molecules on the outside of the cell are sodium (Na).

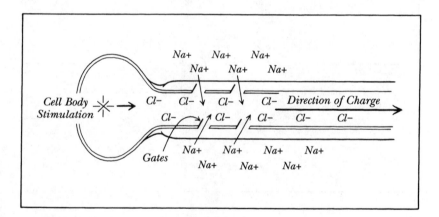

When a nerve cell is stimulated at one end, the cell becomes excited. For this stimulation to be conveyed along the neural network, these molecules start dancing in and out of the cell walls, creating an electrical charge. As the sodium is allowed into the nerve cell, more gates open, one after the other, like dominoes falling forward. As the exchange of positive and negative molecules continues down the nerve fiber, the charge creates a flow of *action potential.* Its contagious nature is referred to as its *self-*

propagating property. The speed of the action potential differs from 0.4 to 260 miles per hour, depending on how large a nerve is (the larger ones are faster) and how much myelin is present (myelin is the fatty substance that acts like an insulator to the cell, like the rubber that covers your electric cords).

Your nervous system is not made up of one long nerve cell, but a matrix and bundles of nerve cells that connect to one another like a giant set of extension cords that plug into one another. These plugs or junctions are called *synapses* and they really do not interlock, but are fields in which the charges are carried over from one cell to the next by substances called *neurotransmitters.* Again, a minimum strength of the charge is required in order for the charge to move from one cell to the next, as well as the charge of the neurotransmitters.

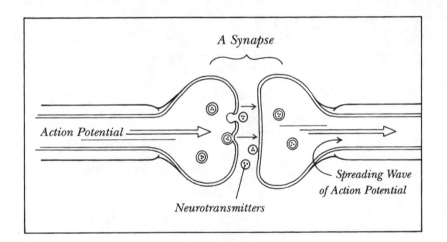

Most neurologists think of the connections as a telephone system, with all of these lines routing from one part of the brain to tissues, and back again. Moreover, the dense interconnections of the brain combine their powerful charges so that they produce enough electrical charge to measure with electroencephalograms.

If the brain's electric system is short-circuited, how can magnets fix them? No one seems to have a clue. Yet for nearly twenty years there have been claims that these magnets help bones and wounds heal faster.

This is not new science, nor is it new medicine. Since the discovery of electricity, doctors have been attempting to harness its power for healing. In 1794, Luigi Galvani, an anatomy professor at the University of Bologna, started conducting experiments when he discovered that the muscles of frogs' legs would react to electric current. Actually the frogs were intended for dinner, but the vision was born and continues to interest medical researchers. There is even a museum of electromagnetic medicine established by Dr. Earl Bakken, who patented the first external cardiac pacemaker in the United States. For all of this interest, physicians have yet to fully grasp how electromagnetic waves work as healing tools. Then again, they still haven't figured out how to cure the common cold, either.

The current theory on electromagnetic waves relates to those gates and neurotransmitters. With the extra power of negative forces from the magnets, the sodium atoms become more excited and enter into the nerve cell with greater enthusiasm, creating greater potential. This action then produces stronger capacities for facilitating the natural networks laid down by the DNA patterns intended from birth. By reinforcing the natural order of neurological structure, enriched alignments of natural healing processes reach their optimal performances.

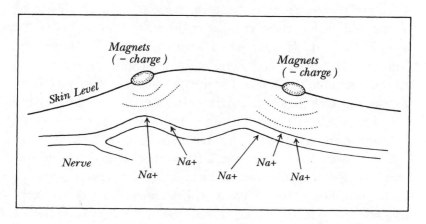

Imagine the greater power and speed as the gates open and create this massive flow, all within the natural limits imposed by the physiology of the body. The neurotransmitters become charged with greater levels of *endorphins,* those feel-good neurochemicals that naturally enhance your mood. Endorphins operate similarly to morphine. They block the transmissions of pain and increase pleasurable feelings. Endorphins interact with other substances, such as serotonin and the neurotransmitters related to depression and euphoria. This one-two pleasure punch has been used to explain the runner's high that occurs during extended exercise. Endorphins and certain neurological tissues are sensitive to the subtle electromagnetic charges that occur during acupuncture. There have been promising experiments in which small transmitters were implanted in the brain to stimulate endorphins and thus control Parkinson's disease, stuttering, and severe pain.

Magnet Therapies

There has not been much scientific research into the effectiveness of magnet therapies. The companies that make them don't do much themselves, since magnets can't be patented or synthesized. This is good news and bad news. The good news is that these devices are available to the public, but the bad news is that they have no scientific research behind them yet.

One of the pioneers in the field of electromagnetic medicine for attention deficit disorder is the pediatrician I mentioned at the beginning of this chapter, Dr. Bernard Margolis of Harrisburg, Pennsylvania. I have tremendous respect for this man's work. He is a dedicated physician who has the best interest of his young patients at heart. He has long searched for ways to allay their symptoms without the use of potentially harmful drugs. His research on electromagnetic techniques and ADD is very interesting.

Dr. Margolis has studied the effectiveness of magnets in mattress pads, pillows, comforters, and medallions, targeting various parts of the body. The mattress pad has magnets sewn into the materials so the forces are equalized over the entire body. Margolis studied the effects of his magnet devices on twenty-eight children with attention problems diagnosed by their parents and teachers. The parents of the children assessed them on physical behaviors, emotional and attention/memory functions before, during, and after using the magnets. Of the twenty-eight children, nineteen showed significant improvement in all scores while using one or more of the magnetic products. Margolis determined that the children who did not respond well were those who'd used only one of his products, indicating that the more magnetic power, the better.

Another of his patients was Ian, eleven, who used the mattress, pillow, and disk magnets. He responded well. He seemed calmer, rested, and focused after their use. His symptoms reappeared when he went just one night without the magnets. His parents noted that while wearing his disk on a visit to a restaurant, Ian behaved much better than he had on previous outings. Typically, he had difficulty staying in his seat and remaining calm and focused. With the disk, he appeared to be in much better control, more focused, and able to converse respectfully.

The reports of Ian's summer camp behavior were remarkable. Previously, Ian had been a terror at the camp. The magnet therapies appeared to change that. But after the magnets were withdrawn, the reports turned negative again.

Thom, fourteen, was an angry, argumentative, and impulsive boy, who was also a bed wetter, averaging once a week. He needed to be told many times to do his chores before they were done, and homework was very unpleasant, with lots of yelling. He had poor study skills. His was irritable toward his younger siblings, and their battles raged constantly.

With the advent of the magnet therapy he became a warm, friendly child and was no longer angry. He became much more empathic to his mother and helped around the house without being asked. His relationships with his siblings improved markedly and he began to take responsibility for their welfare. He began to enjoy his studies and he stopped wetting the bed. His mother considers the change "a miracle."

Dr. Margolis's patient Jan, eleven, had severe attention and impulsive problems. She'd been on medication for two years. He took her off the medication, which is known to retard growth, and treated her with magnet therapies. Since then, she has grown four inches, gained fifteen pounds, and is doing very well in school.

Probably the most dramatic case that Dr. Margolis has told me about involved a five-year-old boy named Timothy who'd been diagnosed with eighteen psychiatric syndromes, including a disorder related to Tourette's syndrome. The essential features of Tourette's syndrome are multiple motor and verbal tics that severely impair social and academic functioning. The physical tics usually involve rapid movements of the head, although various parts of the body can be affected. Verbal tics may involve clicks, grunts, yelps, barks, sniffs, snorts, and coughs.

This poor boy had been in and out of twenty-two schools. Since he could not be controlled by his parents, he was living in a foster home. He'd been in seven by the age of five.

Needless to say, medications were of no help. Dr. Margolis gave Timothy a magnet pad and pillow as well as a comforter blanket with magnets sewn inside. It changed his life. His parents took him back. His symptoms have completely disappeared. At last report, he was leading a normal life.

Dr. Margolis has also used magnet therapies with adult patients. He told me of Ali, forty-five, who had suffered a brain injury three years before coming to him. He was having problems concentrating and focusing because of damage to his brain. Medication had not helped. After using magnet therapies, he has recovered his abilities to concentrate, though he has reported that in periods of high stress the problems sometimes recur.

Magnetic Action Plan

If magnetic therapy is something you'd like to try for your ADD child, all of the doctors I've interviewed recommend Nikken products. Rest assured, I do not own stock in this company. It's simply the one brand name that seems favored by physicians I spoke with. There has been no demonstration that any one magnetic therapy product is better or worse than others. You are welcome to get your magnets at the hardware store to see if they have any effect.

Opinions vary on where the magnets are best located for maximum use in pain therapy. The approach I have used, supported by every doctor with whom I have discussed attention deficit disorder remedies, is a general stimulation with magnets inside mattress pads and comforters. The use of the magnetic disk on the chest has been successful, especially during the day. It can be used under the shirt so it is not noticeable.

Be prepared for your child to take some teasing from friends, and maybe pointed questions from your family physicians if they do not have faith in magnet therapies. The magnets will not harm your child. The only danger is that you might build up expectations that are not fulfilled. The magnets are not a cure-all and there is no guarantee they will work for your child.

I've been told that multiple levels of magnet stimulation give the most powerful results. If you purchase a brand designed specifically for healing treatments, be sure to read the directions carefully so you will know how to use the magnets most effectively. My wife complains that I never read the instructions when I attempt to put something together. I figure that I will read them when and if things don't work out my way first. Don't be like me.

I recommend also that you go through a thorough behavioral checklist (include the items in the audit if you wish) and that you get several additional behavioral checklists from sources such as the teacher, counselor, and friends. Maybe some of your child's behavioral problems will be eliminated. Learning problems may linger. In my experience, a combination of approaches works best.

Dr. Margolis first studies the child's behavior without medication or magnets. Then he studies them while using the magnet therapies. If there is behavioral change in ten days, you may want to extend the time in order to see if it is only a temporary change—maybe another ten days. If the behavior remains on an even keel, take the magnets away and see if the ADD symptoms return.

The brand-name magnets for healing treatments are not inexpensive but this benign treatment has worked in many cases and there is really no downside that I've found. Even if they do not work for your child, you've not lost any ground.

Electromagnetic medicine is a long way from replacing traditional approaches because no one has yet to explain the interactions of the human body to the satisfaction of science. However, no one knew how to explain how aspirin relieved pain. We just used whatever worked. Maybe that will be the way of this new (and old) approach for ADD. However, at present more than seventy research studies (cited in *Mosby's Complementary and Alternative Medicine*) clearly support efforts to be made in this field.

Please do not come to the conclusion that you have to understand the mechanics of electromagnets. Possibly the secret is that no one really does, and my lack of ability to make sense of it should not be taken as a lack of aptitude on the reader's part. This stuff gets as maddening as quantum physics and multiple universes if you try to make an equation of perfect predictions. Even Einstein admitted that the electrons of the atom seemed to have a consciousness of their own.

As a practitioner and scientist, I have seen success and lack of success with these electromagnetic devices, which means that just as there are many causes of ADD, there are many remedies. For the purpose of this book I am asking the parent and child to become the practitioners and scientists with these tools. As such, everyone has to think outside the envelope of existing theories, especially if the current approaches are not working. This may be one of those possibilities.

THIRTEEN

Spiritual Healing

J erry was out of control by the age of eleven. Ritalin was no longer effective in controlling his ADD symptoms. His parents brought him to me as his military school was preparing to boot him. He was hyperactive and rebellious to the point of self-destruction. I worked with Jerry for three sessions without seeing any improvements. He wasn't motivated at all. I don't give up easily, but privately, I wasn't sure I could help him.

It happened that Richard, a friend from California, was visiting me. California seems to be a place that inspires experimentation of all kinds, particularly in spiritual things. Richard practiced a form of healing that approached therapies from a spiritual aspect. His stories of his successes had intrigued me.

Religion and faith have always been a part of my life. I believe that we all have a spiritual side, no matter what faith we practice or how we express it. I'm not alone in that. Most thoughtful people seem to consider themselves to be both physical and spiritual beings.

About 95 percent of Americans profess a belief in a power higher than themselves, and that figure has not dropped below 90 percent in the last fifty years. Nine out of ten people say they pray—most of them (67–75 percent) on a regular basis—according to a Gallup poll. Many Americans have stated that their faith is a central guiding force in their lives, with two-thirds reporting that they are members of a church or synagogue. There are also indications that religion is becoming "more important" in our lives, an increase of 7 percent from ten years before; the increase in "personal need" is up 24 percent.

I try to consider all factors in searching for therapies to help my patients. Before Richard came along, I hadn't done much to address spiritual aspects because my training had always been in the treatment of the body and mind. Yet attention deficit disorder is a devastating problem that affects all aspects of a patient's life and that of his family too. And it is also true that although modern medicine has moved away from spiritual matters, the history of the healing arts is deeply rooted in addressing mind, body, *and* spirit.

I told Richard of my frustration with Jerry's case and he offered to talk with the boy and his parents. They agreed to give it a try. During their first meeting, Richard had Jerry lie down on a massage table. He instructed the boy's two older sisters and parents to form a circle around him. Richard asked us to silently "connect our hearts" for Jerry. I was nervous about this process and fearful of what it might do to my reputation in the conservative medical community, but the boy's family seemed to be accepting Richard's approach, so I stuck it out too.

After putting his hands over the boy in silence for what seemed like an hour (it was probably more like three minutes), Richard the healer spoke. "Jerry would like for you to know that he is sorry for all the grief and shame he has caused you, and asks your forgiveness."

The mother broke out in tears and murmured something like, "We do not care. We only want what is good for you." (I could not hear her well because of her sobbing.)

Richard repeated again, "Jerry would like for you to know that he is sorry for all the grief and shame he has caused you, and asks your forgiveness. Do you forgive him?"

The father and younger sister nodded, the mother and the older sister said in unison, "Yes, yes, yes." I observed a large exhalation of breath come from Jerry's body and a slight shudder, as if he was weeping.

After some more placing of hands on Jerry's head, Richard said quietly, "Let us pray for the wisdom to rise above our selfish ways and learn to love each other in the way God intended us to do. Do you agree, family?" He waited until each of the family members spoke to this conviction. Then he continued, "Let each of your hearts be open and speak a blessing and commitment for Jerry."

Again, each of the members spoke a sentence or two about how much he or she cared for Jerry and wanted to be of aid whenever he needed it, but the oldest sister seemed to be most intent on examining her motives aloud and was moved to tears.

After some time, Richard finally asked Jerry to rise, but first he gave a quest. "Jerry, as you arise, you will begin your life as from the beginning. You are to walk the way of a teacher and honor your path as a healing teacher."

Jerry sat up and smiled. He seemed relieved and relaxed. I was amazed at the difference in this boy's demeanor. He spoke in slow and deliberate sentences, much different from the fast, high-toned pitch I had observed before. He was a different person.

After that strange session in my office, he returned to military school and became a model student. I lost touch with his family, but at the last report he was doing well and presented no problems other than the usual adjustment to life as a young man.

After that experience I asked Richard, "Is this something you have a special gift for, or can the rest of us do it?"

Richard laughed. "No, I am not magical. This is just common sense wrapped in some mystery." He explained his approach and the spiritual basis of the things he'd done. He explained that he sensed Jerry's symptoms were related to family conflicts and an "imbalance" of love. He worked to restore the spiritual balance by having each family member declare love and devotion to the other. This gave Jerry the forgiveness he'd been seeking. He'd felt guilty for disrupting the family.

Richard had also picked up on a "negative force" coming from the oldest sister. It's not unusual for the oldest sibling to resent the birth of a second child, who displaces her as the center of attention. He had focused on getting her to forgive Jerry and to help him heal.

Playing the devil's advocate, I asked, "Do you think you cured the boy's ADD?"

Richard shrugged his shoulders and replied, "ADD is only a bunch of bad attributes you have given to a set of symptoms, and I do not know what I have done for that. But you place too much emphasis on the disease and not enough on the healing power of the family.

"It would do you good to put more trust in the family, Jerry, and yourself," he told me.

Spiritual Matters

Richard was not my first contact with this form of healing, which I've come to think of as *transpersonal medicine* because it transcends the person and what we can do as individuals. It is based more in the spiritual realm of faith and hope, drawing upon human capabilities that have not been fully explained or explored by science.

Transpersonal medicine might easily be dismissed as *weird* science. People have no rational understanding of it, although most individuals will acknowledge that at some point in their lives they've experienced or witnessed or sensed some aspect of it. Maybe a family member appeared to beat a deadly cancer by praying and maintaining a positive attitude, or someone in the community has exhibited healing powers that no one can explain, or a sick and dying old man was rejuvenated by the attentions of a neighbor child.

Each experience is different yet the same. Words cannot articulate the process but somehow it works. My guess—a highly educated one because I've studied this for many years—is that human beings have been healing one another through spiritual means for much longer than the science of medicine has been practiced.

In the 1970s, as I became more and more involved on the front line of medical practices, I developed a large toolbox. That is, I was comfortable with a wide variety of approaches to patients with symptoms now identified as attention deficit disorder. I had tried hypnosis, individual psychotherapy, group therapy, relaxation therapy, bioenergetic therapy, Gestalt therapy, and several others in which I had gained expertise. Yet I wasn't all that successful in curing people of those symptoms, and that bothered me greatly.

I had patients with other challenges as well, and one of them was a woman dealing with chronic pain from an automobile crash that left three of her cervical vertebrae fractured. Although she had undergone surgery, her pain was still intense. I'd been working with her for a week when she returned after a weekend of treatments and told me that her pain had subsided almost entirely.

She had visited a healer, she said, explaining that she'd released her fears and suffering to God. Naturally, I was suspicious, though curious too because she did seem to be feeling much better. I'd taken courses in psychosomatic medicine and learned that some patients can create symptoms, including pain, because of repressed anger or depression. If that was the case with this woman, it was possible that she felt cured after her session with the healer. Still, I'd seen this woman's X rays. She definitely had a persistent misalignment that would have caused her pain.

My second thought was that she had indeed been healed through the power of suggestion. We know that when a person holds an image very strongly in mind, the body can respond accordingly. Maybe it was all the effect of a powerful suggestion and there was no "real" bone healing anyway.

The bottom line was that my patient was ready to go home and restart her life without pain. Something happened to help her, and I wanted to know what that was. I made an appointment to meet her healer. I prepared myself to meet a quack, charlatan, or fanatic of some sort. My hackles were up.

The healer met me at the door of her home—not an office—and before I could go on the attack, she disarmed me with her serenity and warmth. She laughed easily, and without trying to impress me, she revealed an impressive and sophisticated knowledge of medicine and psychology. This was a very smart and educated woman.

As I discussed my patient's experiences with her, and then talked of several other problem cases, she chuckled and gently chided me. "They cannot do it by themselves, and that is what you are asking them to do. They know they can't, and you are just annoying them. Help them find their sources of the healing path and they will find a way."

Briefly, my hackles went up again. It was an instinctive reaction brought on by years of teaching, in five medical schools. You don't hear a term like *healing path* in those institutions of reductionistic reasoning to the gene or DNA. It's the sort of touchy-feely phrase that medical professors might openly scorn. Yet it is also a phrase that goes back centuries, particularly in Asian cultures. The healer claimed that each of us has a set of forces around us—other forms of spirit that can be healing sources. She was spooking me again, but I kept listening.

She said there are a number of healing sources around us: the love of another, the power of another person's words or touch, a spiritual connection, internal healing that is triggered by an outside source. "This healing power simply needs to be recognized and embraced," she said.

She made me nervous because her belief in spiritual healing was well outside the accepted mainstream of medicine, but as I realized even then, her sources were rooted in philosophies that were developed centuries before Ritalin and Prozac hit the market.

I am a religious person and I certainly believe in the power of prayer, so I couldn't easily dismiss her belief in the restorative powers of spiritual things. After some soul-searching, I decided to test some of the approaches she suggested with my patients.

My first experiment was the "Western-hospital-style group prayer meditation." I tried it with one of my chronic pain therapy groups with whom I'd developed a strong rapport. I took a member of the group, Jan, into the biofeedback room and hooked her up to monitors for internal and external temperature, muscle tension, heart rate, and EEG. I left Jan with instructions to read or just relax, and I returned to the group. I then led the group in a relaxation exercise before asking them to focus on Jan in the biofeedback room. I told them to help her heal her pain by raising her body temperature. We did this for ten minutes, took a break, and then did it again for another ten minutes before bringing Jan back into the room with us. I also had a technician bring in the records from the monitors that we'd hooked to Jan.

The results of our experiment were fascinating and I've duplicated them in many exercises since with other patients. Everyone in the group reported benefits from being part of a healing process, but Jan benefited most of all. The readings from the monitors showed that in the exact periods of the group's healing thoughts, Jan's physiology changed for the better. Her finger temperature rose from 91.3 degrees to 94.2 degrees and her muscle relaxation correlated to higher Alpha readings on the EEG.

Afterward, Jan said she felt a sense of gratitude and grace during the process and after it. She felt as though her guardian angel had shown its presence for the first time, she said. She also reported a profound sense of being part of something greater than herself.

Key Elements of Spiritual Healing

I've studied Richard's approach and those of other spiritual healers. I've found that there are commonsense aspects to what he did that day, and there are also elements derived from the belief, shared by most people, in the spiritual nature of all men and women. The primary aspects that I've identified as significant include

- positive regard for self (worthiness)
- awareness of being a part of a bigger force or power
- the power of touch
- the power of ritual

Positive Regard for Self (Worthiness)

Most ADD patients, regardless of age, have low self-esteem. Many say they feel worthless. This is as much a spiritual problem as it is a mental health problem. And it can result in physical problems. The symptoms of ADD isolate people, contributing to loss of self-worth, social isolation, and loneliness. The critical component of this underlying dynamic is that they feel abnormal and unworthy. I've heard them say, "I don't deserve to be healthy." Often they feel responsible for anything negative that happens to family members or others they know.

The path to healing will be hindered if ADD children do not follow it. If they feel so unworthy of being healthy, then they cannot embrace anything but disease, and no treatment will be effective.

Awareness of Being Part of a Bigger Force or Power

There is nothing more frightening to the human being than isolation. A diagnosis like ADD can make your child feel like the only one in the world with a problem. A child's friends can be unintentionally cruel, thoughtless, and even just plain mean about the symptoms and the resulting problems.

Humans are a social species. Since the earliest days of man they've lived, hunted, and fought together to survive. We developed language so that we could communicate with one another. Most of our survival skills are based on group interaction and co-operation. It is no wonder, then, that a sense of isolation and loneliness can debilitate a child, as well as an adult. We are not wired to be loners, and children in particular need the security of a group. It goes to the very core of our nature.

Children with ADD often ask, "Why me?" because they feel it isolates them from their peers and their families. The question "Why me?" underscores the basic need to be a part of something larger than themselves because that gives them perspective and security.

The first step in any twelve-step program is the awareness that you have some external support unique to you that is always available. I have studied healing groups and healing stories from around the world, and I'm always struck by the healing power of a restored sense of security, a sense of being loved, and a sense of belonging.

The Power of Touch

Two nurses, Dolores Krieger and Janet Quinn, pioneered the field of therapeutic touch in the 1970s. They produced a wealth of scientific data that cannot be denied. In one of their most creative experiments, each participant consented to receiving a minor cut on the arm. Then the nurses monitored the healing rates of each subject. They were all instructed to extend their arms through a small hole in a screen so they could not see what was happening. Each was then touched either by a nurse trained in healing touch or with a warm pad. The participants did not feel the difference. The healing times were twice as fast for those who received the human touch.

I have trained parents to touch their children with ADD in specific areas, and there has always been a positive response. The alternative touching therapy philosophies of Shen or Reiki postulate that there is an energetic flow (or flux) that occurs within the body that has been disrupted with ADD. Healers hold that the natural energy can be restored through the touch of another person.

If you want to try this method, hold your palms close to each other, almost a half-inch space apart, palm to palm. Relax and breathe for a period of time and see if you can feel any warmth or magnetic pull. This is called *chi* in Asian medicine. The next step would be to place your hands on the head and neck of your child. This loving touching is usually instinctive to parents, particularly mothers. It is one of the many rituals of child rearing that can also be observed in other mammals.

The Power of Ritual

Whenever human beings gather to ward off danger or to cope with threat, to worship, or to honor one of life's major transitions, they develop rituals. Rituals are common activities we plan and conduct with conscious intentions. Wedding is our marriage or mating ritual. Thanksgiving dinner is a meal ritual. Graduation is a learning ritual. The retirement dinner, baptism ceremonies, the bachelor's party—these are all rituals, rites of passage.

My research into the healing power of rituals has shown the following results for participants, especially those who may be the focus of a ritual such as a birthday, a graduation party, or a bridal shower:

- higher self-esteem
- more hope and encouragement
- a sense of connectedness
- feelings of empowerment and support
- a sense of being transformed

If these benefits occur on the psychological level, the physiological impact is also substantial. We know there is a linkage between stress and adrenal stimulation that leads to lowered immunity functions as well as an array of neurological and cardiovascular issues. If this pattern were reversed, the total impact would have a positive influence on cognitive and biological performance.

There is another aspect that is important to acknowledge and that gives some credence to the whole concept of rituals and relationships. Researchers recently discovered a remarkable feature of our neurological system, which may explain some of the ways we think *and* feel: there is an independent order of communication between human nerve fibers. Researchers have shown that there is a vibrational field around each person, in the shape of an a egg. These vibrations are contagious. If you place one person next to another, soon both of them are in resonance. This may explain how one person's energy can influence another person's emotional or cognitive states. Isn't it true that if you are with a group of high-energy people who are happy and upbeat, you tend to feel the same way? And since music is a sound vibration as well, this principle might explain the power of music to affect our moods and cognitive states as well. Is there a reason that the large majority of spiritual rituals include music? Dancing is the oldest form of medicine known in recorded history, and its use of rhythmic stimulation for improved mood and cognitive abilities has been substantiated in over a hundred research studies.

Taking the Next Step

Science and spirituality may be more closely linked than we now generally understand. Quantum physicists have identified invisible forces on the atomic level that may one day explain the presence of "spirits." I'm not trying to persuade you one way or the other. My only intent is to encourage you to consider spiritual healing as another therapy available in treating your ADD child.

Touch Exercise

Have your child find a comfortable place to lie down and relax. Her job is easy because all she has to do is lie there and receive the treatment. The child can even talk if it is not too distracting. The toucher, usually the parent, begins by centering herself and releasing any expectations or thoughts of failure. (Thoughts of failure often cancel out positive energies.)

In a relaxed posture, hold your hands facing palm to palm about a half inch from each other. Breathe deeply and focus on the energy between the palms so that there is a heat or tingle felt. Using your imagery, create a powerful vision of your love and caring extending out through your hands and develop an intention for the best outcome for your child.

With these thoughts in mind, place your hands on the child, your right hand over the navel area and the other over the heart area. Remain in this position for at least thirty seconds. Then with your right hand remaining on the navel area, put your left hand over the forehead. Remain at that position for about thirty seconds. After those initial steps, follow what your intuition directs.

Ritual Making

Rituals are generally created with three specific phases in mind: the *separation* from ordinary reality, the *transition* from one status to another, and the *return* to life.

The separation phase can be accomplished in a number of ways. You can decorate the environment with flowers or drapes as well as dressing yourself or your child in special clothes. Smells are very powerful agents in this regard. Basically the idea is to change the child's state of mind from ordinary to a heightened, or at least different, reality. Too often we perceive life as a humdrum or routine, day-in-and-day-out experience. But rituals break up the routine and offer new possibilities. Your child might be able to do things you thought he couldn't do during a ritual because barriers tend to disappear. Your child might be a different person afterward. In order to create new possibilities, you have created the empowerment of expectation.

The second phase is one of change. What new life is your child planning to forge? What new roles are you and your child going to play? What will be the new responsibilities in the life ahead? Most important to healing rituals, how is your child's life going to be if there are no longer these limitations? The transition phase can be marked by gifts or pledges. There can also be specific changes in behaviors, such as silence, mood changes (being happier), and reciting vows of intent. Often there is a decisive step one takes to symbolize this decision (such as wearing new jewelry or new clothing).

The third phase is usually the step back into everyday life with the new role or title. This is usually met with celebration. In the case of ADD rituals I have witnessed the setting of new goals, plans to change one's diet, the decision to use certain aids, and expressions of appreciation for others.

Love

Love has true healing properties, especially with children with ADD. Rather than define love sensually or romantically, I would like to consider it as an attitude. This exercise can be undertaken by two or more people, including the child. If there are more than two, form a circle around the child with ADD. Although most people prefer to hold hands to form a bond within the group, this is not necessary. The most critical requirement is to focus on the child with the intention of helping him. Close your eyes and hold his image. Members of the group might also touch the child lightly to convey caring.

The next step is to bring focus by humming, chanting, or singing together. The key is to feel a common voice. Think of concerts you've attended where the entire audience sang along with the performer. Wasn't there comfort in that communal experience? Didn't you feel, however briefly, close kinship with all the others singing the same words in the same harmonies? That's what you are aiming for here, except there is more to it because your goal isn't just to experience pleasure, it is to heal with love.

Everyone has an opinion about the mysteries of healing, and there are certainly dangers in expecting too much from spiritual approaches. My advice is simply to consider it as one of many tools to be wielded. There is still much to be learned about the healing power of spirituality and faith. I hope someday to be able to justify all my experiences in some form acceptable to science. For now, all I can say to you is that you should not disdain the possible benefits of spiritual healing for your ADD child.

Transpersonal Audit

The need for transpersonal medicine appears to me to be universal. This audit can help you to determine if these approaches might be useful for your child.

Determine whether the following ADD symptoms relate to your child:

	Always	Usually	Rarely
1. He feels that things are out of his control.	2	1	0
2. He feels lonely and feels no one understands.	2	1	0
3. He asks himself, "Why me?"	2	1	0
4. His biggest need is to be normal.	2	1	0
5. He wants to stay away from people more.	2	1	0
6. He hates to tell anyone else about his problems.	2	1	0
7. Your family is being disintegrated by this problem.	2	1	0
8. Your family is becoming a victim of this problem.	2	1	0

Scoring

Sum up the numbers marked for each item (2 or 1) for a total score in a range of 0 to 16, and compare it to the interpretations below. It is important to administer this audit to all the family members so that you can get a better understanding, for further discussion, of the impact of ADD on the cohesion of your family unity.

10–16: The family is suffering from the impact of ADD, and that may be eroding some trust and balance of assurance for each of you. The recommendations are for you to begin some transpersonal medicine approaches, although they may be more appropriately exercised in accordance with your traditional values and rituals.

5–10: The family has some sensitivities to the impact of ADD on the needs of assurance and mutual understanding of one another's needs. Effort needs to be extended for more discussion and action for the comfort of one another in the expression of love and caring.

0-4: The family is apparently dealing with the problems of ADD in a mutual and constructive approach. These approaches should be encouraged and supported.

Transpersonal Medicine as a Verb

Transpersonal medicine is a term coined to identify the invisible forces of healing and caring that mainstream medicine has neglected to articulate or simply forgotten. The emphasis of modern approaches has been so highly focused on the magic pill and fears of litigation that natural healing has been demeaned to the status of superstition. As a nation and culture we have lost the skills, and we no longer trust in our inner resources; it has become almost a secret that the body has the capacity to heal itself.

The belief that "God doesn't make junk" has particular relevance in the sense that most of us are born whole without serious problems that cannot be overcome. And even if there were malformations, such as heart or brain abnormalities, this does not mean that we do not deserve respect for our authentic selves. The majority of our problems come as a result of our lifestyle, the environment in which we live, and the internal damage we do to our passion for life, namely fear responses.

The fact that most physicians would agree on is that the body heals itself if given a chance, and medical science helps it to this end as much as possible. If you break your leg, it will heal and even straighten the bone if placed inappropriately. Moreover, the break will mend so that it is stronger than before. You will regain health from most diseases unless overwhelmed by sheer force, and if you succeed, your immunity will be stronger for the effort. At least two-thirds of infected people will survive the invasion of a bacteria or virus, even if the exposure is to syphilis or tuberculosis.

Leonard Sagan, in his book *The Health of Nations,* analyzed historical health statistics and discovered that there was no time in history when medicine alone significantly affected the rate of any disease in a nation. According to his research, medicine didn't wipe out tuberculosis. Instead, once families learned how to prevent its spread through public health campaigns, it was all but wiped out.

There is no sense, then, in hoping that a magic pill will someday cure all children of ADD. Instead, we should try every possible therapy and treatment at hand, including those that have existed for centuries as ancient healing arts.

FOURTEEN

Healing Family Conflicts

R ob was a rebel with a cause no one could fathom. At thirteen, he was on a downward spiral of self-destruction and delinquency. He'd been diagnosed with ADD in the first grade. His parents had been giving him Ritalin since then, but he'd stopped taking his pills in the third grade. He was selling them as speed to high school kids instead. He'd built up a bankroll of three thousand dollars, and a record of disciplinary problems culminating in his arrest.

Rob had "borrowed" his aunt's car at about one o'clock in the morning. He was ripping down the street, smoking one of his father's cigars, with a group of friends in the car, when he lost control. He had dropped the lit cigar and was looking for it when the car spun out into the parking lot of a convalescent home. It wiped out several wheelchairs and sideswiped a van, but luckily no one was hurt.

After his parents picked him up at the police department, they brought him to me. He threw himself into a chair as if he were jumping off a bridge backward. He knew the drill and he was ready to play the game. But I threw him off by asking him something he'd never heard before.

"Rob, before we talk about what happened, I would like to know more about you. How did your parents come up with your first name, and do you like it?"

The question threw him off so much that he couldn't think of a smart-aleck or defiant answer. "My dad named me after his brother—my uncle—and I really never thought much about it."

"Where is your uncle?"

"He's dead. He died before I was born from some disease of the liver. I think he was a drunk, but I have never asked. Every time I have tried to talk about him, my dad gets tears in his eyes and he just leaves the room."

I told Rob that I didn't believe him when he said he'd never thought about it, especially when his father reacted so strongly to his uncle's memory.

Rob smiled and relented. "Yeah, I guess I have. Sometimes I feel that I was supposed to do something special in my life to make up for something my uncle did, or didn't do, but I don't know what. It's like an obligation, but I haven't lived up to it. I'm always disappointing people that way."

Family Issues

The problems of attention deficit disorder are often masked by personality clashes within a family and by faulty assumptions family members have about their individual roles. The causes of ADD are many and varied. It is often diagnosed because of a child's behavior, but some cases are more related to emotional problems, both those of the child and within the family. That doesn't make treatment any less challenging, but it calls for a different approach.

In many cases, the emotional problems that contribute to ADD symptoms arise from situations like Rob's. He had no neurological damage. Instead, he was confused and emotionally out of balance with his family. I developed a treatment approach consisting of specific phases that have been effective in resolving family issues associated with the symptoms of ADD.

Although there is no typical case, Rob's ADD symptoms were related to emotional problems rather than neurological issues, and my approach to his case illustrates how those sorts of problems can be addressed by working with the entire family. I first helped Rob root out the source of his emotional turmoil, and I then worked with him and other family members to ease the burden that was causing so much stress in his life.

"Would you like to take another name and get this burden off your back?" I asked him.

Rob sat up in his chair as if I had slapped him in the face. "Can you do that?" he asked. "I mean . . . I don't want to hurt my dad's feelings, or anything, but . . ." Then he hung his head down, as if in despair. "Aw, I know you were just asking. I know you can't do that."

I told him it was entirely possible to do that if he wanted help. "It will mean that you can start your life over with a new identity. Is that what you want?" I asked him.

Rob's eyes widened. I could almost hear the wheels turning in his head as he considered the possibilities. Finally he grinned, and whispered, "Why not?"

As Rob considered the possibilities of starting a new life, I probed the old one. To help him, I had to determine the source of his emotional problems. With some gentle questioning, he told me his story. At times, he'd stop and cry. The boy was carrying around a lot of hurt.

He felt he'd failed his parents to the point where he'd never be able to please them. His first memories included his failure at potty training and the shame of bed-wetting. He felt he'd failed his parents in school, in sports, and even in doing things like taking out the trash. His older brother, Junior, picked on him, as older brothers tend to do. But Rob felt that his brother was relentless and his parents unforgiving.

He recounted a story about the two of them playing in a pond and getting wet and dirty. Junior ridiculed him even though both of them were a mess. And his parents sided with Junior and praised him for chastising his little brother, according to Rob. That incident was typical, he said. Rob felt that his brother was idolized by his parents because he was named after their father, while Rob was named for an alcoholic uncle.

At thirteen years of age, Rob had already reached some profound conclusions about how his life was going to be, according to his role within the family. That is not unusual for emotionally troubled children, and unless they get help in working out those issues, it can affect their entire lives.

As Rob gave his perspective on his family's dynamics, it became apparent to both of us that his behavioral problems and bad attitudes were rooted in family issues. He'd felt trapped in the role of the failed son and he saw no way out of it until I suggested the name change. Identifying the root of Rob's emotional problems was just the beginning.

Role Identification

My next three sessions were spent talking with his mother, father, and brother, Junior. The mother was a quiet, shy person whose lack of vitality was striking. The mother was so detached that she did not know exactly what her husband did for a living, other than that he went off to the office every day. She talked in soft, submissive tones, almost in whispers, as she explained that she had been raised in poverty. She was the ninth of ten children. Hunger and need had dominated her childhood. She'd shared a bed with four other siblings. She married at age fifteen, but her husband was killed in a hunting accident two years later. She'd returned to the family and worked as a grocery store sacker to help out. She'd met Rob's father at a church function. She was pregnant with Junior when they married.

Rob's mother had little to say about her needs or her desires for herself. She was bewildered by his behavior. Her own parents had been so occupied with mere survival that she had no real role models for parenting. She loved her boys but wished for a girl with whom she could find more in common. She said she'd been diagnosed with cancer, but she did not know what type, nor did she have any idea of the treatments that had been suggested.

As anticipated, the father was the dominant force in the family. He was a large, intimidating man. He'd lost faith in any efforts to help Rob. After so many therapists and treatment programs, he didn't want to spend much time with me. He was the second son in a family of five. He'd dedicated himself to outshining his older brother through persistent hard work, higher grades, and stauncher religious practices. A civil engineer, he was the first college graduate of his family and he prided himself on being the first to own a home.

The father acknowledged that he probably would not have married had he not been forced to, but he said he had no conflicts with his wife. There seemed to be very little emotional attachment. "My work is my mistress," he said. That comment resonated in my mind throughout my session with him.

The father also acknowledged that he was very proud of Junior because his oldest had traits he considered to be most noble. He portrayed Junior as hardworking, obedient, ambitious. And he did not conceal his disappointment in Rob. He could not remember being proud of him on any occasion. I asked why he had named his son after his older brother, but he did not answer. He looked away from me, but I saw that tears were welling in his eyes. To change the subject, I asked the father about his parenting style, which he described as authoritarian.

My interview with Junior, who was very much his father's son, was short and shallow. His answers to my open-ended questions were "yes sir" or "no sir." When I asked what he thought of his little brother, he smiled slyly and said, "He's a klutz. I get by with what I want, and he takes the blame. I think he likes it."

He seemed to feel safe in admitting that he used his younger brother, so I pressed on. "This is what I am seeing, so tell me if I am wrong. You were the first son, so you can do whatever you want. If you get into trouble, you manipulate your little brother so he takes the hit. Am I right so far?"

Junior grinned and nodded.

"As long as you can keep him in the doghouse with your father and mother, you can get away with almost anything, right?"

He was enjoying this. He was so manipulative and cocky that he didn't think anybody would ever spoil his game.

"I guess I have been pretty hard on old Rob, but it is just so easy," he said.

Family Treatment

Step I: Turning On the Lights

Obviously, Rob had good reason to feel wronged within his family. He was the fall guy for his manipulative brother, who could do no wrong in the eyes of the domineering father. In other families, the mother might step in and act as the protector and supporter of the second son, but Rob's mother was so emotionally detached she didn't have a clue. She had claimed the victim's role for herself.

Rob was also correct in seeing that there was significance in his name. His father was projecting memories of his older brother— and his own fear of failure—onto him. Junior was the family manipulator who pulled everybody's strings, and he was the chief beneficiary of all the dysfunction.

Actually, the more I learned of this family, the higher was my regard for Rob. The second son was in better shape than might be expected considering the environment he'd grown up in. He had adopted the role of "bad kid," which at least gave him some control and power within the dysfunctional framework. He'd figured out that his father's low expectations had some benefits. Since he'd been a loser at birth in his father's eyes, he had nothing to gain by improving his behavior. Frankly, I am surprised that he didn't already have "Born to Lose" tattooed on his arm.

If a child knows that he is never going to get praise or support, why should he try? By getting into trouble, he was only living down to low expectations, and the consequences were no worse than the disdain and emotional distance he faced every day.

While it appeared clear that Rob's ADD symptoms were primarily the result of his dysfunctional family situation, I ruled out any other factors before I began a counseling program. Rob had no neurologically related problems, which explained why he had maintained passing grades even while spending most of his time in detention.

Rob's psychopathology tests were also telling. He tested high for depression and low self-regard. He was very confused about his identity and his goals. Understandably, he had a high need for acceptance. Rob was a prime candidate for recruitment by a street gang, but fortunately, he'd escaped that fate.

This boy did not have ADD, but he did have many symptoms associated with it. He had been right in rejecting the Ritalin. It was only making him hyperactive. As a confused child, he was treating his symptoms as best he could. He needed help in finding a way out of the self-destructive patterns he'd developed in order to survive.

Step II: You Cannot Change What You Do Not Acknowledge

I called the family in for the first group counseling session, wondering how they would respond. Their faces were grim as they filed in, like students walking into the principal's office after being thrown out of class. I told them that I'd come to some conclusions about how they treated one another. I explained that these conclusions were just my opinion, and they were free to challenge me on them.

I have a very direct style of counseling, so I minced no words as I offered my view of the family dynamics. I offered no damning judgments but I told them that things would have to change within the family if we were going to help Rob.

As I expected, Rob's father was the first to respond, and he was on the defensive. "Doctor, I respect you and your opinion, but Rob has been a problem from the day he was born. Are you saying that I have been a part of this for thirteen years?"

I told him that all families have areas of stress and conflict, some of which they don't even discuss openly, some that may go back generations. I told him that there was obviously an issue between him and his own brother, and that it had affected his relationship with his second son. Rob hadn't been a problem since birth; he'd *made* him one because of his troubled relationship with his own brother. Rob had been carrying the burden of that history all his life.

The father sat in silence when I'd finished speaking. No one in the family dared to break the silence. Finally I said: "Why don't you tell me what happened to your brother."

It was as if I'd stabbed him in the chest. He began to choke, almost collapsing on the floor. After a drink of water and a short administration of relaxation and breathing instructions, he tried again to speak. "My brother was a failure and a shame to my parents. He was disrespectful and caused great harm to my mother by his defiance. He died in a plane crash when he was only twenty-four, and my mother died a year later. He caused it by his selfishness, and I was grateful that he died." These words were spoken with such vehemence and anger that his body trembled. His fists were clenched so tightly his knuckles went white.

He looked at me and then at Rob. "I promised myself that I would never allow any of my children, especially my sons, to be so disrespectful. It seemed that when I named him Rob, he began my brother's life all over again."

His stare lowered to the floor and he began to cry.

Rob looked more perplexed than threatened. "Dad, why did you name me Rob, then, if you hated him so much? Were you trying to put a curse on me?"

I spoke up, addressing the father. "This is not unusual for families to revive the memory so they can finally put an end to unresolved emotional issues. You had unfinished business with your own brother. Is that right?"

The father was in no shape to answer. He was sobbing uncontrollably. The mother started to comfort him, but I shook my head and she settled back. The father needed to handle this himself in order to get past it.

I turned my attention to Junior. "What do you think, Junior? You seem to have been the lucky one in this family."

Junior smiled and said, "Yeah, but I think I need to take care of my brother now. This has gone too far."

The mother quickly said to me, "I didn't know. Believe me, I didn't know. I saw all of this and I thought Rob was just a strange child. But I did not protect him, either, because . . . I just didn't know." Now she was crying, kneeling as if begging forgiveness. The father patted her as he tried to regain his composure.

Finally I turned to Rob and asked, "Are you surprised?"

Rob was the only person in the room who appeared utterly at peace and happy. He was smiling. The burden had been lifted.

"All I can say is that I need to lose this name, fast. It has caused me trouble for too long."

His smile was so infectious, I began to snicker. Junior joined in and before long, all of us were holding our bellies and laughing out loud. It must have sounded like a party. And it really was a celebration. All the tension in the family had been broken.

The father got up and hugged Rob and said, "I am sorry, so sorry. I love you." Rob returned the words and patted his dad's back. Then the mother did the same. Everyone was hugging everyone. Even I got a family hug.

As we ended the session, I said, "My assignment for this family is to continue talking openly about how things went wrong. Each of you played a part, including Rob. You do not need a therapist to do this, but you've got to keep talking it through. I suggest that you write down your ideas before you gather, but be sure to arrange at least two sessions before I see you again. Do not try to solve the problems, just discuss your thoughts and feelings freely."

The light of truth has a powerful effect on people. Too often families live in denial. It's as though an elephant is sitting in the living room but no one wants to acknowledge it. Even when family members recognize that their relationships are dysfunctional, they won't acknowledge it for fear of making things worse. They hide from one another and deny their love for one another.

Rob's family had faced some pretty powerful truths. That was a huge step, but it wasn't the end of their problems. It would take some time for them to adjust to new ways of relating to one another. Insight is helpful, but the journey does not stop there. The next required step is forgiveness and release of the past.

Step III: Stepping Out of the Past and into Forgiveness

Regardless of anyone's best intentions, forgiveness doesn't come easily. One counseling session can't erase years of scarring. This phase of the treatment process is one of the most dangerous. Those who feel victimized often seek revenge at this point. Sometimes, the parents feel so guilty for the pain they've caused that they quit parenting. Venting anger, even when it is justified, only builds more rage. Righteous anger is no less destructive than rage, for all parties.

I advise families to put the hurt behind them in order to move forward. It doesn't help to lash out at one another or to summon up every unpleasant and hurtful memory of wrongs done in the past. There must be some agreement to bury the hatchet and to focus on doing better in the future.

When Rob's family returned for their next session, there was a tendency to focus on how unfairly Rob had been treated. Rob was reveling in the victim's role and in his father's new vulnerability. Junior, whose survival instincts were well developed, had taken on the new role as his brother's defender and champion now that his parents were more submissive because of guilt.

I called a halt to it. I told them it wasn't going to work. No one could erase what had happened, but it wasn't going to get any better if they continued to pick at the scabs. Rob's dad said he wanted to move on immediately. Rob's mother was willing to do whatever everyone else wanted. Junior too. Rob was still mad and looking for revenge.

Finally, I laid it out for them. I told the father he could continue the fallen leader role. I asked the wife if she was content to be submissive and administer to the wounded. I told Junior that his ability to switch sides was amazing. And I told Rob to stick with his new role of avenger for as long as he thought it was helping the family.

Rob struggled to get his anger in check but then I saw him let go of it. "I guess we are through," he said. "But you sure took the fun out of it."

What I'd done is called *spitting in the soup*. I'd put into words the new and equally dysfunctional dynamics of the family, and in doing that, I pulled the plug. They were finally ready to start building a future.

Step IV: There Is No Cure for Life, Only a Plan

The next step was for this family to chart a more positive course. First they had to decide and express what they wanted as a family. Then they had to determine how they were going to get it. In other words, they had to name it to claim it.

As expected, Rob no longer wanted to be the family's whipping boy. Nor was he going to be administering the whip. He wanted a new name and a new start. After some discussion and suggestions from the family, he chose the name Bobby. It seemed to fit. And he figured that it would not be hard to get his friends to use it. He also requested a new start, so the family promised never to bring up problems he'd caused, such as the stolen car incident. In addition, the new Bobby was given the responsibility of deciding what traits went with his new name. Junior wanted a new name too. He admitted that he hated being a Junior because it implied that he was a replica of someone else. He apologized to his dad, and the family went along with it. He chose Jay R., which I thought was pretty creative.

The father decided to join in the spirit of new beginnings. He didn't want to always be the disciplinarian. I suggested that he adopt the "contractor's role," in which he assigned privileges and chores. For example, if Bobby wanted to stay out late one night, he'd have to earn the privilege by doing an assigned chore, such as washing Mom's car. There would also be a penalty or consequence if he abused the privilege. It sounded complicated, but it took some of the pressure off the father and gave the boys some control over their own fates.

They all agreed, and I was given the role of appeals judge, just in case someone didn't like the chores or penalties handed out.

The mother, who was comfortable in the role of conciliator, said that she wanted her husband and children to look to her for support. And so, the family set off on a new direction. They hit the expected bumps along the way, but all in all, they found a healing path. Bobby honored the traits he ascribed to his new name—integrity, joy, and music. He shut down his Ritalin-dealing operation and began doing things in which he could take pride.

New bonds were formed. Bobby discovered that his dad could play the harmonica well, and they jammed together every Tuesday night. This was not only a changed boy, this was a changed family.

REVIEWING THE PHASES OF FAMILY TRANSITIONS

I: Turning On the Light in the Darkness. Bring the awareness of the family secrets and assumptions into the light, without judgment and with love. These may involve uncovering layers upon layers of repressed thoughts and secrets.

II: You Cannot Change What You Do Not Acknowledge. Look beyond your own perceptive and distorted judgments. Find other views for truth and insight into your lives.

III: Stepping Out of the Past into the Future: Forgiveness. Release the bondage of continued resentment and anger toward one another. There is no event worth serving a life sentence for.

IV: There Is No Cure for Life, Only a Plan. Relationship is a process of helping one another. Name your needs and allow the family to meet them with you.

An Audit for Defining Family Roles

To help your family examine how it functions, use the two lists of self-descriptions on the following page. On each list, have family members circle the words that they think apply to their roles in the family most of the time. If someone cannot make up his or her mind, ask another family member to help.

List 1: Externally Oriented Vs. Self-oriented

- makes decisions easily by himself
- self-focused
- direct with others
- uses internal feelings, instead of others', as guide in decisions
- high leadership abilities
- comfortable being by herself
- willing to fight for "right" regardless of consequences
- stubborn
- action oriented
- follows self-rules instead of others' rules
- sees simple explanations for problems
- does not mind giving talks to groups
- usually feels a special mission in life
- usually feels "different" from others
- thinks in ways different from others

List 2: Tradition-minded Vs. Pioneer-minded

- concerned for the welfare of others
- considers parents and elders are always right
- feels comfortable giving advice
- feels that there is "a right way"
- respects family traditions and values and attempts to maintain them
- believes that some people are sheep and others are leaders
- believes that answers can be found with enough study
- believes in the importance of knowing his place in life
- feels that rules are good
- believes that it is sometimes hurtful to expect too much from life

- wants to live up to the expectations of others
- believes older people are wiser than younger people
- thinks discipline is the way to achieve something
- agrees that people should do what they are told by the person in authority
- believes children should be taught to behave

Scoring

Total the number of circles you have on List 1 **(0–15),** and circle that number across the top of the square below under the title "Externally Oriented—Self-oriented." Now count the number of circles you made on List 2, which should be in a range of **0–15** as well. Circle that number on the vertical list labeled "Tradition-minded—Pioneer-minded."

Draw a line (imaginary or real) down from the number across the top and another line across from the side number. Where those lines cross will place you in one of four boxes—A, B, C, D. For example, if you scored a **3** across the top and a **13** on the side, your lines would cross in the A box. Or if you scored **11** across the top and **5** on the side, you would score in the D box.

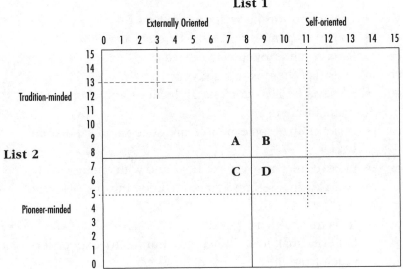

The combination of your two scores will place you in one of four boxes, and your personal category will be based on the collections of those general descriptions. Box A defines those people who see themselves as externally oriented, with traditional values, which indicates they are natural Teachers. They tend to be mother hens with those they care for, giving advice and attempting to steer their chicks along traditional paths, even if their chicks are older than they are. The most important part of being a Teacher is that the Teacher is the carrier of wisdom and past truth. The negative aspect is that that wisdom and truth may no longer be relevant.

A Teacher in the context of family is one who provides context and direction to help others. However, a Teacher also runs the risk of smothering the family and restricting innovation and self-determination.

If you landed in box B, you would be classified as the family Warrior. Warriors are often directed by a sense of mission. They often set goals and establish guiding values early in life. The positive attributes include a deep sense of commitment. On the negative side, they can sometimes be so determined that they lose perspective on whether their mission is a wise one. A family Warrior can be an inspiring leader but sometimes he loses sight of individual needs in his zealous efforts to complete a mission.

If your two scores had a cross-coordinate in the C box, you would fit the family role of a Democratic Leader. This type of family member has a pioneer spirit and is very extroverted. The Democratic Leader builds consensus, forms teams, and leads efforts to change things for the better. Good features of the Leader are the enthusiastic efforts made for change and the conviction that everyone can handle the change. The negative aspect is that any action can be bogged down by anyone's fears and lack of trust.

In family units, Democratic Leaders are very positive forces because of their willingness to try new things, but the downside is that they often try too many things at once. They may go from one guru or book after another, trying to enlist everyone's support, without giving one method enough time for change to be effective. This may cause confusion and depression.

The block entitled D is the Inventor box. Inventors are those people who live in their own world with little long-term interest in others' opinions. Inventors are like children in the sense that they are fascinated by new ideas and concepts, and thus are fun to be around. The downside is that they are usually too interested in fun and their ideas to participate seriously in the family's needs. They are seen as not being *team players*.

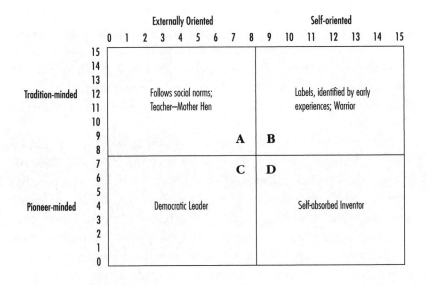

In families, Inventors are often perceived as rebels and immature, but they can be enormously creative. They are usually very eager to participate in problem solving, but they tend to be intolerant of tradition and have little respect for authority. This can lead to major conflicts because of differing values and styles.

The Family Dance

Being trained in family counseling and having the experience of observing the dynamics of families around the ADD issue, I must admit that most of the time the manipulative behavior of the child with ADD is fostered and perhaps initiated by unconscious family behavior. However, which comes first, the chicken or the egg?

Children with ADD will press a family's emotional resources and any kid will naturally behave to serve his own needs.

On the other hand, children with ADD will also influence their families' behaviors. Because of their children's accident-proneness and lack of success, parents will often begin to obsess over their lack of parental abilities to prepare for this problem. Because of the lack of direction and suitable models in their own families of origin, the parents will begin to lose confidence in themselves and become dysfunctional.

Rather than blame family dynamics for problems, the mission of this book is to turn this around and give resources and tools for the families. No one takes the time to educate families in meeting challenges, especially ADD. This chapter is a start toward a healthy problem-solving process.

FIFTEEN

Educational Strategies

My boyhood buddy, Spook, was a man of many talents. By the age of fifteen, he was famous across west Texas for his talent as a horse trainer. He was a horse whisperer who had a way with both mustangs and Mustangs. Spook was good with horsepower too. I swear he kept my 1947 Plymouth running with a pair of pliers and baling wire.

For all his varied skills, Spook wasn't much good with numbers. One of the reasons we got to be such good friends was that my father helped Spook with his algebra homework almost every night. My buddy was a genius when it came to working with things he could put his hands on, but he could never get either his hands or his mind around concepts like $x + y = z$.

It frustrated him no end, but I remember my father telling him, "Spook, you aren't stupid or dumb, you just learn differently than the others. And you might even want to be proud of that fact." My father was a wise man. He helped Spook get through algebra, and last I heard, my buddy was working as a county judge.

Children diagnosed with attention deficit disorder whose symptoms are related to neurological problems are not dumb or stupid either. Like Spook, they simply learn in different and unique ways. But they too must find patient and willing teachers who understand their challenges. ADD students learn differently because their brains operate on more limited frequencies. They don't respond well to the regimented approaches typically used in a classroom of mainstream students.

The parents of an ADD child have to be vigilant in monitoring their child's education. Your child will likely have more than thirty different teachers in his school career. It is up to you to make certain that his teachers are aware that ADD presents special challenges but also opportunities for innovative teaching. Most teachers have received some training for dealing with students with ADD, but because teachers generally have to deal with a roomful of young people, they tend to go with what works for the majority of them. The parents of the student must make sure he gets the special attention and assistance he needs to learn.

Because of the challenges students with ADD present to most public school systems, more and more of their parents appear to be turning to homeschooling. In the parent groups I work with, virtually every one who has had a child finish high school advocates homeschooling instead of public school. Not every family has the resources to do this, of course. And not every parent is suited to the role of teacher, especially day in and day out.

But whether you wish to homeschool your child or send him to a public or private school, it is important that you understand how his mind works and the best and most efficient ways he learns. I've found that most children with ADD learn best when family members are involved in their education, whether as teachers or as backup tutors.

Special Needs Vs. the Assembly Line

Most public school teachers will tell you that today they are saddled with having to teach for mandatory progress tests required by school systems. These requirements and the ever-growing number of students in their classrooms have robbed teachers of the little time they once had to give special attention to individuals with special needs. Sadly, children with ADD don't do well at all in assembly-line educational systems. Because they demand extra attention and cause disruptions, they are often seen as threats to quality control by those teachers who are under intense pressure to make on-time delivery of their students to the next stage of the process. I am not being facetious.

A superintendent of schools in a Texas school district set up an elaborate televised teaching system for each classroom. The video-taped curriculum is standardized for high test scores. Teachers serve as little more than monitors.

This mass production approach to education presents an enormous challenge to the ADD child and his parents. Instead of working with children's special needs and teaching to their highest expectations, teachers lower the bar, which further lowers the self-esteem of vulnerable ADD children. These children can learn and thrive, but only if they are taught in a manner suited to their needs.

Five Bridges for Teaching over Neurological Gaps

Children and adults with ADD have neurological gaps that interfere with the cognitive processes of memory, concentration, and attention span. Their more limited brain functions also affect muscular coordination and mental energy. Teachers, then, have to deal with

- ineffective motor output
- insufficient memory
- weak production control
- low mental energy
- language dysfunction

Ineffective Motor Output

When children are referred for possible neurological problems, one of the common assessment tools is for them to draw geometric figures, such as a circle, a square, and a diamond. The delay in fine motor development becomes apparent in the drawings of these simple figures. In fact, this is probably the most telling test. Some of the distortions come from the fact that the children's internal visual perceptions are distorted (this is usually related to learning disabilities). Many of these children cannot draw anything resembling a circle or a square because of the lack of fine motor dexterity in their hands. This lack of motor control reflects the neurological confusion of coordination, pacing, and planning required in every subject in school.

Most of us don't give much thought to the neurological complexities involved in drawing simple figures and forming letters, but they are tremendous. For the child with ADD, it takes trial and error with lots of patience to reach that level of coordination. The operative word is *patience*. Even mainstream first-graders have difficulty learning their ABCs at first. The learning process involves training the brain, or *grooving* a neurological sequence.

Children with ADD can do this, but they must be allowed to do it slowly because of their slower neurological processes. It works to give them some paper and have them trace the letters over and over again, letting them examine their own work, and encouraging them to do it better and better. It is best not to make this a *quantitative* exercise, so that they have to write two hundred *a*'s and two hundred *b*'s. Make it a *pride* exercise; let them determine when they have accomplished the task of writing their letters right, with the hope of instilling a source of accomplishment.

Practice is the best teacher for students with ADD. Don't put time limits on them, and allow them, to work in informal settings too. Try to stress the fun and pleasure of creating something beautiful.

Insufficient Memory

Memory is a neurological function. Some people have greater capacities than others, but to a certain extent, memory capacity can be improved with exercises and even a few tricks. If you really wanted to, you could learn to remember every name in the phone book, or the birth dates of everyone you know. It doesn't take genius. Yet children with ADD often beat themselves up for having poor memories in the mistaken belief that they'll never be able to do any better.

Memory training is based on the physiology of brain function. The brain requires oxygen to function and memory is influenced by how much oxygen you have circulating around the bloodstream. But the symptoms of ADD tend to limit oxygen flow. Children and adults under stress don't breathe deeply. They also tense their muscles. Both of those behaviors withhold oxygen from the brain and, when done habitually, limit memory capacity. That is why it is important for ADD students to learn in a relaxed setting.

LEARN TO RELAX, RELAX TO LEARN

Step one. The deeper your child breathes, the better his memory will be—as long as he doesn't take it too far and hyperventilate. Tell your child to think of it in this manner: your breath is the fuel of memory, and the more you relax and breathe, the more you can remember. I have taught kids this strategy and their test scores consistently go up at least ten points.

Step two. Instruct the child to use all of his oxygen fuel to focus on what he needs to remember. If the stored information does not automatically come back, have him think of all the associated information that goes with it. For example, if he is trying to remember the date Kennedy was shot, think of everything else that was going on during that era, like the Cuban missile crisis or the civil rights movement. Memory associations are a great trick for learning. Children can teach themselves to remember things even by associating the study material with the clothes they are wearing or the food they are eating as they study. Muscle memory can be taught in the same way. I had a friend who was a pastor, and the last four digits of his phone number were 8–2–4–6. When you dial them, you make a cross pattern. I never memorized the numbers because my muscles were trained to make a cross when I wanted to call him.

It also is helpful for ADD students, and most others too, to write down material that must be stored in the brain. When you write something down, it engages your muscle memory too. Confession: in high school, I tried to cheat in my physics class by writing down all the formulas on a small piece of paper that I was going to sneak into the test. The formulas were long and I had trouble fitting them on a small enough piece of paper. I had to rewrite them several times, smaller and smaller each time. By the time I had perfected my tiny writing, I didn't need the cheat sheet. I had the formulas memorized!

Reading material out loud is also very helpful when a child is trying to remember something, perhaps because he is committing it to muscle memory too. My recommendation is to entice your child to talk through problem solving in math too.

Weak Production Control

Production control is how you show what you know. Many times I hear children with ADD explain that they know the answers, but they just don't know how to express them. This is the result of cognitive limitations that cause poor organization skills. It's especially intimidating for ADD children to express complex thoughts, so they often rush the process, trying to tell all they know at once.

When I was in high school I worked part-time for my father as a mechanic's assistant, mostly as a brake specialist. I was supervised by Dud, a wise man—in spite of his nickname—who laughed at my many mistakes. Like the typical ADD child, I'd get nervous and try to rush through a process that required a step-by-step approach.

"Frank, you try to do everything at once," Dud once told me. "There is a beginning and an ending, with steps in between. Try that and see what happens."

The lesson for students with ADD is to divide any task—whether it's a brake job or a homework assignment—into parts: a beginning, a second part, and so forth, until the end. This applies to reading, spelling, writing, and math problems. It might be helpful to remind your child of the best way to eat an elephant: one piece at a time.

Instruct your child to approach an assignment by first thinking of the steps that he must go through. It might help to craft a story around the problem. This can be fun and it will help in understanding as well as production. This is called the Socratic method of teaching, after the Greek teacher Socrates. He used to engage in dialogue and questions so that his students would learn to think in methodical ways. This is the best way to teach a child with a diagnosis of ADD. It offers the opportunity to expand the possibilities while allowing the student to exercise problem-solving skills.

Low Mental Energy

Often ADD children will begin a task with great enthusiasm that quickly fades into fatigue. One of my patients, Nancy, did well in her morning classes and made good grades but was failing in her afternoon classes. Another patient, Frances, had the opposite problem. She was an afternoon person, who did poorly in morning classes and excelled later in the day.

We all have highs and lows in mental energy, and these patterns are fairly consistent for each one of us. Some of us are morning people, who arise each day in a chipper mood, bright-eyed and ready to learn. Others are night people, who don't come alive until after sunset. Scientists refer to these energy cycles as *circadian rhythms* and brain research has verified their existence.

Unfortunately most elementary and high schools don't offer both day and night shifts. Even normal teens tend to be night people because of hormone flows associated with adolescence. ADD children tend to have fluctuating cycles that add to their learning challenges. Their energy ebbs and flows in high peaks and low valleys. It is difficult for them to sustain mental energy throughout an entire school day.

One of the best solutions to the fluctuating energy levels of ADD kids is *teenage torment.* The teen is not tortured, but the people around him might be. I want to break this to parents gently, but there is no gentle way to say it: the blaring music your ADD child plays might be just what this doctor would order. As I've noted earlier, ADD kids instinctively try to stimulate their sluggish brain activity in a number of ways that are often judged to be antisocial, irrational, and dangerous by others. Risky behavior is one such behavior. And playing blaring music with heavy bass and drumbeats is another.

The brain is stimulated by these forms of music. When your ADD child listens to music while studying, it may well be helpful to him. It energizes his neurotransmitters even as it drives you and the neighbors bananas.

I've got more shocking news. Chewing gum is another way for an ADD child to stimulate his brain, though you don't have to tolerate him leaving it on the bedpost overnight. Chewing, leg bouncing, foot tapping, and other repetitive and rhythmic behaviors are all typical ways that ADD kids try to self-stimulate their lethargic brains. The explanation is interesting. A substance called collagen connects each tissue in the body, and when a person moves, tensions set up within this fabric of the body create electrical charges. This is called the *piezoelectric effect*. The individuals are supercharging their brains by pumping up their mental energy. This mechanism also explains why physical exercise aids in problem solving and memory.

Body postures can stimulate emotional states too. In our research, we asked college students to assume a slouched posture common to depressed individuals for a period of ten minutes. After that period, each reported feelings of depression regardless of his mood prior to the test. There is a scientific explanation for this. Crystalline components located at the ends of the muscles radiate electromagnetic signatures that signify imbalances in body chemistry that are communicated through emotions, such as depression. We found other postures that produce emotional states, including the "victory" posture, in which a person sticks out the chest and chin and flings the arms back. This gives a feeling of elation.

It is believed that children with ADD actually benefit from getting up and moving around in class—even though it normally would bring a reprimand from a teacher. The posture typically assumed while sitting in a classroom is probably detrimental to learning for an ADD child because of the emotional state it puts him in. When a child's shoulders are stooped and his head is down, the chest cavity is compressed, inducing lethargy in ADD children. We've demonstrated to teachers that when they allow the ADD kids to move around more freely, it helps them learn.

Language Dysfunction

In studies of criminals and other antisocial personalities, one of the most consistent personality attributes is these individuals' difficulty in expressing their emotions verbally. It is believed that they act out their emotions through violence and risky behavior to compensate for their inability to express those feelings verbally.

In my anger management therapy classes, we often note that the participants have limited vocabularies. When we give those in the program words or phrases that help them express their feelings verbally, it often dissipates their anger without violence. Children with ADD have similar problems because of their reduced vocabularies. In fact, some studies have found that more than 50 percent of those convicted of violent crimes or antisocial behavior have been diagnosed with ADD.

The good news is that ADD kids also benefit from therapies that improve their ability to express themselves. The power of words can be amazing. I learned that back in the third grade. The school bully was harassing me one day and we were squared off in the school yard. Kids were crowded around us hoping to see a fight. My older sister was in the crowd. She came to my rescue but in a very interesting way. As the bully and I circled each other, she peppered him with questions: "You look pretty pissed to me, all right. You look pretty mean to me, so I guess you are going to beat the stuffin' out of my little brother, right?"

The bully did not take his eyes off me, but he spoke to her. "No, I ain't pissed. I'm just messing with him."

This was welcome news to me. It was such a relief, I couldn't help but offer a spontaneous wisecrack. "Well, I guess I will consider I have been messed with, and now we can do something else."

The bully got a kick out of that. "I guess you can say you have been messed with, then." We all laughed. End of conflict.

From that point on, whenever he messed with me, I'd announce that he'd accomplished his purpose of scaring me, and that was all it took.

Years later, I saw another example of the healing power of words when my colleague Richard Wall taught elderly women patients dealing with depression to vent their anger with curse words. They took to it like marines, but only within the confines of his office, where the walls fairly shook with the words of foulmouthed matrons. It was quite a sight, and quite a sound too. And it worked. Words do have power, and given the power, children and adults can find paths to their potentials.

Innovative Teaching Gifts

I've learned other creative methods for stimulating the minds of students with ADD from innovative teachers I've met over the years. I was raised by teachers, so I respect them deeply. Some of the most dedicated people I've ever met were on the faculty at the public school in Andrews, Texas, where I had my first teaching assignment after college. The principal, Vernon Payne, had a teaching staff of naturals. They had the training but much of what they did was instinctive. I marveled at their skills. They were excited about their students' potential. No student lacked for attention at that school. And in my three years there, I never saw a student fail. Below are a few of the innovative methods for students with ADD that I learned from teachers there and around the country.

246 The ADD Answer

Token Rewards/Big Returns

This is a reinforcement method in which students are given a to-ken of redeemable value for appropriate and productive behavior. One of the steps in this procedure is to break down the desired behavior into small parts so that the individuals will learn in incre-ments. For example, if you wanted to use tokens such as dimes for reading behavior, you might want to begin the procedure by re-warding your child first for just looking at a book as the first step. After the child is rewarded for that, the next step might be to re-ward him for reading the first page, then the first five pages, ten pages, and so on. The final reward would be for answering ques-tions to test for comprehension.

This approach is very effective for ADD children, in part be-cause the step-by-step approach to tasks works well with children who have difficulty focusing on the big picture. The system of in-cremental rewards also works well in building a sense of ac-complishment for children with low levels of confidence and self-esteem.

I've also seen this method used successfully for group therapies for ADD children. They were divided up into small groups and given tokens redeemable at the local music store. This not only in-creased student productivity and built self-esteem, it also fostered greater teamwork among ADD kids, who generally do not per-form well in group situations.

I highly recommend the use of a token reward system for teaching ADD children. So often these kids feel isolated. They are also highly self-critical. Imagine the consistent frustration of never completing a project or being rewarded for a good job. These chil-dren are often battered emotionally because their ADD symptoms get them in trouble. The token reward system makes learning much more enjoyable for them. It is not the value of the tokens; it is the recognition of a step forward. And it is the underlying mes-sage that says, "We care."

Multiple Sensory Learning

The more of the five senses used in learning, the better and faster the process. Research shows that if a class is presented with a subject orally, the learning rate is only 17 percent. But if that material includes a visual presentation, the learning rate increases dramatically to 75 percent. If the material is acted out with the participants speaking dialogue, the learning rates increase to 95 percent.

Because of the neurological gaps experienced by a child with ADD, multiple sensory learning is a vital tool. A child's ability to comprehend and learn increases dramatically when teachers use methods employing a variety of visual, audible, kinesthetic (body-movement), and even smelly exercises. Who can forget the rotten egg experiments in chemistry class?

One of the research teaching methods we've tried used lemons, oranges, and cinnamon as memory enhancement tools. There was no inherent relationship between the words to be memorized and the fruits, but we had the students associate each word with a particular smell as the items were presented. If a series of eight words was to be repeated, such as *chair, cat, weather, pliers, man, picture, coat,* and *yellow,* a picture of each item was presented on a slide projector as the students were given a taste of a particular fruit. Not surprisingly, the students performed at a higher rate.

A common lament among critics of education is that teachers are not adequately rewarded for innovation. But teachers who use innovative methods with ADD kids are rewarded by the fact that their students often become much more attentive and cooperative in class. Teaching them with a multiple sensory approach has enormous benefits, regardless of the age of the student.

During my public school days as a math teacher, I would bring blocks of wood of various sizes to the class and distribute them to the students. I would use these blocks as audiovisual aids to present lessons on fractions, ratios, geometry, and quadratic equations. I also used apples, which I'd cut up for early discussions of calculus. Since my classroom had been a choir room, I even brought in a piano and used chord progressions to discuss number series and hierarchical equations. These were average seventh- and eighth-grade students with the usual array of behavioral issues and distractions, but I was able to teach them college-level material because I engaged their brains with all sorts of materials. I know my methods worked because I tested the students for specific knowledge. And my class scored, on average, in the ninetieth percentile on the achievement tests. Let's hear it for wood blocks and apple slices!

Pump Up the Class

All students benefit from regular exercise but ADD kids in particular need to be physically active to keep the blood flowing to their brains. I recommend three key exercises, borrowed from martial arts training, before each class. These exercises help the brain ramp up, which enhances attention span and focus. The steps are based on common sense, but young people enjoy the martial arts ritual. Some teachers even award colored belts for classroom concentration.

Begin these exercises by having your ADD students do *relaxation therapies like deep breathing*. Instruct them to make themselves comfortable and then to focus on an object or particular space on a wall. Have them focus their energy and mental focus on their beating hearts. I tell students that the heart is the source of pure energy, devoid of fear or anxiety, and it is a powerful tool.

After about three minutes, I have the students do a few *muscle stretching exercises*. The exact exercises are not critical, as long as the arms, legs, and back get some attention. My favorite is what I call the flower awakening. I use music for this. Everyone starts curled up on the floor, and slowly stretches out the arms and neck as if she is a flower growing from the floor and reaching for sunshine or rain. Eventually the students stand and extend their arms and legs. They also bend and stretch according to their own needs. Some of these movements become humorous. Laughter is encouraged. It is stimulating too.

The stretching period should take about three minutes. The next phase is *toning exercise*. The students are asked to hum a tone (or even a song) that wakes up the brain. They try to find a tone that causes vibrations in their heads. The room may sound like a beehive within minutes. That's OK if they are breathing and concentrating on their empowerment. These physical exercises eat up a little class time but they pay dividends in increased focus and energy.

Love and Learning

The best teachers find ways to reach all their students. The family is a valuable part of the teaching and educational process, both in imparting direct instruction and in sharing values. In particular, an ADD student needs to learn these things from family members:

- They love and respect him.
- They have faith in him.
- They support him at all times.
- They are interested in his feelings and thoughts.
- They value academic progress as a positive tool for the student.
- They are willing to help.

ADD students need to know these things and they need to hear them repeated to them—every day. Hang them on the refrigerator, slip notes in their books and lunch boxes. The greatest contribution a family can make to an ADD child is to let him know that his parents and siblings are in his corner at all times.

SIXTEEN

The Game Plan

As a former high school coach, I couldn't leave you without a game plan. Your opponent is attention deficit disorder. Because ADD can attack and impact on your child's life in a variety of ways, I've provided assessment tools to help you determine the best game plan (or plans) for your child. ADD affects children and adults in six areas, so I've designed defenses for each of them. Because each child's ADD symptoms are different, let's first assess how your child is affected within each of these six areas:

- self-concept
- behaviors
- home relationships and harmony
- social relationships
- spiritual life
- school life

I realize that each of these areas has been covered in previous chapters, and I would certainly hope that you will look back to those chapters for guidance and direction. But you cannot just follow one approach at a time. That creates confusion, and if there is not a major success with one approach, it might be thrown in the dump as unusable when it could be very powerful in conjunction with another. The message is that your child needs an integrated plan that includes a mixture of approaches. ADD is not a single problem and it cannot be helped with a single solution. That is the reason for this chapter, to start with the *big picture*.

For each category of assessment there will be a 1-to-10-point rating scale, with 1 meaning no impact of ADD in that area, and 10 meaning that the effects of ADD are having dysfunctional impact in that area of life. Each of the rating scales has different relevancies to determine how well your child is functioning; however, the underlying ratings are based on the general scale below.

TEN-POINT DIMENSIONAL SCALE OF ADD
IMPACT ON LIFE FUNCTIONS

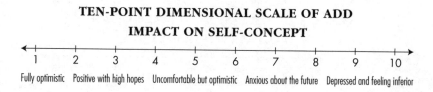

| 1 | 2 | 3 | 4 | 5 | 6 | 7 | 8 | 9 | 10 |

No impact Minor impact but coping well One significant life area impacted Two life areas impacted Three or more life areas impacted

Self-concept

In this category we'll look at how your child feels about himself by looking at his self-esteem, self-assurance, and self-sufficiency. There are many ways to determine a child's self-concept but I've found the best method is to simply ask the child basic straightforward questions: "How strong do you feel when you are facing tough problems?" or "How confident are you in your own abilities?" or "How well are you going to do on a test next week?" Have your child respond to those questions using the ten-point scale below.

TEN-POINT DIMENSIONAL SCALE OF ADD
IMPACT ON SELF-CONCEPT

| 1 | 2 | 3 | 4 | 5 | 6 | 7 | 8 | 9 | 10 |

Fully optimistic Positive with high hopes Uncomfortable but optimistic Anxious about the future Depressed and feeling inferior

Behaviors

Behavioral areas include the ways parents and children cope and react. These reactions can be divided into *reflexive* reactions, which usually do not include any thought processes about consequences (impulsivity), and *consequential* responses, which include some processing before action. The assessment of forecasting and expecting the consequences of his or her behavior is a feature of self-control (impulsive behavior). The child with little awareness often creates more significant consequences out of the frustrated need for impact from external sources, such as teachers, parents, and law enforcement. The general dimension is not necessarily "good" behavior (accommodating to regimens), but appropriate and flexible behavior (behavioral adaptations to conflicts and demands). In the family meeting consider a variety of situations in which the child reacted without regard to the consequences (teacher responses, peer responses, and so forth).

TEN-POINT DIMENSIONAL SCALE OF ADD
IMPACT ON BEHAVIORS

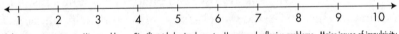

Behaviors age consistent   Minor problems   Significant behavioral events   Has caused reflexive problems   Major issues of impulsivity

Home Relationships and Harmony

ADD can affect a child's home relationships and family harmony by triggering rebellion by the ADD child toward parental authority or tension with siblings who resent all of the attention demanded by the ADD child.

TEN-POINT DIMENSIONAL SCALE OF ADD
IMPACT ON FAMILY

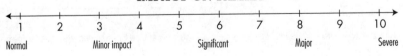

Normal   Minor impact   Significant   Major   Severe

Social Relationships

How does your ADD child get along with others? This includes friends and siblings, teachers, and other adult authority figures. Does your child make friends easily, or does he tend to be a loner? Does he welcome interaction and human contact, or shy away from it? Do others seek him out, or do they shun him?

TEN-POINT DIMENSIONAL SCALE OF ADD
IMPACT ON SOCIAL RELATIONSHIPS

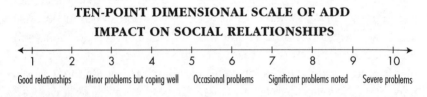

1	2	3	4	5	6	7	8	9	10

Good relationships | Minor problems but coping well | Occasional problems | Significant problems noted | Severe problems

Spiritual Life

A child's sense of spirituality may be limited to talk of guardian angels or fairy godmothers, or when faith is more a part of a family's life, it can be well defined in the context of organized religion. In many cases, children who feel disenfranchised because of ADD search for reasons that may lead them to question or refute their spiritual beliefs. Often this is merely an act of anger and frustration rather than a conscious rejection of their spiritual beliefs. They may lack sophisticated philosophies about a supreme being, but that will not stop them from asking questions about why they've been chosen to suffer. Some may embrace their faith and pray for help. Others may question their faith and ask how a loving God could allow them to suffer.

Use the 1–10 scale to determine how much ADD has affected your child's spirituality, the sense of specialness and assurance.

TEN-POINT DIMENSIONAL SCALE OF ADD
IMPACT ON SPIRITUAL LIFE

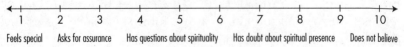

1	2	3	4	5	6	7	8	9	10

Feels special | Asks for assurance | Has questions about spirituality | Has doubt about spiritual presence | Does not believe

School Life

Children with ADD are most often evaluated in this area because the symptoms are commonly first noted by teachers. Too often teachers assume that the child with ADD would learn in the same manner as other students if not for the symptoms. I strongly encourage parents to investigate how their children best learn and to make certain their difficulties in school are truly related to ADD rather than other factors. Parents have to serve as advocates for their children because teachers and school officials are more likely to focus on their own needs and the needs of a class or a school instead of the individual needs and circumstances of ADD children. Although the schools may have the responsibility to assess each student, especially those with learning difficulties, resources are limited. It is also true that in many school systems, ADD is poorly understood and the reflex response is to demand that children be medicated to control their symptoms in class. I urge parents to seek expert advice and counseling before they medicate their children, whether from a psychologist, psychiatrist, neurologist, or rehabilitation therapist.

The list below contains the major areas of challenges for children with ADD sypmtoms.

Auditory Memory (Immediate, Recent, and Remote). This is an assessment of how well your child remembers items told to her, such as numbers or words.

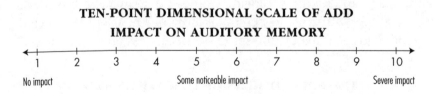

**TEN-POINT DIMENSIONAL SCALE OF ADD
IMPACT ON AUDITORY MEMORY**

1   2   3   4   5   6   7   8   9   10

No impact   Some noticeable impact   Severe impact

Fine Motor and Pacing Coordination. This area of learning relates to how well the child can perform skills such as writing, drawing, and producing appropriate outputs.

TEN-POINT DIMENSIONAL SCALE OF ADD
IMPACT ON FINE MOTOR AND PACING COORDINATION

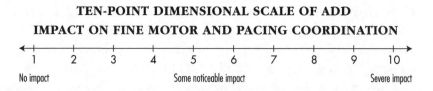

Visual Memory. This assesses the areas in which the student is required to remember what she was taught in visual presentations such as reading, observing concepts on the chalkboard, and understanding spatial relationships.

TEN-POINT DIMENSIONAL SCALE OF ADD
IMPACT ON VISUAL MEMORY

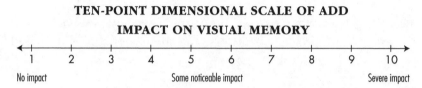

Embedded Audio Acuity. This skill is usually very difficult for children with ADD because it calls for a person to listen to a wide variety of signals and pick out the important ones, as in listening to a story and hearing the main points of relevance.

TEN-POINT DIMENSIONAL SCALE OF ADD
IMPACT ON AUDIO ACUITY

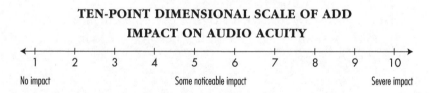

Arithmetic Sequencing. Although simple arithmetic problems usually represent no obvious challenges, they do require the student to remember to sequence the operations correctly, such as adding the columns in proper order or maintaining the numbers in proper arrangement.

TEN-POINT DIMENSIONAL SCALE OF ADD
IMPACT ON ARITHMETIC SEQUENCING

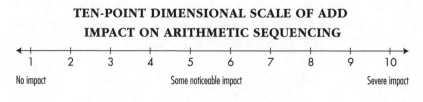

Listening Concentration. Probably one of the most difficult for children with ADD, this assessment requires the student to grasp the theme of a story and maintain the memories of characters and circumstances imparted by auditory presentation.

TEN-POINT DIMENSIONAL SCALE OF ADD
IMPACT ON LISTENING CONCENTRATION

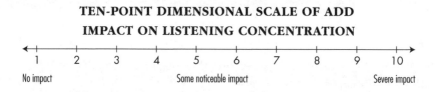

Reading Concentration. This learning skill enables the student to remember the facts, characters, and themes of stories imparted by visual presentation.

TEN-POINT DIMENSIONAL SCALE OF ADD
IMPACT ON READING CONCENTRATION

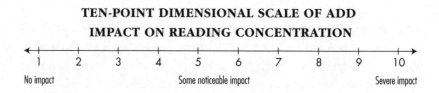

Auditory Abstraction and Logic. This skill enables a person to organize facts and questions in her head by receiving auditory information.

TEN-POINT DIMENSIONAL SCALE OF ADD
IMPACT ON AUDITORY ABSTRACTION AND LOGIC

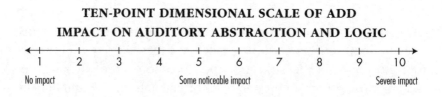

Visual Learning Capacity. These tasks measure how quickly a student can remember important visual information and reproduce the information in appropriate ways.

**TEN-POINT DIMENSIONAL SCALE OF ADD
IMPACT ON VISUAL LEARNING CAPACITY**

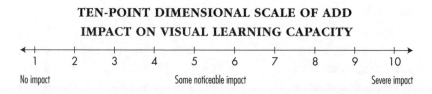

Abstract Tolerance. This is the measure of the level of tolerance and endurance a student has in pursuing a solution to a problem that requires long-term commitment (the answer requires some long-term processing, similar to a mystery).

**TEN-POINT DIMENSIONAL SCALE OF ADD
IMPACT ON ABSTRACT TOLERANCE**

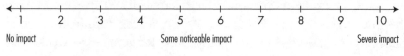

Summary Audit for Action

It might be useful to use a summary form in order to formulate an action plan. I have listed the areas mentioned above for an overview of the areas that need to be addressed.

Assessment Area	Rating									
Self-concept	1	2	3	4	5	6	7	8	9	10
Behaviors	1	2	3	4	5	6	7	8	9	10
Home Harmony	1	2	3	4	5	6	7	8	9	10
Social Relationships	1	2	3	4	5	6	7	8	9	10
Spiritual Life	1	2	3	4	5	6	7	8	9	10
School Life										
Auditory Memory	1	2	3	4	5	6	7	8	9	10
Fine Motor Control	1	2	3	4	5	6	7	8	9	10
Visual Memory	1	2	3	4	5	6	7	8	9	10

Assessment Area	Rating									
Embedded Audio Acuity	1	2	3	4	5	6	7	8	9	10
Arithmetic Sequencing	1	2	3	4	5	6	7	8	9	10
Listening Concentration	1	2	3	4	5	6	7	8	9	10
Reading Concentration	1	2	3	4	5	6	7	8	9	10
Auditory Abstraction	1	2	3	4	5	6	7	8	9	10
Visual Learning	1	2	3	4	5	6	7	8	9	10
Abstract Tolerance	1	2	3	4	5	6	7	8	9	10
OVERALL IMPACT	1	2	3	4	5	6	7	8	9	10

Game Plans

From the assessments you make in the areas listed above and from the ones from the preceding chapters, you can formulate a game plan for treating your child's symptoms. Remember to work with the child's strengths, but find ways to build up her more limited areas. Any area in which your child scores above a 6 suggests a need that should be addressed. Attention deficit disorder just doesn't go away. Your child will need treatment and counseling, perhaps for many years. I know of fifty-year-old adults still using therapies they learned more than thirty years ago.

Based on your findings with the evaluations, make a priority list, with the most severe issues at the top. Get your entire family involved in the process. Enlist the help of siblings in looking for resources as suggested throughout this book. The following are basic approaches you might want to take in specified areas:

Self-concept Issues

Action Plan #1: Daily Positive Hits. ADD children get so much negative feedback that it needs to be actively countered by positive hits of encouragement and support. Parents and family members get so wrapped up in treating the *problem* they sometimes lose sight of the *individual,* his needs and feelings. Too often parents forget to tell their ADD children that they are loved and appreciated. Children need to hear that just as adults do. Make a point to say something positive every day to your child. Let your child know that you appreciate him regardless of the trouble he has caused.

In my hospital programs I have always insisted that each patient be given a positive stroke every day. It is part of any healing process. I believe the body responds, sometimes in miraculous ways, when patients feel they are in a supportive and positive environment.

Action Plan #2: Counseling. Often ADD children develop negative inner conversations. They take on the labels others affix to them, calling themselves stupid or worthless. It is difficult for an ADD child to break free of that negative thinking, especially if it has been reinforced by teachers, friends, parents, or other family members. Parents sometimes slip up when they become frustrated with a child. If it happens often, however, the child may take disparaging words to heart. Once such comments have been made repeatedly, it can be difficult for the parent to rebuild a child's wounded psyche. This is where the extended family can be of enormous value. Grandparents, aunts, and uncles can be great healers. Their kinship gives them a bond that can open the door to healing with an ADD child. On a different level, professional counselors and psychologists are exceptionally helpful in reshaping a kid's self-concept into constructive modes.

Behaviors

Action Plan #1: Behavior Modification. Often children misbehave because they are getting payoffs from it. They want attention, even if it comes in the form of punishment—a payoff they can easily earn. Mostly, I see ADD children act out because they are confused. These children, with their slowed brain functioning, usually cannot prioritize their activities very well. Since they have difficulty doing one thing at a time, they go into hyperactive mode as they attempt to do everything at once. It actually makes sense when you understand what is going on in their heads, but that doesn't always make it any easier for the child or the parents to deal with.

By reinforcing positive behaviors in very concrete terms and developing better methods for expressing their frustrations, ADD children can learn more acceptable behaviors. Too often I have observed that a parent or teacher will tell a child what to do once, and then become frustrated when the child does not immediately respond. It takes more time to get that message into the mind of an ADD child.

Action Plan #2: Get Professional Help. There is no shame in getting a professional consultant to help you and your child. There are wonderful counselors, psychologist, psychiatrists, and support parents, and even a network of online counselors. They don't have all the answers, but they've probably heard nearly all the problems.

Home Harmony

Action Plan #1: Have a Huddle with the Family and Make Some Joint Decisions. Try some of the tools in this book and together develop a plan that calls for family participation. Agree to meet regularly to assess how this is working for each family member. Remember the steps in Chapter Fourteen as you approach each issue. Openly discuss each topic and reveal your feeling and desires; listen to the others; work out contracts on how all of you can help one another to bring about what you want to happen (not what you don't want), and make a plan.

Action Plan #2: Family Counseling. This is the stuff that marriage and family counselors are so good for. Get some help, even if it is for a one-shot consultation, because, unlike psychotherapy, you don't have to dig up your whole past and wallow in the bad stuff. You can just deal with the current problem, get some creative solutions, and move on. See the counselor down the street or one on the Internet at www.mytherapynet.com.

Social Relationships

Action Plan #1: Groups. Support and therapy groups help children with ADD heal. They offer a positive path to understanding and acceptance. I've never heard of an ADD child solving his problems or developing a workable plan by himself. It just doesn't happen. Isolation and seclusion only foster depression. As a family you cannot allow this to happen. Find a group that has a common interest, such as chess, dancing, sports, or even helping build a house or car. Boy Scouts and athletic clubs can be great resources for children with ADD. Children with ADD need organizations that foster teamwork and harmony.

Action Plan #2: Develop a Class. We humans are social animals who have developed advanced societies because we come together to solve problems. The modern manifestations of this are therapy groups or classes. These come in all forms and address all problems. If your ADD child is having trouble with social skills, there are all sorts of classes available through schools, colleges, churches, social service agencies, and private counseling services. If your child balks at attending them with a parent, have a favorite sibling, aunt, or uncle take him.

Spiritual Life

Action Plan #1: Talk to Your Child About How Special He Is Spiritually. We are spiritual beings too. Whatever your faith or beliefs, find a way to talk to your child about his spirituality and let him know that he is valued on that level too. The first step for your child is to discuss his special and unique place in the universe. Aside from focusing on the negatives of sin and retribution, emphasize for the child that each soul is different and precious. Songs and poems have special impact at this age.

Action Plan #2: Stories. I just reread *The Little Prince* (by Antoine de Saint-Exupéry) and was reminded of the strong messages told us through metaphor. This is a story of a child who comes from another dimension and discovers that love is what makes each of us unique and special, worthy of attention. There are many stories we can read to our children that convey how important love is and the inherent protection from isolation and fear it supplies. It is your responsibility to find these and read them to your kids. Excellent resources can be found at your library, school, or religious center, and from friends.

School Life

Action Plan #1: Become the World's Leading Expert on Your Child. No one knows more about your child than you. Educate yourself on his needs in every area so that you can be his champion in dealing with doctors, teachers, counselors, and psychologists. Take your child in for a thorough physical examination and insist that the physician look for hormonal imbalances, toxins, vitamin deficiencies, and all the possible factors that could possibly affect learning. Consider the use of medications carefully, and allow their use only as part of a holistic treatment program rather than as a total solution.

Invest in a thorough neurological assessment for cognitive issues with a professional neuropsychologist, rehabilitation psychologist, clinical or counseling psychologist, neurologist, or an educational assessment specialist. Ask that person to prepare a written report and make sure you understand everything in it and what it means for your child's educational needs. The areas below can serve as a base for your requests from the evaluators:

auditory memory	fine motor control
visual memory	embedded acuity

arithmetic sequencing	listening concentration
reading concentration	auditory abstraction
visual learning rate	abstract tolerance

Action Plan #2: Become an Advocate for Your Child to the School. These action steps take courage and enormous energy, but remember, your child's future depends on your being his champion. Become a pest if that is what it takes. Some of the greatest people in history were pests who did the right thing when no one else would. The old adage that the squeaky wheel gets the grease should be your motto. Remember that most schools do have programs for attention deficit disorder, but sometimes they haven't been implemented. Stir the pot. Be the burr under the saddle.

Be a presence in your child's school. Volunteer for school activities so you'll know what is going on. Sit down with counselors and teachers regularly to let them know you are involved. Tell them what works, to make their jobs easier. Write out recommendations. Give the teachers literature, review your child's work, and above all, reinforce the teachers' efforts positively. They work hard and put forth tremendous effort for all their children, so you can be their best friend and colleague by telling them when they are doing a good job. Write letters to their principals or superintendents when they bring about progress in your child.

You absolutely do not want teachers to lower standards for your kid. That would be a disaster. But make the learning experience as positive as possible. I must warn you: this is a very tough assignment. Most parents tell me that they would probably do homeschooling if they had to do it over.

Persistence is the key. Do everything you can to make this a family effort. Family unity will get you and your child through this, and the bonds that form will be dividends for many years to come, for all of you.

Good News

Life is rarely what we plan it to be. Things happen, and there seems no reason or cause, especially related to something you have done. Dr. Joseph McGraw, father of Dr. Phil McGraw and a longtime friend of mine, used to say, "Most people spend 95 percent of their time deciding if they got a bad deal or a good deal, and 5 percent figuring out what to do about it, when it should be the opposite."

So you may still be deciding whether you, as a parent, got a good or a bad deal in a child with a diagnosis of ADD, but the time for worrying about that 5 percent has long past. It is time to look at your child for who she is, and start on a plan to help instead of worrying about what won't. And that plan may work or not work at first, but you do not have the right to reverse field and start rehashing the injustice of the world. If one approach doesn't make a difference, that is the time to work out another plan. Your kid deserves it. After all, you are the hero in this scenario.

And the interesting piece to the puzzle is that the answer may not lie directly with the problem. It might be in the things that you consider unimportant, such as getting to know your child's world, and listening for those subtle needs for understanding, and dealing with their frustrations. Dealing with the school yard bully or learning to be "cool" might be breakthroughs.

The good news is that if you have followed this book this far, you will be successful because you care to see the many options available. And there is more. I mentioned only those approaches that have a history of scientific findings, but there are many that will be new resources in the near future. Laser therapy that can be applied with a handheld applicator will soon be offered. This laser is safe and will be very reasonable.

Eyeglasses have been developed that influence the brain through specific use of light. There is still some research needed to make sure there is no negative long-term residual impact, but these may be offered within a year. I am doing research on these as this book is being written. Specialized neuroprogramming through the use of acoustical devices is also in the works, with implications not only for ADD but for other problems as well, such as Parkinson's and Alzheimer's. Maybe Star Trek medicine will happen sooner than we think.

These new developments are mentioned because I want you, as parents, to know that you have a partner in trying to help your child. I am working to assist you to be the most informed parent you can be, and to know that there are always options for helping your child become the best kid he or she can be.

Afterword

When my favorite musician, Mark Rider, had the opportunity to look this manuscript over, he made an interesting statement. He said, "This is not a blues song or an orchestra concert, but it could be a gospel." He was right. Although attention deficit disorder is a very sad circumstance for families, and understanding it requires a multidisciplinary score of experts, there really is a simple message underlying this book. My belief is that with courage and faith, even mountains can be moved. A gospel is defined as anything that is accepted as true and in the "good news" category. This book was based on a promise that attention deficit disorder could be managed and overcome. I can only hope that the reader took the journey with me and indeed found sources of hope, information, and empowerment. As with all challenges that appear to limit us from actualizing the extraordinary potential we have, those individuals who discover their paths to success realize that all we truly need is the core we call our authentic self.

For every door that closes, there are at least three that open, and that is true with neurological complications. As the brain is sabotaged and its forces subdued, we must find resources to infuse the stimulations required to bring about the latent capacities within us. Hopefully I have brought forward some of these very powerful tools and encouraged each of you to venture into the challenges presented.

Medicine is at the threshold of revolution, and management of most diseases is not far away. However, regardless of progress on the part of surgical or internal balance therapies, the primary ingredient will always remain the patient because it is the heart of the individual that foretells the result of any intervention. Medicine currently has few avenues for the child with ADD; this places the responsibility for his management squarely on the shoulders of the family as the advocate.

Being a health care professional, I could say that I wish for a medical treatment that would wash away all disease for all humankind, but this is only partly true. I resent seeing people suffer, especially my own family, yet I see how challenges can make our lives richer and help us realize how vulnerable we are. Our arrogance is constantly being tested by those forces that illuminate our weaknesses. By learning to use our true strengths we may learn how divine we really are.

While I was writing this book, I was contacted by the Angel Foundation (www.AngelFoundation.org), and was amazed that they were willing to help me develop a research center to study and design treatment for ADD, and would fund a world-based training program for children's hospitals and orphanages based on approaches discussed and studied at the center, including those presented in this book. As I researched this foundation, I found that its mission, set forth by its founder, Prince Romanov, and supported by many donors, has been to serve the children of war-torn countries. More than 1 million children are orphaned after a war, and there is obviously multiple trauma to their souls and bodies. I gladly joined the foundation's mission with the additional focus on ADD that would be significant in these circumstances.

As if there is some kind of divine force aiding in this book, many people have anticipated the guidance offered and have requested professional treatment resources, so I have contacted the best child psychologist I know and partnered with her to develop clinics for the children and parents in need of assessment and consultation. With some long soul-searching hours, we have conceived of the PsychoNeuroPlasticity Programs to cover all the protocols for ADD described in this book as well as to deal with future issues of other neurological diagnoses in which a multilayered approach is required. *Neuroplasticity* is a relatively new term that refers to the way the brain can create new avenues in the nervous system for tasks, both cognitively and physically. For example, children whose brains have been injured in areas that are associated with writing can learn to write using another part of the brain. That is what we think we can do with ADD.

These new clinics have just been funded as of the writing of this book, and for those interested parents who need some direction from a professional, you may contact us at http://www.gfranklawlis.com/ADD-PsychoNeuroPlasticity.

This book appears to have a life of its own. It has grown from a hope to a reality, from a set of observations to a guide for future successful interventions on a global basis. This is not my doing, but I would be the first to serve in such a mission. The one thing I am certain of: this book is just the beginning.

Resources

The process of writing and publishing a book can take months and years to do it right. Since this one required breadth and depth of information from many sources, it was no exception. And to write a book with all the areas covered in their deepest applications would take volumes. I would be the first to admit that many of my approaches and insights stand on the shoulders of other pioneers in the field, and I would be negligent if I didn't reveal some of the best sources for learning more about the arenas noted in this book. These are my top picks for the reader who wants more direction and guidance into the approaches addressed.

BOOKS

Amen, Daniel G. *Healing ADD: The Breakthrough That Allows You to See and Heal the Six Types of ADD*. New York: The Berkeley Publishing Group, 2001.

Breggin, Peter. *The Ritalin Fact Book*. Cambridge, Mass.: Perseus Publishing, 2002.

Campbell, Don. *The Mozart Effect for Children*. New York: HarperCollins, 2000.

Freeman, Lyn, and G. Frank Lawlis. *The Mosby Textbook on Alternative and Complementary Medicine*. New York: Mosby, 2001.

Greenwood-Robinson, Maggie. *20/20 Thinking*. New York: Penguin Putnam, 2003.

Hendler, Sheldon S., and David Rorvik. (Eds.) *PDR for Nutritional Supplements*. Montvale, N.J.: Thomson, 2001.

Levine, Mel. *The Myth of Laziness.* New York: Simon and Schuster, 2003.

Lyon, Michael K. *Healing the HyperActive Brain.* Calgary, Canada: Focused Publishing, 2000.

Schwartz, Jeffery M., and Sharon Begley. *The Mind and the Brain.* New York: HarperCollins, 2002.

Stevens, Laura J. *Twelve Effective Ways to Help Your ADD/ADHD Child.* New York: Avery, 2000.

Zimmerman, Marcia. *The ADD Nutrition Solution.* New York: Henry Holt, 1999.

ASSOCIATIONS

American Academy of Pediatrics (AAP)

http://www.aap.org

Organization of pediatricians dedicated to the health, safety, and well-being of infants, children, adolescents, and young adults. Provides a roster of physicians and information about ADD/ADHD.

Association for Applied Psychophysiology and Biofeedback (AAPB)

http://www.aapb.org

This association is the professional organization for information and professional resources in biofeedback and neurobiofeedback.

Attention Deficit Disorder Association (ADDA)

P.O. Box 543

Pottstown, Pennsylvania 19464

484-945-2101

http://www.add.org

Contact Person: Robert M. Tudisco, Esq., Vice President (robert. tudisco@verizon.net)

The Attention Deficit Disorder Association is a national nonprofit organization as defined by 501 (c) (3) of the Internal Revenue Code. It has been in existence since 1989. The mission of ADDA is to provide information, resources, and networking to adults with ADHD and to the professionals working with them. In doing so, ADDA generates hope, awareness, empowerment, and connections worldwide in the field of ADHD by bringing together science and human experience. The information and resources provided to individuals and families affected with ADHD and professionals in the field of ADHD focuses on diagnoses, treatment, strategies, and techniques for helping adults with ADHD lead better lives.

Attention Research Update

http://www.helpforadd.com

Contact: David Rabiner, Ph.D., Director

The Attention Research Update Newsletter *is a tool to help parents, professionals, and educators stay informed about new research on ADD.*

Children and Adults with ADD (CHADD)

8181 Professional Place, Suite 150
Landover, Maryland 20785
301-306-7070, Ext. 102
http://www.chad.org

CHADD was founded in 1987 in response to the frustration and sense of isolation experienced by children with ADD and by their parents. At that time, there were very few places one could turn to for support or information, and ADHD was seriously misunderstood by many people. Indeed, children and adults with ADHD were often wrongly labeled as "behavior problems," "unmotivated," or "not intelligent enough"—and many clinicians and educators knew little about ADD. CHADD is a national organization with more than 32,000 members and more than 500 chapters nationwide, providing support and information on ADHD.

The National Dissemination Center for Children with Disabilities (NICHCY)

http://www.nichcy.org

This organization is a clearinghouse for information on disabilities and issues pertaining to individuals (birth to age twenty-two) with disabilities.

Sparktop.org

Charles and Helen Schwab Foundation
1650 South Amphlett Boulevard, Suite 300
San Mateo, California 94402
650-655-2410
http://www.sparktop.org

Sparktop.org was developed by Schwab Learning, a service of the Charles and Helen Schwab Foundation. (Charles Schwab is the founder of the financial services company that bears his name.) Both Mr. Schwab and his son have been identified with dyslexia (difficulty with reading and basic language skills). Learning from those experiences, they established Schwab Learning in 1988 as a nonprofit organization helping to direct parents toward information and resources while providing expert answers to important questions. Schwab Learning's mission is to assist kids who learn differently become successful in learning and life.

OTHER WEB SITES OF INTEREST

http://www.infoadhd.com
This Web site is very informative about dietary recommendations that have been found useful for children and adults suffering from the effects of ADD and ADHD.

http://www.add.about.com
For those students who need some assistance with scholarships that are specifically for those with ADD and ADHD, this Web site could be a big help.

http://www.fmsnutrition.com
Another nutritional approach to ADD/ADHD.

http://www.adders.org
A very important Web site for information about support groups and advice from other parents.

JOURNALS

Since I am a nut when it comes to looking through a zillion journals and even scouring the popular press for any information about ADD and ADHD, I have found pearls in a variety of places. Being a psychologist, I am most familiar with the journals of the American Psychological Association, all of which can be accessed through http://www.apa.org/journals. A list of publications with which parents would likely find relevance is as follows:

Alternative Medicine Review
American Psychologist
Behavioral Neuroscience
Canadian Journal of Psychiatry
Consulting Psychology Journal
Developmental Psychology
Families, Systems & Health
Health Psychology
Journal of Abnormal Psychology
Journal of Biological Psychiatry
Journal of Clinical and Experimental Neuropsychology
Journal of Consulting & Clinical Psychology
Journal of Counseling Psychology
Journal of Educational Psychology
Journal of Family Psychology
Journal of the American Academy of Child and Adolescent Psychiatry
Neuropsychology

Index